Praise for
The Natural Gas Revolution

"Robert Kolb has written an excellent and comprehensive volume on the changing energy landscape. Both specialists and non-experts will benefit from the deep analysis he provides."

—**Gawdat Bahgat**, Professor of National Security, National Defense University's Near East South Asia Center for Strategic Studies

"...a very comprehensive scan of the gas landscape with associated shifts from unconventional developments."

—**Matthew Hulbert**, Chief Political Advisor, Saudi Aramco

"I have gone over [this] fine effort and can find no reason to be critical or even add anything! Very well done and easy to understand. I enjoyed [the] sections on shale plays and China very much."

—**Randy Brown**, Managing Partner, Tremont House Enterprises (Energy Group)

"I was very impressed with the in-depth information and historical data the book provides. It should be required reading for anyone in the industry now and in particular new employees coming into the energy business to help them understand the 'big picture' when it comes to energy in the world."

—**Paul Belflower**, Vice President, Marketing & Supply, Mustang Fuel Corporation/Mustang Fuel Marketing

"In this crisp and compact book, Robert Kolb pulls together the fast, world-changing transformation in energy across the globe. As dessert, we get a delicious treat of maps and charts that make the new picture visually clear. If you want to understand how your world may change, read this book."

—**Steve LeVine**, author of *The Oil and the Glory*

"This book is a 'must read' for anyone working in or interested in the natural gas industry. Kolb's discourse is eloquent and very insightful as he takes the reader through history up to present day of the natural gas revolution. The book is a pleasure to read!"

—**Betty J. Simkins**, Professor of Finance and Williams Companies Professor of Business, Spears School of Business, Oklahoma State University

"In *The Natural Gas Revolution*, Robert Kolb presents a thorough yet readable insight into the natural gas industry and its prospects for the future. While he does not shy away from explanation of the technical aspects of natural gas production, he does so in a manner that makes the concepts understandable to a reader with no background in the industry. Neither does he avoid the controversy surrounding fracking and other environmental concerns. The book is well researched and documented and a compelling read even for those of us who are familiar with the energy sector. Anyone concerned with the future of energy on a domestic or global scale should find a few hours with this book as time well spent."

—**James L. Williams**, WTRG Economics

The Natural Gas Revolution

The Natural Gas Revolution

At the Pivot of the World's Energy Future

Robert W. Kolb

Vice President, Publisher: Tim Moore
Associate Publisher and Director of Marketing: Amy Neidlinger
Executive Editor: Jim Boyd
Development Editor: Russ Hall
Operations Specialist: Jodi Kemper
Marketing Manager: Lisa Loftus
Cover Designer: Chuti Prasertsith
Managing Editor: Kristy Hart
Senior Project Editor: Jovana San Nicholas-Shirley
Project Editor: Elaine Wiley
Copy Editor: Kitty Wilson
Proofreader: Anne Goebel
Senior Indexer: Cheryl Lenser
Senior Compositor: Gloria Schurick
Manufacturing Buyer: Dan Uhrig

Pearson offers excellent discounts on this book when ordered in quantity for bulk purchases or special sales. For more information, please contact U.S. Corporate and Government Sales, 1-800-382-3419, corpsales@pearsontechgroup.com. For sales outside the U.S., please contact International Sales at international@pearsoned.com.

Company and product names mentioned herein are the trademarks or registered trademarks of their respective owners.

Printed in the United States of America

First Printing August 2013

ISBN-10: 0-13-335351-6
ISBN-13: 978-0-13-335351-8

Pearson Education LTD.
Pearson Education Australia PTY, Limited.
Pearson Education Singapore, Pte. Ltd.
Pearson Education Asia, Ltd.
Pearson Education Canada, Ltd.
Pearson Educación de Mexico, S.A. de C.V.
Pearson Education—Japan
Pearson Education Malaysia, Pte. Ltd.

Library of Congress Control Number: 2013940896

To Lori.

Contents

Acknowledgments

Like any other author, I have a variety of debts that it is my plea-sure to acknowledge. First, I would like to thank my home institu-tion, the Quinlan School of Business at Loyola University, Chicago, for its continuing support of my research program and for giving me the freedom to pursue my interests, wherever they lead. Ira G. Liss in Boulder, Colorado, prepared the many maps and diagrams that appear in this book. I believe they add considerably to the clarity of the story I have to tell. I wish I had had access to them as I did the research for this book! I would also like to thank Jim Boyd and Russ Hall at Pearson/FT Press. Jim was committed to the book from first hearing, or at least so it seemed. Russ was always prompt and helpful in shepherding the book through its development. I would also like to thank the editor of the *Journal of Social, Political, and Economic Studies*, Roger Pearson, for his continuing interest in my work.

A number of people have been very helpful in reviewing a pre-liminary draft of the text and making helpful comments. I would espe-cially like to offer my sincere appreciation to: Steve LeVine, author of *The Oil and the Glory*; Betty Simkins, the Williams Energy Com-panies Professor of Finance at Oklahoma State University; Matthew Hulbert, Chief Political Advisor for Saudi Aramco; Randy Brown at Tremont House Enterprises; Paul Belflower at Mustang Fuel Corpo-ration; Gawdat Bahgat at the National Defense University; and Jim Williams, at WTRG Economics.

About the Author

Robert W. Kolb holds two Ph.D.'s from the University of North Carolina at Chapel Hill (philosophy 1974, finance 1978) and has been a finance professor at five universities. He is currently a professor of finance at Loyola University Chicago, where he also holds the Considine Chair of Applied Ethics.

Kolb's recent writings include *Futures, Options, and Swaps 5e*, and *Understanding Futures Markets 6e*, both co-authored with James A. Overdahl. Recent edited volumes are: *Lessons from the Financial Crisis: Causes, Consequences, and Our Economic Future, Sovereign Debt: From Safety to Default*, and *Financial Contagion: The Viral Threat to the Wealth of Nations*, both published by Wiley. Kolb's most recent books are *The Financial Crisis of Our Time* (2011) and *Too Much Is Not Enough: Incentives in Executive Compensation* (2012), both published by Oxford University Press and both selected for the Financial Management Association's Survey and Synthesis Series.

Preface

We live in the midst of a revolution in energy that has already changed the energy future of the United States and now is beginning to transform the rest of the world as well. Because energy is so vital to all modern economies, these developments are rearranging the relative strengths of many of the most important nations in the world. This book tells the story of how this revolution began, where it stands now, and how it is likely to transform the world.

Less than 10 years ago, the United States faced what appeared to be a permanent fate of massive imports of oil and natural gas. In the ensuing years, the country has suffered a massive financial crisis, has endured a deep and persistent recession, and currently struggles through a period of less-than-satisfying anemic economic growth. This malaise has been accompanied by the dynamic rise of China and the perception of many that the United States is on an irretrievable path toward losing its customary preeminence and, perhaps, even to becoming a second-tier nation. In addition, environmental problems in the form of climate change have been gaining increased world attention. Compared to many other leading nations, the United States has done little to address its carbon footprint. There has been almost unanimous agreement that reducing carbon emissions is going to be extremely difficult in an economy used to relying on hydrocarbon energy sources.

Much—perhaps all—of that anticipated dismal future is no longer part of the forecast for the United States. Because of remarkable technological advances in accessing energy and a continuing wave of new discoveries of gas and oil, it now appears almost certain that the United States will soon become a reliable net exporter of energy. Largely benefiting from improved methods in petroleum geology, major new discoveries are occurring almost monthly around the world, even in areas long thought to be bereft of oil or gas, such as the eastern Mediterranean and the shores of Tanzania and Mozambique.

In the United States, geologists have long known of enormous quantities of gas and oil trapped in deep strata of shale and other sedimentary rocks that have held them inaccessible and beyond the reach of existing technology. But the twin technological innovations of hydraulic fracturing ("fracking") and horizontal drilling have unlocked these resources and led to an energy renaissance in the United States. Over the same time, the world has extended its ability to ship gas in liquid form around the world, opening economic possibilities that have long been closed and freeing some nations from the grasp of limited supply options.

For 40 years, many of the world's large economies, including those of the United States, Western Europe, and Japan, have been held as virtual energy hostages, a precarious circumstance of deep concern to policymakers and much of the public. This dependency of the West has been made worse by the nature of the countries that have been the world's energy jail keepers: Russia and the exporting nations of the Mideast. Following the United States, other nations are starting to extract their own shale gas and oil resources that appear to be abundant and widely distributed around the globe. Even nations that truly possess no gas or oil, such as Japan, can now at least look forward to a variety of suppliers, including many allies.

Chapter 1, "To the Brink of Innovation," examines the U.S. energy situation just after the turn of the twenty-first century. It was not a pretty picture. U.S. oil production peaked in 1970 and fell steadily for almost 40 years, until 2008. The United States also faced a serious deficit of natural gas and a future of gas imports. The longstanding failure to develop alternative energy sources, an inability to confront the problems of global climate change, and a general environmentally inspired hostility toward hydrocarbon sources of energy all conspired to create quite a serious energy situation. Yet unknown to almost everyone, the United States was about to enjoy a sudden large increase in energy production. In 2008, as if from another planet, came the first significant increase in oil production.

In contemporary public discourse in the United States, few topics generate more passion than the technology behind the new wave of energy production. Chapter 2, "They Call It a Revolution," explains this technology in nontechnical terms. Opponents of hydraulic fracturing fear that the process will taint aquifers on which populations depend for their very lives. The technique requires the pumping of water, sand, and chemicals into a well under high pressure to fracture the shale beds in which the gas or oil has been locked. Doing so frees the gas or oil to flow into the well and to the earth's surface for capture and use. While hydraulic fracturing has been in use for decades, what makes the technique so newly powerful is its combination with horizontal drilling. The sedimentary rocks containing the gas or oil lie in horizontal beds. To reach into them, the driller sinks a vertical well for some distance and then turns the drill to operate at a 90-degree angle and to traverse the shale bed. From any point of view, the ability to drill horizontally at a depth of a mile or more below the earth's surface is a marvelous technological tour de force.

Merely acquiring energy without a means of transporting it to the point of use remains only a half-achievement. Chapter 3, "Liquid Natural Gas and the World Gas Revolution," explains the long, slow, and now-maturing development of a worldwide transportation network that allows natural gas to be liquefied by chilling, pumped onto ships, transported to its destination, re-gasified, and then taken to the ultimate consumer. This aspect of the gas revolution is important because it allows producing nations to cash in on their newly discovered bounty, and it also makes it possible for receiving countries to secure needed energy resources at a more favorable price and to diversify their suppliers.

Chapter 4, "Environmental Costs and Benefits," considers the very real environmental challenges of the natural gas revolution. As mentioned, these include the danger of polluting critical water sources. But there are a number of other issues as well, including water consumption, the disposal of water laced with chemical and other pollutants generated in the production process, the disturbance of the land around the well site, and the changes that are brought to communities rich in these newly accessible resources. If all these challenges can be addressed successfully, we still face the issue of relying on hydrocarbons as opposed to once and for all, somehow, making a rapid transition to truly renewable and carbon-neutral sources of energy. There is another side to the environmental balance sheet, however. While waiting for the perfect world of completely renewable energy to arrive, substituting natural gas for coal and oil promises significant environmental benefits. Generating electricity by burning natural gas rather than coal is much cleaner. China derives 70% of all its energy from coal, and the environmental costs of that policy are well known. Also, as the United States moves ever more away from coal and toward natural gas for electricity generation, the large economies of the Eurozone are becoming more coal dependent as they close gas-fired plants and accelerate the building of coal-fired power plants.

Chapter 5, "The United States and China," begins an extended treatment of the effects of the world energy revolution as it will play out around the world. The United States and China have the two largest economies in the world, and both stand to be major beneficiaries from the natural gas revolution. The United States has already begun to cash in, while China sits atop the world's largest shale gas reserves, waiting to be tapped once China succeeds in assembling the necessary expertise and infrastructure. Chapter 6, "The World's Other Large Economies," turns attention to the other eight countries that make up the world's 10 largest economies: Japan, Germany, France, Italy, the United Kingdom, Brazil, India, and Russia. As we will see, most of these countries are beneficiaries of the natural gas revolution, but Russia almost certainly will be a big loser.

Beyond the big 10 economies, many other nations have a stake in the natural gas revolution, and Chapter 7, "The Other Contending Nations," explores the role that these countries will play. Iran, Qatar, and Turkmenistan, occupying second through fourth places in total world reserves of natural gas, following Russia in first place, have different problems and opportunities. But many other countries are also dramatically affected, ranging from Argentina to Australia, Turkey to Tanzania, and Malaysia to Mozambique. Developments in the world energy revolution have brought many small or even previously insignificant producing countries into the energy spotlight.

Chapter 8, "The Next Energy Revolutions," the book's concluding chapter, considers two further energy revolutions that are on the horizon. The first of these is the development of shale oil on parallel with what is already well under way with shale gas. The chapter also introduces a completely new and untapped resource that is the world's largest hydrocarbon resource—the mysterious and previously inaccessible "fire ice"—or methane hydrates.

A Note on Energy Values and Conversions

Quantities of energy are expressed in a variety of measures and forms, due in part to our continuing reliance on both the metric and English systems. Also, hydrocarbon energy comes in a variety of forms—solid, liquid, and gaseous—and different measures are suitable to each. But in whatever form, these energy sources are all reducible to a common measure—their energy content. These brief notes are intended to help you understand and compare the basic measures.

We begin with a measure of energy, the British thermal unit (Btu). 1 Btu is the energy required to raise 1 pound of water by 1 degree Fahrenheit. To make the Btu more salient, we can note the following approximate equivalences of energy content:

1 food calorie ≈ 4 Btu

So a normal daily intake of 2,000 food calories is equivalent to about 8,000 Btu.

1 gallon of gasoline ≈ 139,000 Btu

1 barrel of crude oil = 42 gallons ≈ 5,800,000 Btu

1,000 cubic feet of natural gas ≈ 1,023,000 Btu ≈ 8.05 gallons of gasoline

Quantities of natural gas are expressed both in metric measures and English measures. The typical unit of measurement in the metric system is the cubic meter:

1 cubic meter ≈ 35 cubic feet

In the United States, the average residence uses about 75,000 cubic feet, or about 2,100 cubic meters, of natural gas per year:

75,000 cubic feet ≈ 76,725,000 Btu ≈ 13 barrels of crude oil ≈ 618 gallons of gasoline

Quantities of crude oil are often expressed in metric tonnes:

1 metric tonne = 1,000 kilograms ≈ 2,205 U.S. pounds

1 metric tonne of crude oil ≈ 7.33 barrels ≈ 4,000,000 Btu

A standard term of measuring large quantities of energy is in millions of tonnes of energy equivalent (MTOE), meaning the energy equivalent to 1 million tonnes of crude oil.

Large quantities of natural gas are often measured in billions of cubic meters (bcm), a quantity of gas sufficient to serve 468,000 U.S. residences for one year.

When gas is liquefied, it is called LNG, for liquefied natural gas. Liquefying gas reduces the volume of gas by a factor of about 600, so that LNG is much more energy dense than gas:

1 tonne of LNG ≈ 1.22 tonnes of crude oil

1 tonne of LNG ≈ 1,360 cubic meters of natural gas ≈ 48,000 cubic feet of natural gas

PLATES

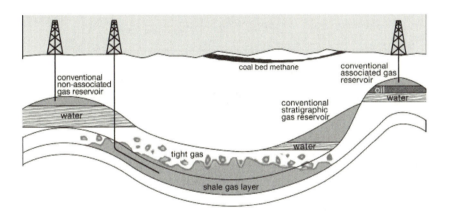

Plate 1 The Structure of Oil and Gas Reservoirs

Source: Adapted from Christopher J. Schenk and Richard M. Pollastro, "Natural Gas Production in the United States: National Assessment of Oil and Gas Fact Sheet," U.S. Geological Survey, January 2002, Figure 1. Artwork prepared by Ira G. Liss.

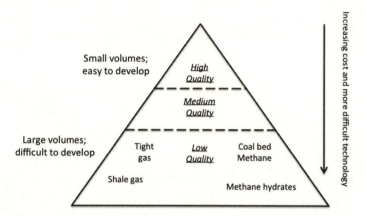

Plate 2 The Natural Gas Resource Triangle

Source: Slightly adapted from Stephen A. Holditch, "Tight Gas Sands," *Journal of Petroleum Technology*, June 2006, 84–90. Figure 1, p. 84.

Plate 3 Unconventional Natural Gas and Oil Plays in the United States

Source: Adapted from U.S. Energy Information Administration, "Review of Emerging Resources: U.S. Shale Gas and Shale Oil Plays," July 2011, Figure 1, p. 6. Artwork prepared by Ira G. Liss.

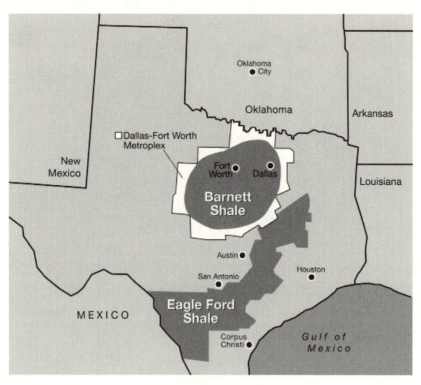

Plate 4 The Barnett and Eagle Ford Shale Formations

Artwork prepared by Ira G. Liss.

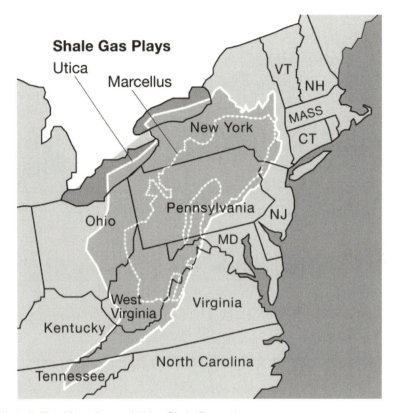

Shale Gas Plays

Plate 5 The Marcellus and Utica Shale Formations

Artwork prepared by Ira G. Liss.

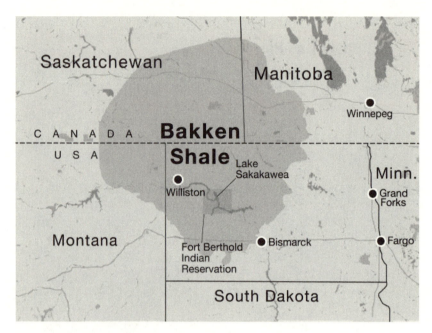

Plate 6 The Bakken Shale Formation

Artwork prepared by Ira G. Liss.

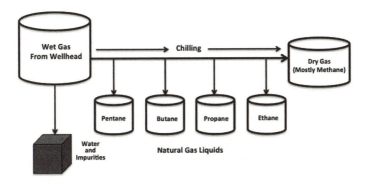

Plate 7 The Process for Liquefying Natural Gas

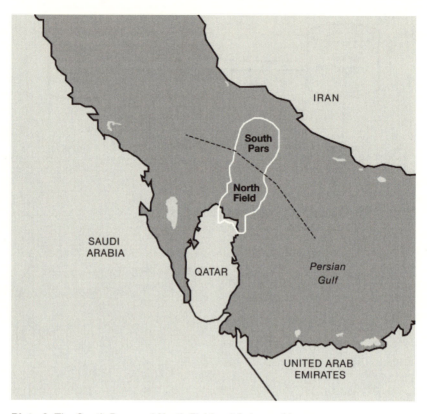

Plate 8 The South Pars and North Fields of Qatar and Iran

Artwork prepared by Ira G. Liss.

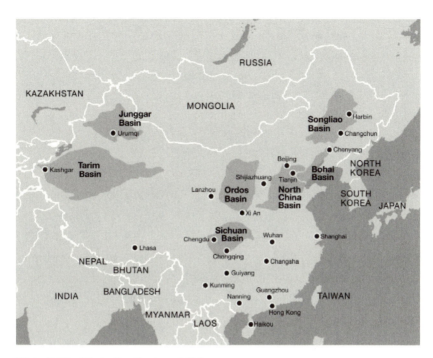

Plate 9 The Shale Gas Basins of China

Artwork prepared by Ira G. Liss.

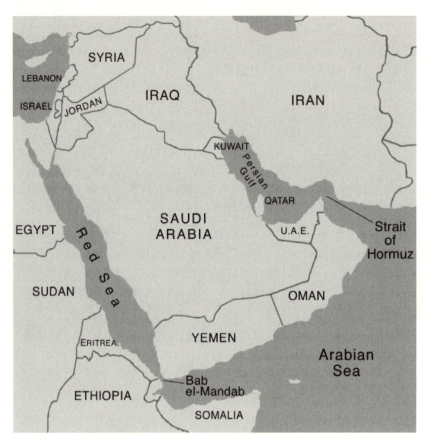

Plate 10 The Constricted Sea Lanes of the Middle East

Artwork prepared by Ira G. Liss.

Plate 11 The Constricted Sea Lanes of Southeast Asia

Artwork prepared by Ira G. Liss.

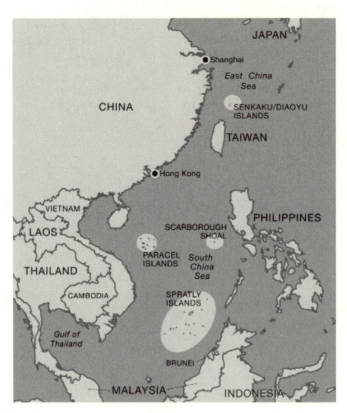

Plate 12 The South China Sea and Its Contested Regions: Paracel Islands, the Spratly Islands, the Senkaku/Diaoyu Islands, and the Scarborough Shoal

Artwork prepared by Ira G. Liss.

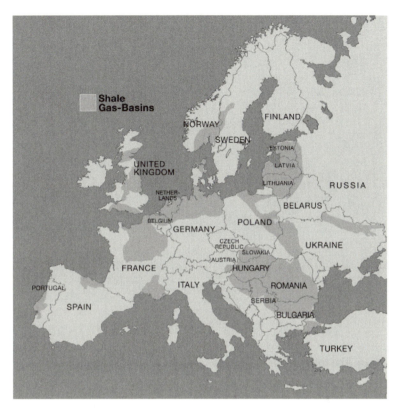

Plate 13 Principal Shale Basins of Western Europe

Artwork prepared by Ira G. Liss.

Nord Stream

Plate 14 The Nord Stream Pipeline

Artwork prepared by Ira G. Liss.

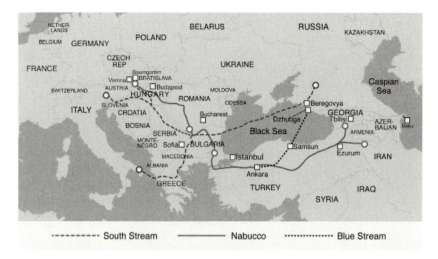

·········· South Stream   ——— Nabucco   ················· Blue Stream

Plate 15 Pipelines of the Southern Corridor

Artwork prepared by Ira G. Liss.

Plate 16 Gas Fields of Southern South America

Artwork prepared by Ira G. Liss.

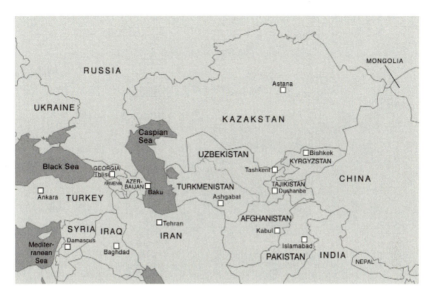

Plate 17 General Map of Central Asia

Artwork prepared by Ira G. Liss.

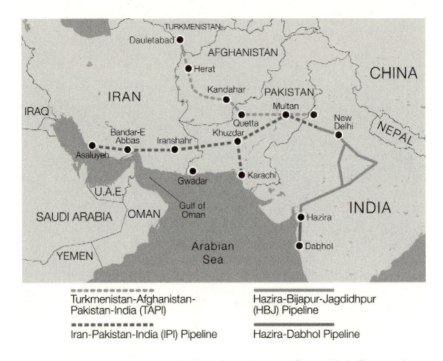

Plate 18 Major International Pipelines from Iran and Central Asia Eastward

Artwork prepared by Ira G. Liss.

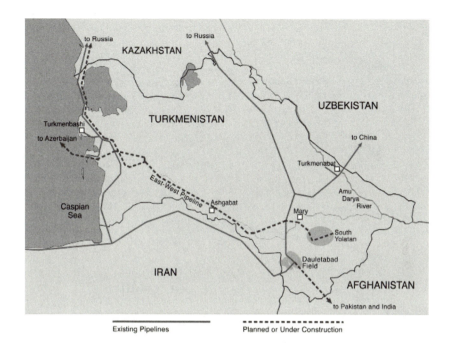

Existing Pipelines   Planned or Under Construction

Plate 19 Turkmenistan's Key Pipelines

Artwork prepared by Ira G. Liss.

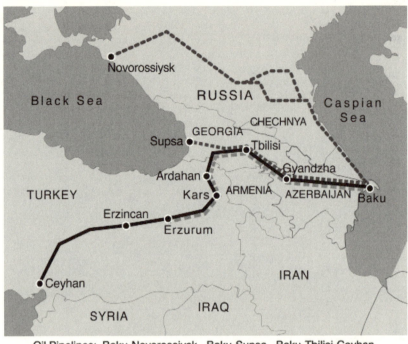

Plate 20 Pipelines from the Caspian Sea Westward

Artwork prepared by Ira G. Liss.

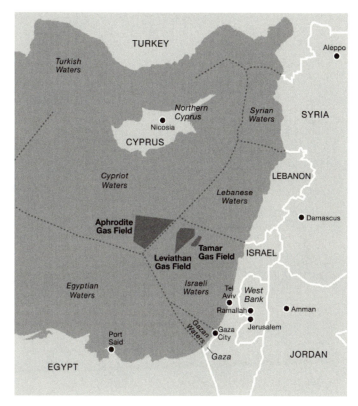

Plate 21 Gas Fields of the Eastern Mediterranean

Artwork prepared by Ira G. Liss.

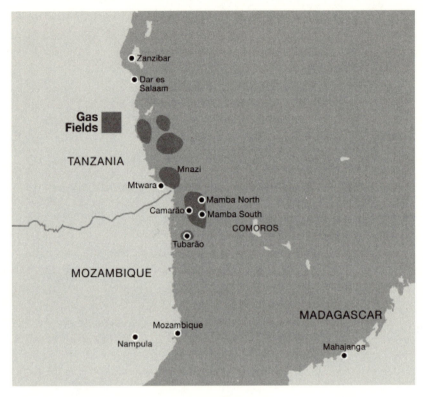

Plate 22 Gas Fields of Tanzania and Mozambique

Artwork prepared by Ira G. Liss.

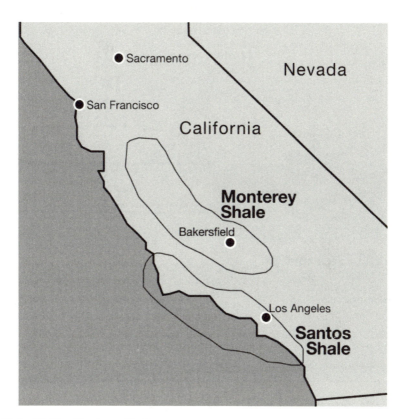

Plate 23 The Monterey Shale

Artwork prepared by Ira G. Liss.

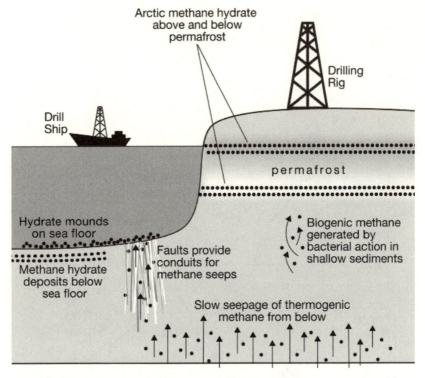

Plate 24 Typical Methane Hydrate Deposits

Source: Adapted from National Energy Technology Laboratory, "Energy Resource Potential of Methane Hydrate," U.S. Department of Energy, February 2011, p. 10.

Artwork prepared by Ira G. Liss.

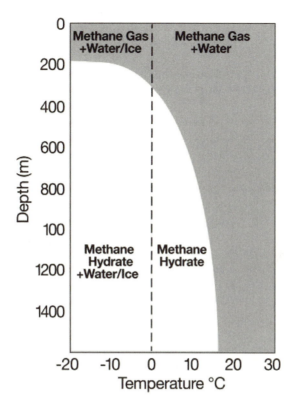

Plate 25 The Pressure and Temperature Interface for Methane Hydrates

Source: Adapted from National Energy Technology Laboratory, "Energy Resource Potential of Methane Hydrate," U.S. Department of Energy, February 2011, p. 8.

Artwork prepared by Ira G. Liss.

1 —————————————

To the Brink of Innovation

World Energy—A Rapid Tour of the Past 200 Years

From the beginning of human history until about 1750, a common date for the start of the Industrial Revolution, the world was poor, and societies were equal—or at least very roughly so, and dramatically so compared to the state of the world today.[1] Over the past 250 years, some nations have succeeded in building economic institutions and deploying technological innovations to facilitate economic growth. These movements have been the primary drivers of a rapid increase in wealth that was initially concentrated in the United Kingdom and soon spread to other early-moving nations. More recently, other societies have adopted institutions and technologies that permit economic progress, and wealth has spread to many other nations. The original Industrial Revolution has been superseded by further industrial and societal revolutions.

Some historians emphasize the role of the rapid technological changes that occurred starting about 1750, while others emphasize what they see as the greater importance of improving institutions that guarantee property rights and propel economic growth.[2] Whatever the ultimate cause of the prosperity that began some 250 years ago, the world's new wealth arrived on a drip, then a trickle, and finally a flood of energy derived from hydrocarbons. Pre-industrial societies consumed relatively little energy, deriving virtually all energy from organic sources. These sources were either human or animal muscle power, or substances that were burned for energy, like wood and peat. Before about 1700, power derived from wind, water, and hydrocarbons played only a negligible or nonexistent role.[3] No matter the sophistication of intellect or the brilliant organization of society, a total reliance on these organic energy sources placed an upper bound on human consumption and wealth, so the almost universal condition of poverty "did not arise from lack of personal freedom, from discrimination, or from the nature of the political or legal system, though it might be aggravated by such factors. It sprang from the nature of organic economies."[4]

Only the past few centuries have seen a significant increase in energy use. The increased exploitation of new energy sources has paralleled the development of technologies that have been able to actually make productive use of that newfound energy. Without industrial technologies, new energy sources could only be used for heating, and the difficulty of accessing new energy supplies has helped to limit human energy consumption.

The new sources of power that accompanied and made possible the rise of industrial technologies were first coal and then oil. Table 1.1 and Figure 1.1 show the transition of the world's energy sources since 1800, when the Industrial Revolution was already in full swing.

Table 1.1 The Transition of World Energy Usage from the Nineteenth to Twentieth Centuries

Fuel Transition	Decade
Coal overtakes biofuels	First decade of the nineteenth century
Oil overtakes biofuels	1950s
Oil overtakes coal	1960s
Gas overtakes biofuels	1960s

In Figure 1.1, the different sources of energy are expressed in a common unit of energy, the energy contained in 1 million barrels of oil. Perhaps most surprisingly, the entire nineteenth century, with all its rapid technological change and innovation, was still dominantly fueled by organic energy sources—non-petroleum resources including wood, peat, and the muscle power of animals and humans. Coal, however, gained an ever-more-prominent role starting in the middle of the nineteenth century. Nonetheless, coal surpassed organic energy as a world energy source only at the beginning of the twentieth century. Oil surpassed organic energy sources in world usage only in the 1950s, and it did not surpass coal until the 1960s.

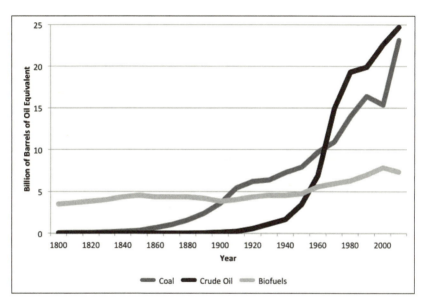

Figure 1.1 The Succession of Energy Sources: Biofuels, Coal, and Crude Oil

Source: Adapted from Vaclav Smil, *Energy Transitions: History, Requirements, Prospects,* Oxford, UK: Praeger, 2010, p. 154.

Coal's slow move to ascendancy over organic energy sources stemmed from the relatively slow spread of the Industrial Revolution to other parts of the world. Only northern Europe and the United States saw rapid industrialization following the breakthroughs in the United Kingdom. In these advanced economies, coal was king, supplying more than 90% of all of England's energy as early as the 1850s.[5] Meanwhile, though it was relatively close to the source of innovation,

Italy had a distribution of energy sources in the 1850s much like England's in the 1550s.[6]

Figure 1.2 shows that the past 200 years of energy history has featured a falling share for organic energy sources, and that trend continues to the present, with biofuels now constituting less than 10% of world energy usage. Nuclear and hydropower are together even less important than biofuels, constituting slightly more than 8% of total world energy usage. Solar power and wind power are both too slight to be factors. Thus, the world currently relies on hydrocarbons—coal, oil, and natural gas—for more than 80% of energy. Focusing on energy derived just from the three main hydrocarbons, oil provides 37%, slightly leading coal at 35%, with natural gas following at 28%. However, the importance of gas is rising and even accelerating. Natural gas supplied 7% of the world's energy in 1950, and it supplies 23% today; its proportion is almost certain to increase.

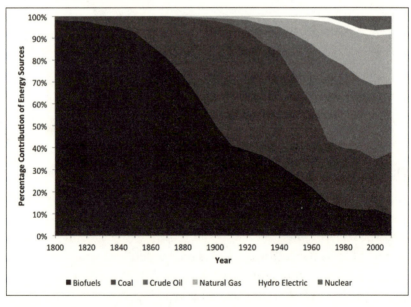

Figure 1.2 Shares of World Energy Sources, 1800–2008

Source: Adapted from Vaclav Smil, *Energy Transitions: History, Requirements, Prospects,* Oxford, UK: Praeger, 2010, p. 154.

That natural gas has gone from a 7% to a 23% share of total world energy in 60 years is all the more impressive when measured against the vast acceleration of world energy usage, as Figure 1.3 shows. In 2008, world energy usage was 10 times as large as in 1900 and 22 times as large as in 1800. Only a relatively small part of this increased energy usage can be attributed to population growth. Rather, there has been a marked increase in energy usage per capita, which has fueled a dramatic increase in per capita gross domestic product (GDP) as well. From 1820 to today, world per capita GDP has risen by a factor of 10, while in the industrialized West, per capita income has surged by a factor of 20 over the same period.[7]

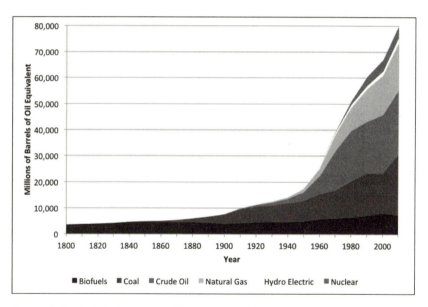

Figure 1.3 The World's Energy Sources, 1800–2008

Source: Adapted from Vaclav Smil, *Energy Transitions: History, Requirements, Prospects,* Oxford, UK: Praeger, 2010, p. 154.

Hydrocarbons: From the Beginnings to Maturity

Today our lives depend so fully on energy derived from hydrocarbons that it is almost impossible to realize how recently these energy sources began to play a significant role in human history. Coal's dominance gave way to oil due in large measure to oil's role in transportation. Today, oil rules the energy day and captures our geopolitical attention. A Russian engineer drilled the world's first oil well in 1848, in Baku on the Caspian Sea. Baku was producing almost the entirety of the world's oil supply around 1860. Today, as the capital of Azerbaijan, Baku continues to be an important hub of hydrocarbon production and transportation. In the United States, oil collected from surface seeps was first used as an ingredient in patent medicine around 1850, but some innovators recognized oil's potential as a source of energy for lighting.

The first oil well in the United States was drilled in Titusville, Pennsylvania, in 1859 by "Colonel" Edwin Drake; it set off the first American oil boom.[8] The following decades saw a competition among several players. John D. Rockefeller's Standard Oil was big in the United States, and the Swedish Nobel family came to be the most important players around Baku. The Nobels were soon joined by a succession of other non-U.S. firms, with the French Rothschilds also playing a prominent role.

It is not too much to say that crude oil made the automobile and that the automobile made oil one of the world's most important commodities. Although it was not the first country to drill, the United States quickly came to lead world production. Over the 1900 to 1950 period, the United States produced more than half of the world's oil. The bounty of U.S. oil played a critical role in both world wars. Within days of the 1918 armistice, the French Senator Victor-Henri Bérenger stated, "Oil, the blood of the earth, has become the blood of victory." Not to be outdone by French metaphors, Earl Curzon of England remarked that the Allies had "floated to victory on a wave of oil."[9] Although obtaining some oil from Mexico and Persia, the real source of the blood, or wave of victory, came from the United States, which supplied 80% of the Allies' oil in the last year of World War I.[10] By contrast, Germany had sufficient coal and natural gas but could draw only on Romania for a secure supply of oil.

Oil from the United States played a similar dramatic role in the winning of World War II, as Table 1.2 shows. Germany had adequate supplies of coal, outproducing every other combatant, even able to convert coal and natural gas to oil and then to gasoline. Nonetheless, the Allied powers outproduced the Axis collective by 63%. But with the war truly being a world war, navies and armies could only get to the front by using oil power, not coal. It was in crude oil production and availability that the Axis suffered the most serious disadvantage. Collectively, the Allies outproduced the Axis in oil by a factor of more than 15. Of that total Allied production, the United States contributed 80%, as it also did in World War I. So if the Allies in World War I rode to victory on a wave of oil, the Allies got to and won World War II on the strength of its massive superiority in crude oil, which was overwhelmingly provided by the United States.

Table 1.2 Coal and Crude Oil Suppliers in World War II (Millions of Metric Tons)

Allies					
	USA	USSR	UK	Canada	Total
Coal	2,149.7	590.8	1,441.2	101.9	4,283.6
Crude oil	833.2	110.6	90.8	8.4	1,042.0

Axis Powers					
	Germany	Italy	Hungary	Romania	Japan	Total
Coal	2,420.3	16.9	6.6	1.3	184.5	2,629.6
Crude oil	33.4	0.2	3.2	25.0	5.2	67.0

Source: John Ellis, *World War II: A Statistical Survey*, New York: Facts on File, 1993. Coal figures are from Table 79, and crude oil figures appear in Table 81.

Note: Approximately two-thirds of German oil production was in the form of synthetic oil derived from coal or natural gas.

A Rude Awakening

U.S. crude oil production continued to increase after World War II, peaking in 1970, at a production of 9.6 million barrels per day. From this high mark, the United States suffered a persistent slide in production for decades.

Coming almost immediately after the peak in U.S. oil production, the Organization of the Petroleum Exporting Countries (OPEC) oil embargo of 1973–1974 was a rude awakening. The United States had experienced other shortages in the many decades of previous oil history, including the West Coast Oil Famine of 1920, probably the first oil shock of the transportation era.[11] But the 1973–1974 experience was several orders of magnitude larger than any previous supply interruption, and it galvanized the attention of the American public, which was forced for the first time in memory to wait in line to fuel its cars.

Within days after the initiation of the oil embargo, President Nixon put the United States on the road to energy independence, declaring on November 7, 1973, "Let us set as our national goal, in the spirit of Apollo, with the determination of the Manhattan Project, that by the end of this decade we will have developed the potential to meet our own energy needs without depending on any foreign energy source." Ever since that time, the nation has been on the long road to that elusive and seemingly ever-receding goal, with every president since Richard Nixon renewing the pledge and commitment to energy independence.[12]

Thus, the three decades that followed the oil embargo were largely unhappy ones for energy in the United States. For oil—the critical energy source—the story was one of ever-increasing usage, ever-falling production, and ever-larger imports, and the same was largely true of natural gas. Even in those times, and continuing to the present day, coal has presented no supply problems. Presently, the United States has about 240 billion metric tons of coal, and even though it is producing almost 1 billion metric tons per year, that is less than one-half of 1% of proved reserves. "Proved reserves" are essentially in-ground resources confidently known to exist that can be extracted profitably under current economic conditions. Generally, "reserves" refers to "proved reserves." Put another way, the United States has almost 250 years' worth of coal at present levels of consumption, and it is actually producing more than it consumes. With oil and gas, the situation has been quite otherwise.

U.S. Oil and Natural Gas at the Turn of the Millennium

Figure 1.4 shows the recent history of oil production and consumption in the United States. Even at the height of production, the United States consumed more oil than it produced, and in the 30 years from 1970 to 2000, the gap generally widened, with increasing consumption and falling production. The situation for natural gas has been superficially different but similar in actual fact. As shown in Figure 1.5, in the United States, the production and consumption of natural gas were in a rough balance initially, but starting in about 1986, consumption increased rapidly, even while production increased. The ultimate result was that the gap between consumption and production grew ever wider toward the end of the twentieth century.

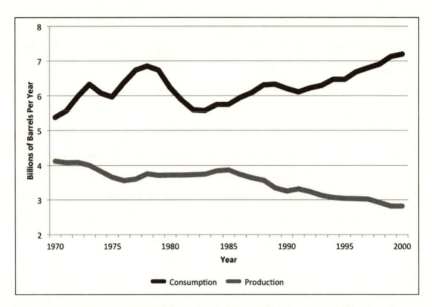

Figure 1.4 U.S. Crude Oil Consumption and Production, 1970–2000

Source: BP, "Statistical Review of World Energy," June 2012.

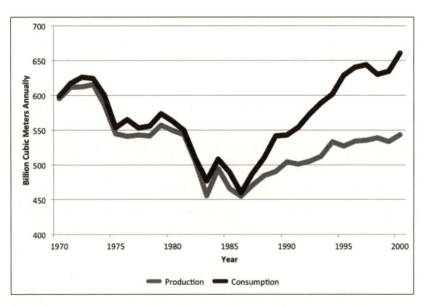

Figure 1.5 U.S. Natural Gas Consumption and Production, 1970–2000

Source: U.S. Energy Information Administration.

Also, U.S. oil and gas reserves fell significantly from 1970 to 2000, as Figure 1.6 shows. From this dwindling resource base, the United States continued to extract more and more of both oil and gas, as shown in Figure 1.7. By 2000, the United States was extracting about 10% of its oil reserves and about 11% of its gas reserves each year. While there had been fluctuation in the production-to-reserves ratio for both oil and gas, the general trend was upward, and this was particularly true for natural gas. Further, part of the reason that these rates of production were not higher was resistance to oil and gas production on environmental grounds. Thus, the energy picture for the United States at the start of the new millennium was certainly perilous.

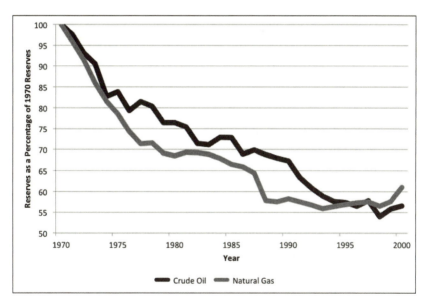

Figure 1.6 U.S. Oil and Natural Gas Proved Reserves, 1970–2000 (1970 = 100.0)

Source: U.S. Energy Information Administration.

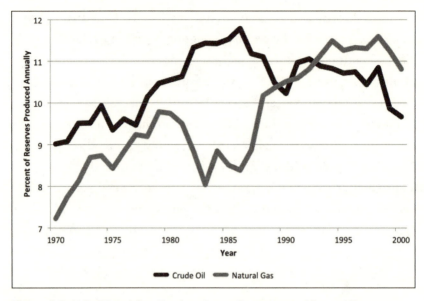

Figure 1.7 U.S. Oil and Gas Produced, as a Percentage of Proved Reserves, 1970–2000

Source: U.S. Energy Information Administration.

The geopolitical situation around the turn of the millennium could only exacerbate reasonable fears about the energy future for the United States and its principal allies. The war between Iraq and Iran had dragged on for almost the entire decade of the 1980s, reducing production for both countries. Iraq's invasion of Kuwait in 1991 only emphasized the turbulence of the Persian Gulf region, with its critical energy supplies. Then came the attack on the World Trade Center in New York in September 2001, ushering in a new era of conflict and supply disruption in the region. In assessing the near- and short-term futures for natural gas in May 2001, the U.S. Energy Information Administration (USEIA) noted that gas prices had more than doubled in the decade 1990 to 2000, and it forecast that prices would rise by 34% in just the next two years.[13] Further, so much gas had been withdrawn from storage that the USEIA saw its replenishment as a challenge that would add to price pressure. The same report noted that some policy analysts were questioning the ability of natural gas to play its expected role in supporting economic growth.

Looking out to 2020, the USEIA predicted that total U.S. energy consumption would increase by about one-third over the period, as would the use of oil. The report also predicted that the use of natural gas would increase by almost two-thirds. As a result of these increases, the USEIA predicted that the United States would have to increase gas imports by about three-quarters and oil imports by two-thirds.[14]

The natural gas supply and demand problems for the United States stemmed from several sources. In the aftermath of the embargo-induced energy crisis of the early 1970s, Congress passed the Powerplant and Industrial Fuel Use Act of 1978 as a centerpiece of President Carter's energy policy. One of the key purposes cited in the act was "to encourage and foster the greater use of coal and other alternate fuels, in lieu of natural gas and petroleum, as a primary energy source." In essence, the law required that new electricity-generating plants that were designed to run on natural gas had to also be capable of using coal or some other non-gas fuel. The act also restricted the use of natural gas in large boilers. In the years following the enactment of the act, demand for natural gas waned, prices fell, gas came into excess supply, and exploration for and development of new gas resources slowed. Given the long lead times for energy development, the disincentives to exploration and development inherent in the act soon caused significant problems.

In recognition of the excess supply that developed right after and partially in response to the 1978 act, Congress voted for repeal of the act in 1987. As the USEIA noted, this repeal "set the stage for a dramatic increase in the use of natural gas for electric generation and industrial processing."[15] Soon after this repeal came "third-generation" combined-cycle gas-fired power plants, which were much more efficient and economically attractive than prior technologies. The repeal of the 1978 act, improved technology, and low gas prices stimulated a switchover to the construction of gas-fired power plants, which contributed to a demand surge for gas. In the next 20 years, the use of gas jumped more than 100%, due largely to the expanded use of gas in generating electricity.[16]

Natural gas sources can be either conventional or unconventional. In short, a conventional natural gas deposit is essentially gas trapped in a single underground reservoir, much like a subterranean pool of water. By contrast, unconventional natural gas deposits consist of gas dispersed over a wider area and held in a variety of rock formations, such as shale, coal, or sandstone. (These types of deposits are explored more fully in Chapter 2, "They Call It a Revolution," as they play an important role in the natural gas revolution.) In 2000, the USEIA published an assessment of technically recoverable natural gas in the lower 48 states, both conventional and unconventional, as shown in Table 1.3. (Technically recoverable oil and gas are resources that it is possible to access with current technology, without reference to the economic viability of doing so.) The total estimate was more than 22 trillion cubic meters, divided almost exactly evenly between conventional and unconventional deposits. This is enough gas to fill the volume of the New Orleans Superdome more than 5 million times.

Table 1.3 U.S. Unproved Technically Recoverable Natural Gas Resources Onshore in the Lower 48 States, as of January 1, 2000 (Billion Cubic Meters)

Conventional		Unconventional			
Region		Tight Sands	Coal Bed	Gas Shales	Total Unconventional
West Coast	623	170	0	0	170
Rocky Mountains	1,557	5,380	1,303	57	6,739
Midcontinent	2,633	425	85	0	510
Southwest	1,586	425	0	198	623
Gulf Coast	4,502	736	85	0	821
Northeast	368	680	227	1,274	2,180
Total	11,270	7,815	1,699	1,529	11,044

Source: U.S. Energy Information Administration, "U.S. Natural Gas Markets: Mid-Term Prospects for Natural Gas Supply December 2001," p. 18.

Thus, there was lots of gas onshore, but it needed to be extracted. However, legal restrictions prohibited the development of much of this gas, particularly in the Rocky Mountain region. Further, while the industry had the technology to develop much of this gas, it was not feasible economically. Often the difference between a proved reserve and a technically recoverable reserve depends simply on the price of the resource and the cost of exploiting the resource. Offshore the United States, there are also vast amounts of technically recoverable gas. The USEIA's analysis divided them into the Pacific, Gulf of Mexico, and Atlantic regions, holding a total of 6.7 trillion cubic meters. However, the entire Pacific and Atlantic regions were legally out of bounds for development, as was one of the three sub-regions of the Gulf of Mexico. These legal restrictions excluded 1.7 trillion cubic meters of offshore gas from production. Thus, with the new millennium, the prospects for natural gas in the United States appeared highly forbidding on both the supply and demand sides of the equation. Far from being a single voice of doom, the bleak future portrayed by the USEIA represented the consensus of wisdom on the subject of hydrocarbons in general and natural gas in particular.

Contrasted with these dire predictions, and not fully understood or anticipated by anyone, the energy future of the United States and the world stood on the cusp of a dramatic change. As we will see, there was soon to be a remarkable jump in estimates of gas resources, and new technologies would make it economically feasible to develop much gas that previously had been only technically recoverable.

Notes

1. See, for instance, Robert E. Lucas, Jr., "The Industrial Revolution: Past and Future," Minneapolis Federal Reserve Bank *Annual Report*, May 1, 2004, p. 1: "Living standards in all economies in the world 300 years ago were more or less equal to one another and more or less constant over time."

2. As Douglass North and Robert Thomas put it, "The industrial revolution was not the source of modern economic growth. It was the outcome of raising the private rate of return on developing new techniques and applying them to the production process." It was, in short, the development of secure property rights protected by a system of laws enforced by a capable government that made

economic growth possible. See Douglass C. North and Robert Paul Thomas, *The Rise of the Western World: A New Economic History*, Cambridge, UK: Cambridge University Press, 1973, p. 173.

3. This is not to minimize or neglect the intellectual achievements of an earlier time. For example, Lynn White chronicles the amazing inventions and technological innovation of the medieval period. Rather, these inventions and technologies were not deployed in a large-scale, sustained, and society-changing way until the advent of the Industrial Revolution. See Lynn White, Jr., *Medieval Technology and Social Change*, Oxford, UK: Oxford University Press, 1966.

4. E. A. Wrigley, *Energy and the English Industrial Revolution*, Cambridge, UK: Cambridge University Press, 2010, p. 239.

5. E. A. Wrigley, *Energy and the English Industrial Revolution*, Cambridge, UK: Cambridge University Press, 2010, p. 37.

6. E. A. Wrigley, *Energy and the English Industrial Revolution*, Cambridge, UK: Cambridge University Press, 2010, p. 92.

7. Angus Maddison, *Contours of the World Economy 1–2030 AD: Essays in Macro-Economic History*, Oxford, UK: Oxford University Press, 2007. See Table 2.1, "Levels of per Capita GDP, Population, and GDP: World and Major Regions, 1–2003 AD."

8. In his Pulitzer-winning book, on which this section largely relies, Daniel Yergin includes a compelling narrative of these early days of oil. See *The Prize: The Epic Quest for Oil, Money, and Power*, New York: Free Press, 1991.

9. "Floated to Victory on a Wave of Oil," *New York Times*, November 23, 1918.

10. "Oil: Oil and World Power," *Encyclopedia of the New American Nation*. Available at www.americanforeignrelations.com/O-W/Oil-Oil-and-world-power. html#b. Accessed October 14, 2012.

11. James D. Hamilton, "Historical Oil Shocks," forthcoming in the *Handbook of Major Events in Economic History*. Working paper, February 2011.

12. "I am recommending a plan to make us invulnerable to cutoffs of foreign oil.... new stand-by emergency programs to achieve the independence we want." (President Gerald Ford, January 15, 1975). "This intolerable dependence on foreign oil threatens our economic independence and the very security of our nation" (President Jimmy Carter, July 15, 1979). "We will continue supportive research leading to development of new technologies and more independence from foreign oil" (President Ronald Reagan, February 18, 1981). "There is no security for the United States in further dependence on foreign oil" (President George H. Bush, August 18, 1988). "We need a long-term energy strategy to maximize conservation and maximize the development of alternative sources of energy" (President Bill Clinton, June 28, 2000). "This country can dramatically improve our environment, move beyond a petroleum-based economy, and make our dependence on Middle Eastern oil a thing of the past" (President George

W. Bush, January 31, 2006). "These are extraordinary times, and it calls for swift and extraordinary action. At a time of such great challenge for America, no single issue is as fundamental to our future as energy. America's dependence on oil is one of the most serious threats that our nation has faced....It falls on us to choose whether to risk the peril that comes with our current course or to seize the promise of energy independence" (President Barack Obama, January 26, 2009). "For decades, we have known the days of cheap and accessible oil were numbered....Now is the moment for this generation to embark on a national mission to unleash America's innovation and seize control of our own destiny" (President Barack Obama, June 15, 2010).

13. U.S. Energy Information Administration, "U.S. Natural Gas Markets: Recent Trends and Prospects for the Future," May 2001, p. viii.

14. U.S. Energy Information Administration, "Annual Energy Outlook 2001: With Projections to 2020," December 2000, pp. 3, 4, 7.

15. U.S. Energy Information Administration, "Repeal of the Powerplant and Industrial Fuel Use Act (1987)," www.eia.gov/oil_gas/natural_gas/analysis_publications/ngmajorleg/repeal.html.

16. U.S. Energy Information Administration, "Repeal of the Powerplant and Industrial Fuel Use Act (1987)," www.eia.gov/oil_gas/natural_gas/analysis_publications/ngmajorleg/repeal.html.

2

They Call It a Revolution

Recent headlines herald the news: Dramatic changes are surging through the world of energy. "Shale Gas Will Rock the World," opines energy analyst Amy Myers Jaffe, and she also declares "The Americas, Not the Middle East, Will Be the World Capital of Energy."[1] The International Energy Agency poses the question "Are We Entering a Golden Age of Gas?" and answers with a clear affirmative.[2] Martin Wolf echoes the answer when he says "Prepare for a Golden Age of Gas," and Tom Gjelten adds his voice with "The Dash for Gas: The Golden Age of an Energy Game-Changer."[3] *New York Times* reporter Clifford Krauss asks "Can We Do without the Mideast?" and answers his own question in another article with Eric Lipton, "U.S. Is Inching Toward Elusive Goal of Energy Independence."[4]

Comparisons of the United States with Saudi Arabia run rife, as Stephen Moore explains in the *Wall Street Journal* article "How North Dakota Became Saudi Arabia," and Brian Milner asserts "'Saudi America' Heads for Energy Independence."[5] In the same vein, respected oil analyst Ed Morse issues the warning "Move Over, OPEC—Here We Come."[6] Steve Levine wonders "Is This Group Think, or Is the U.S. about to Be Energy-Independent?" while a Citigroup report echoes the theme of U.S. energy independence and the death of the "peak oil" hypothesis.[7] Such major changes will create some losers, of course—mainly coal. Wolf Richter writes that "Natural Gas Is Pushing Coal Over the Cliff," and a widely followed oil blog speaks of "Natural Gas and the Brutal Dethroning of King Coal."[8]

The Early History of Natural Gas

Just as with oil seeps at the earth's surface, humans have used immediately accessible natural gas for at least two millennia. Human awareness goes much farther into the past, with lightning strikes igniting surface emissions of gas. At the time of Confucius, about 500 B.C., the Chinese were already collecting gas emerging from seeps at the earth's surface, conducting it with pipes made of bamboo, and using its heat to distill drinking water from sea water.

Natural gas, particularly these ignited surface excrescences, has played an important role in religion. It seems almost certain that the flame at the Greek temple at Delphi on Mount Parnassus was fueled by such a natural gas emission. Plutarch tells us that a goatherd first discovered the Oracle at Delphi. He also notes the emission of a delightful fragrance. Recent geological investigations indicate that the fragrance may have come from a compound related to natural gas, ethylene or benzene.[9] Plutarch tells us also that the emissions were weaker in his time than previously. Today, there is no naturally occurring flame at Delphi.[10]

Zoroastrianism, in which fire plays a central ceremonial role, antedates the Oracle at Delphi, having been established around 1000 to 1500 B.C. From inception, worship was conducted at sites with naturally occurring flames, and the worship of Ahura Mazda spread through most of present-day Turkey, Iran, and much of Central Asia. The three "flame towers," modernistic high-rise buildings completed in 2012 in Baku, Azerbaijan, pay homage to Zoroastrianism and Baku's long-prominent role in fossil energy.

Beyond using naturally occurring gas for practical purposes or to facilitate worship, Great Britain was the first country to use natural gas in an industrialized commercial process. As early as 1785, rather than capture naturally occurring gas, the British used coal to produce natural gas and employed the gas to light homes and streetlamps. The same technology reached the United States in 1816, and Baltimore installed gas streetlamps. Naturally occurring gas was known in the United States around 1626, and the first gas well was also the first oil well, as Edwin Drake captured both from his very first 1859 well. Quickly, a pipeline was run to nearby Titusville, Pennsylvania. William Hart in Fredonia, New York, knew of a natural gas seep in a creek, and he drilled the first well designed to harvest natural gas, which led to the founding of the Fredonia Gas Light Company. Robert Bunsen invented the Bunsen burner in 1885, which allowed gas and air to be mixed in the correct proportions to regulate temperature for cooking and heating.[11]

Without a well-developed pipeline structure, gas remained difficult to transport. So during the nineteenth century, gas was mostly produced from coal and used principally for lighting. In 1891, a 120-mile pipeline brought natural gas from fields in Indiana to Chicago. This same Hoosier gas was used to produce many of the large windows that still adorn Chicago's revolutionary skyscrapers built in the same era, the finest example being the Reliance Building, completed in 1895 and still standing in its window-filled grace at the corner of State and Washington. The fields of gas in Indiana were soon exhausted in this production of the glass for Chicago's windows, and the Chicago *Tribune* declared the "End of Natural Gas" in September 1899.[12]

Having addressed the transportation issue by building pipelines, natural gas was launched for more widespread use, but problems still remained. The United States really only started to develop a significant pipeline network in the 1920s, and the full fruition of this network required advances in welding, pipe-rolling, and metallurgy that emerged from World War II. Following the war, the United States embarked on a pipeline-building boom that lasted into the 1960s. Today, the United States has the most developed natural gas pipeline network in the world, with more than 300,000 miles of interstate and intrastate transmission pipelines. This figure does not count local distribution lengths, which collectively add an enormous number of miles to the total.[13]

The Creation of Oil and Natural Gas

All petroleum resources originate as organic matter. In the typical event, plants and animals die and are deposited in still water—swamps, bays, estuaries, or even deep oceans. The Devonian period, about 416 to 359 million years ago, with its warm, humid climate, was particularly ideal for the creation of this organic matter. But the process has been continuous over many geological periods.

After the organic material is laid down, sediment covers the dead plants and animals, and successive layers of sediment eventually form an overlayer of mineral material that begins to compress into rock. The pressure of the overlaying rocks and the natural warmth of the earth cause the temperatures of the organic material to rise, initially transforming the dead matter into kerogen, the precursor to oil and natural gas. Further cooking with ascending temperatures transforms the kerogen. Under the right conditions, and in a temperature range of 60 to 150 degrees Centigrade, the "oil window," the kerogen becomes oil; with further heating to the range of 150 to 200 degrees Centigrade, "the gas window," the kerogen becomes natural gas.

This preheated mix of rock and organic material can also be found today. One particular example is oil shale, something quite different from shale oil or shale gas. Oil shale is shale that is rich in kerogen, the essential organic precursor and geological building block of oil, that has never been heated and transformed into gas or oil. Oil shale generally lies close to the earth's surface. If it is mined and heated, the kerogen contained in the oil shale can be transformed into oil or gas. Parts of the United States are extremely rich in oil shale, most notably the Green River Basin of western Colorado, southwestern Wyoming, and northeastern Utah. While in principle oil shale can be transformed into oil, such a process requires massive mining of tremendous volumes of oil shale and heating the material to transform it into gas or oil. Such a process has two tremendous pitfalls. First and foremost, the mining would have to be on a massive scale and would cause considerable environmental destruction. Second, heating the oil shale requires a great deal of energy. The environmental destruction, the high cost of mining on a massive scale, and the energy cost of heating the oil shale jointly ensure that deriving useful hydrocarbon energy from oil shale is economically infeasible and likely to remain so for the foreseeable future.

The normal formation of gas and oil requires a process that occurs over millions of years—millions of years to form the sedimentary rock overlayer and additional millions of years to cook the organic matter first into kerogen and then eventually into oil and natural gas. Also, the kind of organic material matters: Wood fragments mostly give rise to natural gas, and algae become both natural gas and oil. This is the thermogenic formation of natural gas and oil, with the gas and oil typically being quite deep in the earth, in the range of 2,000 feet and greater at the time of formation.

Natural gas can also form biogenically. In this case, the organic material lies at a more shallow depth and never receives enough heating to produce oil and natural gas thermogenically. Instead, the gas is produced by anaerobic bacteria. Scientists can use chemical markers to distinguish between thermogenically and biogenically originating natural gas.

Once formed, oil and natural gas do not necessarily stay trapped in the source rocks of their origin. Instead, they can migrate in response to pressure differentials in the surrounding rock. To do so, the source rock must have microscopic pores that create pathways for the oil and gas to travel. If the source rock is too fine-grained, then the petroleum material remains captured within the source rock. Often the rock above the petroleum source rock is saturated with water; in this case, the gas and oil, both being lighter than water, ascend. As a consequence, the typical migration route is upward or lateral, and it continues until the oil and gas encounter a barrier in the form of impermeable rock—rock that is too dense to contain the pores and pathways necessary for further migration. Because the gas is lighter

than oil, it accumulates above the oil and just beneath the impermeable rock that constitutes a seal and prevents further travel.

Plate 1 shows the main structures of oil and natural gas accumula-
tion. Natural gas reservoirs often occur together with oil finds. Gas
that lies in the presence of oil is called *associated gas*, as in the reservoir depicted on the right side of Plate 1, with oil lying above water
and gas resting above the oil, all held in place from above by impermeable cap rock. Gas reservoirs also occur without the presence of
oil, as shown in the left-hand reservoir of Plate 1.

Plate 1 also illustrates the two basic kinds of traps that form oil and
gas reservoirs, stratigraphic and structural. The left- and right-hand
reservoirs in Plate 1 are structural, with the trap consisting of rock layers that have been deformed by folding or faulting. The stratigraphic
gas reservoir results from a trap formed by discontinuous layers of
rock, as in the case of a coastal barrier island. The reservoirs discussed
thus far are all examples of conventional oil and gas deposits.

There are also three main types of unconventional gas and oil
deposits, as shown in Plate 1: shale gas and oil, tight gas and oil, and
coal bed methane or coal bed gas. The bottom layer of petroleum
resources shown in the figure lie in a layer of shale. In this layer, the
lack of pores and pathways keeps the gas or oil in place and prevents
upward migration. Shale gas and oil lie in a layer of shale rock, while
coal bed methane is natural gas lying in coal seams. Tight gas and
tight oil are petroleum resources in which drilling offers very low flow
rates of the resource. Therefore, the term is somewhat imprecise.[14]
Shale gas is closely akin to tight gas, except that it specifically resides
in shale rock. As a working definition, we can think of unconventional
gas and oil as petroleum resources that are difficult to extract economically without using special techniques, a definition that would
embrace shale and tight oil and gas as well as coal bed methane.[15]
Thus, *shale* and *tight* as modifiers of *oil* or *gas* are often used inter-
changeably, even by many experts. Whether the tight rock is shale or
some other type of rock matters little for understanding the energy

revolution, as the drilling processes are similar. One can even say that to a non-driller or non-geologist, the difference in the exact type of rock does not matter. Therefore, we will follow the custom of many and continue to speak of shale gas and shale oil to refer to all types of tight gas and tight oil. As we will see, hydraulic fracturing and horizontal drilling are the two key technologies that now enable access to these unconventional resources.

One other type of gas deserves mention, although it plays no role in today's energy supply. Methane hydrates are natural gas resources trapped in surrounding frozen water molecules that exist primarily at the ocean floor and are trapped in marine sediments. The U.S. Department of Energy observed: "Methane hydrates are 3D ice-lattice structures with natural gas locked inside, and they can be found under the Arctic permafrost and in ocean sediments along nearly every continental shelf in the world. The substance looks remarkably like white ice, but it does not behave like ice. If methane hydrate is either warmed or depressurized, it releases the trapped natural gas."[16] In essence, methane hydrates exist as underwater ice, and the estimate of the resource is some multiple—perhaps a large multiple—of the sum of all other forms of hydrocarbon energy on earth. At present, technology does not allow the production of these resources, yet they are of tremendous interest for the future, as the resource is vast. While the technology to access this resource will not be developed for some time, countries and companies are already jockeying to position themselves to acquire this gas in the future. In addition, these methane hydrates constitute extremely large quantities of presently sequestered carbon, with enormous potential to accelerate global warming if they are released. I return to a discussion of methane hydrates in Chapter 8, "The Next Energy Revolutions."

Plate 2 depicts the distribution of worldwide natural gas resources in the "gas resource triangle." In essence, conventional and easy-to-access resources lie at the top of the triangle, exist in relatively small quantities, and have been exploited commercially for more than a century. Unconventional gas resources—shale gas, tight gas, and coal bed methane—exist in much greater quantities but are more difficult and costly to develop. It is only in the past decade that advanced technologies have brought these resources to commercial production. Finally, the earth holds the most plentiful source of natural gas of all as methane hydrates, but this gas remains too difficult and too expensive to produce, if it can be produced at all.

The Basics of Extraction, Production, and Completion

When Drake drilled his first Pennsylvania well in 1859, he was after oil, not natural gas, but nature gave him both. His exploration investment was minimal, as he was drilling along a stream named Oil Creek; native Americans had known of the oil seeps along the creek since before historical time and European arrivals had been aware of the same thing since the 1600s. Today, such easy-to-find gas and oil sources have been largely exploited. As a result, modern gas and oil exploration requires sophisticated technologies, relies on a profound understanding of geology, and depends on the efforts of many scientists and engineers. Rather than investigate the process of exploration and discovery, we begin our brief account of the process of extraction, production, and completion at the point when a likely discovery has been made. Key to the extraction is the drilling of a gas or oil well.

The basic process of drilling a conventional well is deceptively simple, although it has been refined over the decades to become extremely sophisticated, especially as the industry has sought to access ever-more-remote sources and ever-deeper reservoirs of gas and oil. To begin, the drilling firm must first establish a well pad, an area on the surface of the earth where it can locate the well and assemble the equipment necessary for drilling. The required pad area can range from a fraction of an acre up to six acres, depending on the kind of well that is to be drilled.

As the firm drills each section of a well, it lines the well bore with steel casing and cements it into place. The casing keeps the earth from collapsing into the bore. The first piece of casing is the conductor pipe. The drilling proceeds from one section to the next, with each new length of the well bore being drilled with a slightly smaller drill bit. The driller joins the sections by using guiding shoes on each length of casing and cements it all into place. To cement the steel casing into place, the driller pumps cement down through the well bore. The cement reaches the bottom of the well and flows back up around the outside of the casing into the area between the well bore and the outside of the casing, the annulus. The driller also pushes a wiper plug behind the wet cement to cleanse the interior of the casing and to ensure that the cement has flowed out of the last section of casing and back up into the annulus. In the process, the driller uses drilling muds to lubricate the drill bit and make the process easier.

When the driller completes the full length of the casing, there must be a way for the gas or oil to enter the well and rise to the surface. The driller therefore uses a perforator gun to pierce the casings at the depth of the oil or gas resource. These perforations allow the product to enter the well casing and flow to the surface. In the process, the driller has to control the pressure in the well casing to regulate the flow of gas or oil and to prevent blowouts.

In metaphorical terms, the drilling of a conventional gas or oil well amounts essentially to drilling a hole to reach the pooled resource, inserting a straw of casings into the well bore from the surface to the reservoir, and drinking the resource. The process of making the well ready to secure the gas or oil is called *completion*, and the actual securing of the resource is *production*. Securing unconventional gas or oil is more complicated, and the two key production technologies of hydraulic fracturing and horizontal drilling come into play.

Hydraulic Fracturing

No oil or gas reservoir provides a complete separation between the surrounding rock and the gas or oil. Even in the best conventional reservoir, the rock surrounding the pool or gas or oil always contains additional product held in the rock. Near the end of a conventional well's life, the driller can obtain additional gas or oil through the process of hydraulic fracturing or *fracking*.

In hydraulic fracturing, the driller creates hydraulic fracturing fluid, a mixture of water and chemicals, and pumps the fluid down the well under pressure. The pressure exerted by the fluid fractures the rock surrounding the reservoir. Fracturing amounts to opening new pores or cracks in rock that contains the gas or oil and then holding the cracks open with small grains, called proppants, that are mixed in with the fracturing fluid. A *proppant* is a grain of sand or some other material that holds open the fractures in the rock, allowing the gas to escape into the well. With the proppant holding the fractures open, gas or oil can seep out of the rock, flow into the well, and rise to the surface.

Hydraulic fracturing has antecedents in the nineteenth century, when drillers exploded nitroglycerin in hard rock wells to stimulate production. This rude technique was soon surpassed, and drillers have been utilizing hydraulic fracturing in the United States since the 1940s, both for conventional and unconventional wells.[17] Already by the 1950s, there were some months with 3,000 recorded fracturing treatments. According to one estimate, by 2010, there had been 2.5 million fracture treatments worldwide, with a given well receiving more than one fracture treatment in many instances. About 60% of all wells drilled today are being fractured.[18]

Since the early days of hydraulic fracturing, the technologies involved have been constantly revised and improved in effectiveness. There are three essential features of the hydraulic fracturing fluid to consider. In almost all instances, a tremendous proportion of the fluid consists of water. But there are two other essential ingredients. If the fluid can be made to flow more smoothly and quickly into the surrounding rock, it travels further into the rock and requires less pressure from the pumps above. As a result, the fracturing treatment can be more extensive and more effective. As a second element in the fracking fluid, drillers add chemicals to the water to modulate the viscosity of the fluid. With these chemicals, the water becomes effectively "slicker," giving rise to the name "slickwater" fracturing. Other additions to the mix also adjust the viscosity of the fluid to keep the proppants in suspension in the fracturing fluid so they can reach the farthest extent into the rock. One of the primary controversies surrounding hydraulic fracturing focuses on the chemicals added to the water to manage the viscosity of the entire mix. Even though 99% or more of the fluid is typically water, the chemical ingredients can be very nasty, including acids, petroleum compounds, and biocides. Different drillers compete to create the best mix of chemicals to secure the desired results, and different wells in different rock formations require different cocktails to make the best hydraulic fracturing fluid. Chapter 4, "Environmental Costs and Benefits," explores some of these environmental controversies in detail.

The third key ingredient of the hydraulic fracturing fluid, beyond water and viscosity-adjusting chemicals, is the proppant. It is absolutely necessary, as it holds open the cracks created by the fracturing. Initially, and even today, river sand screened to the proper size is the primary proppant, with experiments in differing sand size constituting the technological competition. Matters have also advanced considerably, with drillers employing a variety of materials as proppants, including plastic pellets, steel shot, glass beads, aluminum pellets, nut shells, sintered bauxite, and fused zirconium.[19]

Key to an efficient hydraulic fracturing material is to manage the viscosity to help the fluid travel further into the rock and create more fractures. But the fluid must also be capable of holding the proppants in suspension so that they travel with the fluid into the fractures. In recent years, guar beans and the gum made from them has become an essential ingredient. Guar gum has long been used as an emulsifying agent in foods such as ice cream. But in fracturing fluid, the gum increases the viscosity of the fluid, allowing it to keep the proppant in suspension. Guar beans grow principally in India, with production being highly concentrated in the desert region of Rajasthan.[20] Formerly used as an animal feed and in subsistent human diets, the recently accelerated demand from the energy industry has created a worldwide shortage of guar and driven prices dramatically higher. Between them, the sand proppant and the guar to keep the sand in suspension can constitute three-fourths of the total cost of the hydraulic fracturing.[21] As a result, the profitability of even firms as large as Halliburton has been noticeably reduced due to the run-up in guar prices, and fracking firms are struggling to find a synthetic substitute.[22] Thus, research continues in this area, with new ideas being implemented almost immediately. For example, Shell Oil has developed a fracking fluid that relies on a foam composed largely of carbon dioxide rather than water.[23]

If we think of a conventional well as it appears in Plate 1, the surface area of rock that surrounds the reservoir is small relative to the reservoir itself. As a result, in this situation, hydraulic fracturing can only make a relatively small percentage contribution to the total amount of gas or oil produced. As we see shortly, in an unconventional well, hydraulic fracturing provides the key necessary to producing any gas or oil at all.

Horizontal Drilling

As Plate 1 shows, not all gas and oil collects in compact reservoirs, such as those illustrated in the right-hand and left-hand sides of the figure. For many decades, the energy industry has known of tremendous gas and oil deposits accumulated in horizontal layers of rock, where it has been diffused through sedimentary rock layers such as shale. This gas and oil never percolated up through the surrounding rock to collect in reservoirs accessible with conventional drilling. For a long time, the techniques necessary to produce this shale gas and oil have been elusive.

Horizontal drilling has been a key technology in allowing these resources to be produced, and it is an absolutely essential element in the shale gas (and oil) revolution. The National Petroleum Council goes so far as to suggest defining *unconventional gas* as "natural gas that cannot be produced at economic flow rates nor in economic volumes of natural gas unless the well is stimulated by a large hydraulic fracture treatment, a horizontal wellbore, or by using multilateral wellbores or some other technique to expose more of the reservoir to the wellbore."[24]

Horizontal drilling proceeds by sinking a vertical well partway down to the sedimentary bed, the shale bed, that contains the gas or oil. At this kickoff point, the driller turns the drill bit to enter and traverse the layer of rock that holds the gas or oil. Fully turning the drill pathway to the horizontal requires about 1,000 feet of vertical distances.[25] Even though the process is called *horizontal drilling*, the actual path can be angled, as on the left-hand side of Plate 1. Further, in some instances, called *fishhook drilling*, the path of the well can descend and then turn upward. The middle well illustrated in Plate 1 shows the construction of the completed well path. We have seen that gas and oil wells are encased in steel through the length of the well. Thus, it is clearly a technological tour de force to be able to turn a drill and continue drilling at an angle. The ability to drill horizontally was late to develop and had little practical use without a specific ability to identify the location and depth of the horizontal shale layer containing the gas or oil.

As you have seen, the production of unconventional gas and oil has been made possible by three ingredients. First, any advance required a deep geological knowledge of the location of shale gas and oil deposits, which has been made possible by advances in instrumentation and exploration techniques. Second, the hydraulic fracturing technique might be optional for conventional wells, but essentially all unconventional wells rely on fractures to release the gas or oil. Third, the process of horizontal drilling is essential in order to make the well traverse the shale that contains the embedded gas or oil.

Contrasting Conventional and Unconventional Gas and Oil Production Techniques

The two essential differences between accessing conventional and unconventional wells described previously—hydraulic fracturing and horizontal drilling—imply further differences in the two drilling processes. Table 2.1 provides a summary of these differences. One important difference is the impact on the land. First, the well pad must be larger for an unconventional well. This greater requirement stems largely from the greater amount of water used in hydraulic fracturing. Often the water must be trucked to the well pad from some other source. Further, about 70% of the hydraulic fracturing fluid returns up the well to the surface. As this fluid is generally laced with toxic chemicals, the area of the well pad must have a containment area to hold the fluid until the driller can dispose of it properly. (This returned fracturing fluid is a potential source of serious pollution, as Chapter 4 discusses.) If there is insufficient water already available at the well pad, then the need to truck water to the site and to haul the returned fluid away gives rise to additional road traffic.

Table 2.1 Key Differences Between Conventional and Unconventional Drilling

	Conventional	Unconventional
Well type	Vertical	Horizontal
Well pad footprint	1–3 acres	3–6 acres
Road construction footprint	About 6 acres	About 6 acres
Road traffic	Limited	More extensive
Water required	20,000–80,000 gallons	2–9 million gallons; average 4 million gallons
Chemicals required	Various; perhaps none	Various; surely a variety, almost always some toxic
Drilling time	About 1 month	About 3 months
Hydraulic fracturing	Sometimes	Virtually always
Source rock	Large concentration of resource; easy to extract	Diffused resource scattered through rock; difficult to extract

Source: Adapted from Paleontological Research Institution, "Understanding Drilling Technology," *Marcellus Shale*, January 2012, 6, Table 1, p. 3.

Water requirements differ sharply between conventional and unconventional wells. In all drilling, water carries the drilling mud down the wellbore and smooths the drilling process. While a conventional well might require 50,000 gallons of water, an unconventional well requires about 4 million—or 80 times as much. The extra water in an unconventional well is used for hydraulic fracturing.

As we have seen, the hydraulic fracturing fluid used in unconventional petroleum production requires chemicals in the mix, and these bring with them the risk of environmental damage. By contrast, conventional drilling uses few or even no chemicals that pose ecological hazard. Finally, unconventional production takes longer, due mainly to hydraulic fracturing, so there is more activity for a longer period of time at the drill pad, implying a greater disruption to the surrounding surface area.

Unconventional Gas Resources and Production in the United States

Plate 3 shows the principal unconventional gas and oil resources in the lower 48 U.S. states. They are widely distributed across the continent but tend to occur mostly in a U-shaped arc that runs from Montana down through Texas and then upward along the spine of the Appalachian Mountains into the northeast. Each deposit, typically referred to as a *play*, has its own special characteristics. Four plays deserve special mention and help to illustrate the variety of these resources: the Barnett, Marcellus, Utica, and Bakken plays.

The Barnett Shale lies in north-central Texas and underlies much of the Fort Worth/Dallas metroplex, as shown in Plate 4. (Plate 4 also shows the location of the Eagle Ford Shale, which is discussed in later chapters.) The Barnett Shale has a special historical role because it was the location for the first really viable commercial exploitation of shale gas and provided a proving ground for the techniques of the natural gas revolution. These drilling innovations were pioneered by George Mitchell, a legend in the energy industry and the founder of Mitchell Energy and Development Corporation. Beginning to experiment with shale fracturing in 1982, Mitchell suffered many setbacks but continued working on the problem for 16 years with little success. After initially using heavy gels and nitrogen foams, Mitchell turned to water-based fracturing in the late 1990s, in part to economize on the cost of the fracking agents. Huge success began only in 1998. The techniques pioneered by Mitchell quickly spread and became more intensively exploited in the Barnett and other plays in the United States.[26] As Table 2.2 notes, the Barnett play is at the mature stage of its life, and production is decreasing.[27] Most of the gas withdrawn from the Barnett has been dry gas, meaning that it has little associated natural gas liquids or oil. By 2008, the Barnett had more than 12,000 wells and produced about 44 billion cubic meters (bcm) of gas that year.[28]

Table 2.2 Key Shale Plays and Their Characteristics

Play	Stage	Characteristics	Short-Term Outlook
Barnett	Mature	Mostly dry gas and oil in the Barnett shale combo play	Decreasing
Marcellus	Developing	Mostly dry gas with some liquid	Increasing
Utica	Early	Liquid rich play; associated gas	Flat/slight increase
Bakken	Developing	Oil and liquid rich play with associated gas	Slight increase
Eagle Ford	Developing	Three zones: dry gas, gas condensates, and oil	Increasing

Source: International Energy Agency, "Gas: Medium-Term Market Report 2012," 2012. Adapted and abridged from Table 10, p. 79.

The Marcellus and Utica Shales lie in the northeast, mostly under New York and Pennsylvania, the home of Drake's first well and the petroleum industry in the United States (see Plate 5). These two formations can only be understood together, as the Utica lies under the Marcellus, which is smaller in geographical extent and was developed earlier. The Utica sprawls from southern Quebec south and west, into eastern Ohio, and down the spine of the Appalachians, running all the way into Tennessee. The Marcellus lies at a depth of 2,000 to 7,000 feet below the surface, and the Utica is several thousand feet lower on average, but still ranges from 2,000 to 13,000 feet below the surface.

Exploitation of the Marcellus really started only in 2004 but accelerated rapidly. The geographical extent of the formation is enormous—approximately 100,000 square miles. Estimates of the resource base continue to evolve and remain highly uncertain, but in its 2012 "Annual Energy Outlook," the U.S. Energy Information Administration (USEIA) estimated unproved technically recoverable natural gas as being almost 4 trillion cubic meters. Of course, not all the technically recoverable gas can be economically recovered; nonetheless, this is a truly enormous resource base.[29] As we see in Chapter 3, "Liquid Natural Gas and the World Gas Revolution," the Marcellus Shale has become especially controversial as it underlies some heavily populated regions and has special geological characteristics that frustrate environmental stewardship. While the Marcellus play started to yield only after the Barnett, Marcellus production has ramped up quickly from almost nothing in 2008 to almost 14 bcm in 2010, with estimated reserves twice as large as those in the Barnett play.[30]

Geologists are only now beginning to understand the Utica, and the U.S. Geological Survey released its first estimate of technically recoverable natural gas in the Utica only in the fall of 2012. This first estimate is for slightly more than 1 trillion cubic meters of natural gas, 970 million barrels of unconventional oil, and 208 million barrels of natural gas liquids, contrasted with a contemporaneous estimate of the Marcellus at almost 4 trillion cubic meters of natural gas.[31] Subsequent estimates are sure to fluctuate, but the overall trend in these assessments has been one of upward revisions. To date, production from the Utica has been only modest, but this, too, is sure to expand.

The Bakken Shale, shown in Plate 6, is located in the 300,000-square-mile Williston Basin and centered mainly in western North Dakota and eastern Montana, but it also sprawls into Saskatchewan and Manitoba on the Canadian side of the border. (See Chapter 8 for a more detailed discussion of the Bakken.) The Bakken, like other plays, has its own special characteristics. Whereas the Barnett and Marcellus plays have produced mostly natural gas, the Bakken's special claim to fame is its high proportion of shale oil rather than shale gas. The Bakken also provides an interesting case study on the evolution of resource estimates. In 1995, the U.S. Geological Survey estimated that the Bakken held 151 million barrels of technically recoverable oil. The same estimate for 2008 was about 3.7 billion barrels. Similarly, proved reserves escalated from 573 million to 1.05 billion barrels in a single year from 2008 to 2009. Production of oil in the

Bakken tells an equally dramatic story, escalating from 3,000 barrels per day in 2005 to 225,000 barrels per day in 2010. Recently, North Dakota oil production surpassed that of California and Alaska.[32]

One feature that makes the Bakken so particularly important is its high concentration of oil, which is much more valuable than gas per unit of volume. The Bakken's rich potential was not really appreciated until very recently, and its geographical position is remote from the natural gas pipeline infrastructure. Regrettably, producing oil in the Bakken brings with it significant natural gas that has had no way to reach a market. As a result, a very high proportion of the natural gas being produced in Bakken is being flared away, with a loss of a valuable resource and an increase in emitted greenhouse gases. However, this situation is rapidly changing, as we see in Chapter 8. (Chapter 4 discusses the problem of flaring in some detail.)

As Plate 3 shows, there are many other unconventional plays in the United States, but we may take the Barnett, Marcellus, Utica, and Bakken as exemplifying the range and some of the special characteristics of natural gas plays. Much remains to be learned about these resources, and current estimates of the total potential of the unconventional resources in the continental United States are probably wildly incorrect. One disturbing feature of the unconventional resource experience has been the very substantial decline in the rate of production from a given well. The rate of falloff in production varies from basin to basin and well to well, but it would not be unusual for the production after five years to be less than 20% of the first year's production. However, some believe that these wells can be refractured to restore, or at least approach, previously higher levels of production. Nonetheless, this falloff makes predicting the ultimate recovery of petroleum resources from these plays quite difficult. All in all, however, as time passes, resource estimates for most plays have continued to rise, not fall, even though production for each particular well does seems to fall off quite quickly.

The U.S. Position in Natural Gas

The advent of unconventional oil and gas in general, and the particular discoveries and enhancements in shale gas in particular, have revolutionized the U.S. position in recent years. Figures 2.1 and 2.2 reflect some key effects of this revolution. As Figure 2.1 shows, proved reserves in the United States fell starting in 1970. The discouragement on using natural gas for electricity generation that was in effect from 1978 to 1987, as discussed in Chapter 1, "To the Brink of Innovation," contributed to this falloff by removing incentives for exploration. But even after 1987, reserves were moribund and bumping along a bottom until 2000. Starting in 2000, reserves surged dramatically, increasing by about 90% in a single decade. As the natural gas revolution is in its infancy or perhaps early adolescence, U.S. reserves are almost certain to continue their dramatic growth. Figure 2.2 shows production rates for natural gas in the United States, which hit a low in 2005 and have accelerated dramatically since that time, increasing a full one-third in just the seven years from 2005 to 2012. Further increases in annual production are almost certain to occur over the next decade.

The price of natural gas continues to be a dramatic factor in the evolution of natural gas reserve growth and production rates. After being near an all-time high in June 2008, at $10.79 per thousand cubic feet, prices fell to less than $2.04 in April 2012, before recovering somewhat in 2013 to around $4.00. If prices remain low, say below $4 to $5 per thousand cubic feet, production at many wells will be unattractive, and further exploration will appear to be unrewarding, which will lead to a slowing of growth in reserves. However, the industry and much of the public understands that the United States has tremendous natural gas that is accessible, and we know how to get it when we need it and when prices make its development attractive.

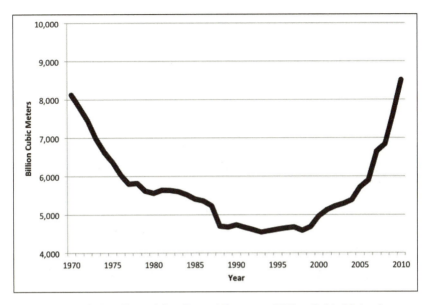

Figure 2.1 U.S. Dry Natural Gas Proved Reserves (Billion Cubic Meters)

Source: USEIA.

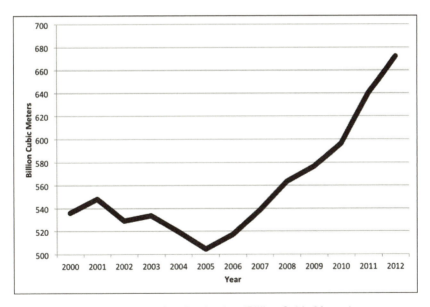

Figure 2.2 U.S. Dry Natural Gas Production (Billion Cubic Meters)

Source: USEIA.

World Natural Gas Resources

While the technology of unconventional petroleum production was almost entirely a creation of the United States, it has surely not escaped world notice. Many nations are now racing to develop their own unconventional resources, or at least to understand them. The geology of the United States is much better understood than that of much of the rest of the world, due in no small part to the more than a century of active exploration and production. While resources elsewhere are not so fully comprehended, there can be no doubt that other geographical locales must be equally blessed. Table 2.3 shows our current understanding of world proved reserves, with 91% being concentrated in the top 20 countries, and with just six countries (Russia, Iran, Qatar, Saudi Arabia, United States, and Turkmenistan) possessing almost 80% of reserves. These amounts are destined to increase and the rankings to change as we learn more about world resources.

Table 2.3 World Natural Gas Reserves

	Proved Reserves (Billion Cubic Meters)	Percentage of World Total
World	186,589	100.00
Top 20 countries	169,593	90.90
Russia	46,962	25.20
Iran	29,239	15.70
Qatar	25,046	13.40
Saudi Arabia	7,687	4.10
United States	7,631	4.10
Turkmenistan	7,408	4.00
United Arab Emirates	6,373	3.40
Nigeria	5,227	2.80
Venezuela	5,004	2.70
Algeria	4,445	2.40

	Proved Reserves (Billion Cubic Meters)	Percentage of World Total
Iraq	3,131	1.70
Australia	3,075	1.60
China	2,991	1.60
Indonesia	2,963	1.60
Kazakhstan	2,376	1.30
Malaysia	2,320	1.20
Egypt	2,152	1.20
Norway	2,013	1.10
Uzbekistan	1,817	1.00
Kuwait	1,761	0.90
Rest of world	16,996	9.10

Source: USEIA, "International Energy Outlook 2011," September 2011, p. 64.

The modest extent of our knowledge about world shale resources is revealed by the title of a publication of the USEIA, "World Shale Gas Resources: An Initial Assessment of 14 Regions Outside the United States," which appeared in April 2011.[33] Due to lack of information, the report excludes enormous swathes of the world: Russia, almost all of the Middle East, virtually all of Africa, and much of Asia. Instead, the assessment focuses on just 32 countries with more reliable, yet still incomplete and partial, information. As shown in Table 2.4, taken together, these countries possess 35.6 bcm of proved reserves, or about 20% of the world's total proved reserves. For these countries, the USEIA estimates total technically recoverable shale reserves as 185,107 bcm. Put slightly differently, the estimate of technically recoverable reserves for these countries just about equals the proved reserves of the entire world. If a somewhat similar ratio were to apply to other areas of the world not included in the assessment, it would imply an even more radically enlarged assessment of resources yet to be discovered. As we learn more, we can only expect the world's proved resources to be increased very substantially, especially as future assessments of shale resources become more reliable.

Table 2.4 33 Countries of the World: Natural Gas Proved Reserves and Technically Recoverable Shale Gas Resources

	Proved Reserves (Billion Cubic Meters)	Technically Recoverable Shale Gas Resources (Billion Cubic Meters)
Europe		
France	6	5,032
Germany	173	224
Netherlands	1,370	475
Norway	2,013	2,320
United Kingdom	252	559
Denmark	59	643
Sweden		1,146
Poland	162	5,227
Turkey	6	419
Ukraine	1,090	1,174
Lithuania		112
Others	76	531
North America		
United States	7,617	24,096
Canada	1,733	10,846
Mexico	335	19,036
Asia		
China	2,991	35,641
India	1,059	1,761
Pakistan	830	1,426
Australia		
	3,075	11,070
Africa		
South Africa		13,557
Libya	1,529	8,106
Tunisia	64	503
Algeria	4,445	6,457
Morocco	3	307
Western Sahara		196
Mauritania	28	

	Proved Reserves (Billion Cubic Meters)	Technically Recoverable Shale Gas Resources (Billion Cubic Meters)
South America		
Venezuela	5,001	307
Colombia	112	531
Argentina	375	21,636
Brazil	361	6,317
Chile	98	1,789
Uruguay		587
Paraguay		1,733
Bolivia	741	1,342
Total of above areas	35,602	185,107
Total world	184,744	

Source: Adapted and corrected from USEIA, "World Shale Gas Resources: An Initial Assessment of 14 Regions Outside the United States," April 2011, p. 4.

Notes

1. Amy Myers Jaffe, "Shale Gas Will Rock the World," *Wall Street Journal*, May 10, 2010; and "The Americas, Not the Middle East, Will Be the World Capital of Energy," *Foreign Policy*, September/October 2011.

2. International Energy Agency, "Are We Entering a Golden Age of Gas?" *World Energy Outlook*, 2011.

3. Martin Wolf, "Prepare for a Golden Age of Gas," *Financial Times*, February 21, 2012; and Tom Gjelten, "The Dash for Gas: The Golden Age of an Energy Game-Changer," *World Affairs Journal*, January 21, 2012.

4. Clifford Krauss, "Can We Do without the Mideast?" *New York Times*, March 30, 2011; and Clifford Krauss and Eric Lipton, "U.S. Is Inching Toward Elusive Goal of Energy Independence," *New York Times*, March 22, 2012.

5. Stephen Moore, "How North Dakota Became Saudi Arabia," *Wall Street Journal*, October 1, 2011. See also Brian Milner, "'Saudi America' Heads for Energy Independence," *Globe and Mail*, March 19, 2012.

6. Ed Morse, "Move Over, OPEC—Here We Come," *Wall Street Journal*, March 19, 2012.

7. Steve Levine, "Is This Group Think, or Is the U.S. about to Be Energy-Independent?" *Foreign Policy*, November 2, 2011; and Citigroup, "Resurging North American Oil Production and the Death of the Peak Oil Hypothesis: The United States' Long March Toward Energy Independence," February 15, 2012.

8. Wolf Richter, "Natural Gas Is Pushing Coal Over the Cliff," *Business Insider*, August 21, 2012; and Testosteronepit.com, "Natural Gas and the Brutal Dethroning of King Coal," August 15, 2012.

9. For recent scientific investigations of natural gas at Delphi, see J. Z. de Boerl, J. R. Hale, and J. Chanton, "New Evidence for the Geological Origins of the Ancient Delphic Oracle (Greece)," *Geology*, August 2001, pp. 707–710; G. Etiope, G. G. Papatheodorou, D. Christodoulou, M. Geraga, and P. Favali, "The Geological Links of the Ancient Delphic Oracle (Greece): A Reappraisal of Natural Gas Occurrence and Origin," *Geology*, October 2006;34:821–824; and Luigi Piccardi, Cassandra Monti, Orlando Vaselli, Franco Tassi, Kalliopi Gaki-Papanastassiou, and Dimitris Papanastassiou, "Scent of a Myth: Tectonics, Geochemistry, and Geomythology at Delphi (Greece)," *Journal of the Geological Society*, January 2008;165:5–18.

10. Plutarch writes: "I think, then, that the exhalation is not in the same state all the time, but that it has recurrent periods of weakness and strength. Of the proof on which I depend, I have as witnesses many foreigners and all the officials and servants at the shrine. It is a fact that the room in which they seat those who would consult the god is filled, not frequently or with any regularity, but as it may chance from time to time, with a delightful fragrance coming on a current of air which bears it towards the worshippers, as if its source were in the holy of holies; and it is like the odour which the most exquisite and costly perfumes send forth." *Moralia*, pp. 495–497. (This translation is from the 1936 Loeb Classical Library edition.   Available   at   http://penelope.uchicago.edu/Thayer/E/Roman/Texts/ Plutarch/Moralia/De_defectu_oraculorum°.html.)

11. This account of the early commercialization of natural gas in Great Britain and the United States relies on Naturalgas.org, "History," www.naturalgas.org/ overview/history.asp. Accessed September 5, 2012.

12. Thomas Leslie, "'As Large as the Situation of the Columns Would Allow': Building Cladding and Plate Glass in the Chicago Skyscraper, 1885–1905," *Technology and Culture*, April 2008;49:399–419.

13. See USEIA, "Estimated Natural Gas Pipeline Mileage in the Lower 48 States, Close of 2008," www.eia.gov/pub/oil_gas/natural_gas/analysis_publications/ ngpipeline/mileage.html.

14. The U.S. Department of Energy defines *tight gas* as "natural gas trapped in a hardrock, sandstone, or limestone formation that is relatively impermeable." U.S. Department of Energy, "Modern Shale Gas Development in the United States: A Primer," April 2009, p. 84.

15. The National Petroleum Council adopted a definition of unconventional gas as "natural gas that cannot be produced at economic flow rates nor in economic

volumes of natural gas unless the well is stimulated by a large hydraulic fracture treatment, a horizontal wellbore, or by using multilateral wellbores or some other technique to expose more of the reservoir to the wellbore." National Petroleum Council, "Unconventional Gas," Topic Paper #29, July 18, 2007, p. 5.

16. U.S. Department of Energy, "New Methane Hydrate Research: Investing in Our Energy Future," August 31, 2012, p. 1.

17. Brad Plumer, "Will the U.S. Export Fracking to the Rest of the World?" *Washington Post*, July 21, 2012.

18. Carl T. Montgomery and Michael B. Smith, "Hydraulic Fracturing: History of an Enduring Technology," *Journal of Petroleum Technology*, December 2010; 26–32. See p. 27.

19. Carl T. Montgomery and Michael B. Smith, "Hydraulic Fracturing: History of an Enduring Technology," *Journal of Petroleum Technology*, December 2010; 26–32. See p. 28.

20. Gardiner Harris, "In Tiny Bean, India's Dirt-Poor Farmers Strike Gas-Drilling Gold," *New York Times*, July 16, 2012.

21. Braden Reddall, "Frackers in Frantic Search for Guar Bean Substitutes," Reuters.com, August 13, 2012.

22. See Gardiner Harris, "In Tiny Bean, India's Dirt-Poor Farmers Strike Gas-Drilling Gold," *New York Times*, July 16, 2012. See also Andrew Callus, "Schlumberger's Clever Frack Takes Aim at Gas Costs," Reuters.com, August 31, 2012.

23. Naturalgasasia.com, "Shell Fracking with Foam," August 15, 2012.

24. National Petroleum Council, "Unconventional Gas," Topic Paper #29, July 18, 2007, p. 5.

25. See Paleontological Research Institution, "Understanding Drilling Technology," *Marcellus Shale*, January 2012, p. 6. This document provides an excellent and more extended discussion of drilling technologies upon which my brief account largely relies.

26. Russell Gold, "The Man Who Pioneered the Shale-Gas Revolution," *Wall Street Journal*, October 23, 2012. See also Martin Wolf, "Prepare for a Golden Age of Gas," *Financial Times*, February 21, 2012; and Daniel Yergin, "Stepping on the Gas," *Wall Street Journal*, April 2, 2011. Even though all observers appear to recognize the key role played by George Mitchell, the ultimate allocation of credit for the shale revolution remains somewhat controversial, with some claiming total success for private initiative, while others stress the constructive role of federal financing. See Alex Trembath, Jesse Jenkins, Ted Nordhaus, and Michael Shellenberger, "Where the Shale Gas Revolution Came From: Government's Role in the Development of Hydraulic Fracturing in Shale," Breakthrough Institute, May 2012.

27. However, part of this decrease in production may be due to slower development, which stems at least somewhat from recently low prices of natural gas.

28. Howard Rogers, "Shale Gas: The Unfolding Story," *Oxford Review of Economic Policy*, 2011;27:117–143. See p. 127.

29. USEIA, "Annual Energy Outlook 2012," June 2012, p. 64.

30. USEIA, "U.S. Crude Oil, Natural Gas, and Natural Gas Liquids Proved Reserves, 2010," August 2012, p. 6.

31. U.S. Geological Survey, "USGS Releases First Assessment of Shale Gas Resources in the Utica Shale: 38 Trillion Cubic Feet," October 4, 2012.

32. Institute for Energy Research, "Bakken Formation Fact Sheet," 2012.

33. USEIA, "World Shale Gas Resources: An Initial Assessment of 14 Regions Outside the United States," April 2011.

3

Liquid Natural Gas and the World Gas Revolution

The paradox of natural gas is its great value for human use coupled with its low economic value per unit of volume, especially compared to oil. A barrel of oil consists of 42 gallons or 5.6 cubic feet. But the energy in one barrel of oil has the same energy as 5,659 cubic feet of natural gas at room temperature. This implies that crude oil has about 1,000 times as much energy as the same volume of natural gas. Oil has high, and natural gas has low, *energy density*—the amount of energy per unit of volume. This fact has enormous implications for the uses of energy in these two forms and for the transportation feasibility of natural gas. The low-energy density of natural gas makes *liquid natural gas* (LNG) critical; LNG dramatically increases the energy density of natural gas and makes transporting gas long distances economically feasible.

As oil tankers around the world give ample evidence, a worldwide seaborne trade carries oil, with much of the world's crude resources flowing out of the Persian Gulf region. By contrast, because of its energy density, natural gas in its gaseous state is uneconomical to transport except via pipeline. Therefore, there has never been a worldwide transportation network for natural gas in its gaseous state. As a further consequence, natural gas has traded in highly localized markets, and gas prices can be wildly different across geographical regions. These market characteristics contrast very strongly with a more-or-less common world price for crude oil, with geographical price differentials being essentially due to differences in transportation costs (and taxes, of course).

The scenario described in the previous paragraph is now changing dramatically due to developments in the liquefaction of natural gas into LNG. When natural gas is cooled to –260 degrees Fahrenheit, the gas liquefies, and its volume shrinks by a factor of approximately 600. With this transformation, the energy value of a barrel of LNG is about 60% of the value of a barrel of oil. This closing of the differential in the value per unit of volume makes transporting LNG much more economically feasible than transporting natural gas in its gaseous state.

The process of liquefaction has enormous implications for world energy commerce and energy markets. Consider the case of Japan, for instance. Japan possesses essentially no natural gas of its own and imports 100% of its natural gas as LNG, making the LNG chain critical to Japan's energy acquisition. After the disaster at the Fukushima nuclear plant in 2011, Japan shuttered its nuclear plants and turned to natural gas to provide a much larger proportion of its electrical power generation. This example shows how critical LNG can be for some nations, and this chapter explores the development of the LNG infrastructure and its implications for the emerging future of natural gas.

Creating and Shipping LNG

At room temperature, natural gas is a vapor, consisting of a mix of hydrocarbons. The primary constituent is methane, the compound that we normally think of as natural gas. However, other related compounds are typically present as well, including ethane, propane, butane, and pentane. Different naturally occurring deposits have different mixes of these compounds. Methane typically accounts for a little more than 80% of the natural gas as it comes out of the ground, and at this percentage, the mix of different constituents is called "wet gas." These gases have different temperatures at which they become vapors or liquids, as Table 3.1 shows. These related compounds consist of hydrogen and carbon atoms, but the number of atoms of each element differs. Gases with more carbon atoms are heavier and have higher boiling points. Methane has the fewest carbon atoms, giving it the lowest boiling point.

Table 3.1 Boiling and Melting Point of Gases (Degrees Fahrenheit)

Gas	Boiling Point	Melting Point
Methane	−260	−297
Ethane	−126	−278
Propane	−44	−306
Butane	+31	−217
Pentane	+97	−201
Water	+212	+32

Source: Bill White, "The Cold Facts about a Hot Commodity: LNG," oildrum.com, October 4, 2012.

If the entire mix of gases constituting wet gas was chilled until methane liquefied, the resulting mix would be a mess that has been characterized as a "slush slurry of product that would muck up the machinery."[1] The pentane, butane, ethane, and propane are natural gas liquids (NGLs), and they are actually a positive feature of the wet gas as it comes from the ground. While the wet gas needs to be purified to increase the proportion of methane, these other compounds can have considerable value if they are present in the wet gas in sufficient proportions.

Plate 7 shows the essential steps in converting wet gas into *dry gas*—gas that is essentially composed of almost only methane. First, the gas is precleaned to remove undesired impurities, such as hydrogen sulfide, carbon dioxide, mercury, and mercaptans (a volatile sulfur compound that smells like rotting cabbage but that is sometimes even found in wine).[2] After pretreatment, the next step is the removal of water from the wet gas. At this point, the gas is ready for chilling to start bringing off the various gases and converting them to liquids, based on their different boiling points. We can think of the basic process as cooling through a very aggressive air-conditioning process. Often some of the NGLs are used to fuel the refrigeration system for chilling the gas, and this consumes about 10% to 15% of the product. If present in sufficient quantities, the various NGLs are captured for sale. As the temperature of the natural gas falls and the various NGLs are siphoned off, the remaining gas becomes almost entirely composed of methane, even though small quantities of other gases remain in the mix; the mix is now called "dry gas." The typical composition of LNG is 91% methane, 6% ethane, and very small portions of other gases, such as helium. (Consumers in Japan and Europe like a bit of ethane in the LNG mix because it makes the gas burn hotter when it is reconverted into gas for ultimate consumption.) The entire sequence of machinery for converting wet gas into LNG is called a *train*, and a typical liquefaction plant often runs several trains simultaneously. Constructing an LNG liquefaction terminal is extremely expensive, ranging from $1,000 to $4,000 per tonne of LNG production capacity.[3] One estimate of the cost of liquefying natural gas pegs it at $1.15 per 1 thousand cubic feet, a cost that reflects the capital costs of plant construction, unavoidable occasional slack in the plant's capacity, and taxes and operating costs.[4]

The understanding of natural gas developed more than 100 years ago, principally in Europe, as an outgrowth of the study of cryogenics, with pioneers in the field being Carl von Linde from Germany and Heike Kamerlingh Onnes from Holland. Much of the technology for liquefying gas developed because of a need for helium for World War I airships. Wet natural gas contains very small proportions of helium—around 1%, depending on the gas field. As a byproduct of extracting helium from natural gas, the U.S. Bureau of Mines produced the first liquid methane in 1924.

The commercialization of LNG dates to 1941, when the East Ohio Gas Company built the first commercial LNG plant, which could process 4 million cubic feet of gas per day into LNG. Here the idea was not to transport the LNG but to store it in insulated tanks to have extra supplies of gas to meet peak heating needs in winter. However, with wartime metals being scarce, the company built its fourth storage tank from inferior metals, and the tank failed in 1944, spilling more than 1 million gallons of LNG. Some of the LNG flowed into sewers, and some found its way into the basements of homes. As the LNG warmed, it turned to gas and eventually ignited, killing 128 people and making 14,000 homeless. Not surprisingly, this disaster rendered the LNG industry dormant for quite a few years. This disaster has made the LNG industry quite safety conscious, and the industry has an excellent safety record on the whole, although there was a fire and a single death at a regasification plant in Maryland in 1979, and an explosion at a liquefaction plant in Algeria in 2004 that killed 27 people.[5]

By the late 1950s, the energy industry was testing the process of carrying LNG by special tanker ships. In 1959, a test shipment traveled from Louisiana to England. The first commercial LNG shipped from Algeria to Canvey Island, an LNG terminal near the mouth of the Thames. The LNG was carried on a purpose-built ship, the *Methane Princess*, which carried LNG equivalent to about 500 million cubic feet of natural gas. The destination for LNG shipments is typically a regasification plant and storage facility. When it reaches its destination, the LNG can be pumped into storage and then used as demand warrants to produce natural gas and to feed natural gas pipelines. Compared to the liquefaction process, regasification is relatively simple. The LNG is allowed to warm under controlled temperature and pressure, and then the gas feeds into a natural gas pipeline. The cost of a regasification plant is only about 10% to 20% of the cost of a comparably sized liquefaction plant.[6]

The LNG Industry

In the 50 years since the first commercial shipment, the LNG industry has flourished and matured, despite its slow initial development. In 1980, there were only five LNG importing and five LNG exporting countries. Table 3.2 shows the countries that currently export LNG, led by Qatar, which accounted for 31% of world exports in 2011. Despite having the world's largest natural gas reserves, Russia occupies only the middle rank among world exporters. Even though the United States was a net importer of natural gas in 2011, it exported a small amount of LNG from Alaska to Japan. Belgium and Spain are also net natural gas importers, but they re-export very small quantities of LNG.

Table 3.2 2011 LNG Exports, Ranked by Total Amount Exported

Exporting Nation	2011 LNG Exports (bcm)
Qatar	102.60
Malaysia	33.26
Indonesia	29.15
Australia	25.93
Nigeria	25.89
Trinidad and Tobago	18.88
Algeria	17.12
Russian Federation	14.39
Oman	10.92
Brunei	9.39
Yemen	8.94
Egypt	8.58
United Arab Emirates	7.96
Equatorial Guinea	5.27
Peru	5.12
Norway	3.97
United States	2.02
Spain	0.74
Belgium	0.61

Exporting Nation	2011 LNG Exports (bcm)
Libya	0.08
Total world exports	330.82

Source: BP, "Statistical Review of World Energy," June 2012.
Note: The United States, Belgium, and Spain re-export a small portion of the LNG that they import.
Note: bcm = billion cubic meters.

Table 3.3 presents information on LNG importing nations, the complement to the exporting countries. Table 3.3 ranks countries in descending order by the proportion of their natural gas consumption that arrives as LNG. The East Asian economic powerhouses of South Korea, Taiwan, and Japan are striking in that they consume large amounts of natural gas and depend entirely on LNG imports for their supply. (The LNG dependence in excess of 100% means that these countries imported more than they consumed in 2011, adding the excess to storage.) A number of major European countries also depend heavily on LNG imports, with Spain, France, and the United Kingdom all acquiring more than 30% of their natural gas supplies as LNG. While the United States is the world's ninth largest importer of LNG, these supplies constitute less than 2% of annual consumption. China is an even larger importer of LNG, but LNG accounts for only 13% of China's demand for natural gas, which is relatively small, given the size of its economy. Not surprisingly, China anxiously seeks new supplies of natural gas, as discussed more fully in Chapter 5, "The United States and China."

Table 3.3 2011 LNG Imports, Ranked by LNG Dependence

Importing Country	Total LNG Imports (bcm)	Total Consumption (bcm)	LNG Dependence (% of Total Gas Consumption)
South Korea	49.31	46.60	105.81
Taiwan	16.31	15.50	105.21
Japan	106.95	105.50	101.37
Spain	24.16	32.10	75.26

Importing Country	Total LNG Imports (bcm)	Total Consumption (bcm)	LNG Dependence (% of Total Gas Consumption)
Chile	3.86	5.30	72.82
Portugal	3.01	5.10	59.06
Belgium	6.57	16.10	40.82
France	14.57	40.30	36.14
United Kingdom	25.31	80.20	31.56
Greece	1.29	4.50	28.76
India	17.10	61.10	27.99
Kuwait	3.18	16.20	19.60
Turkey	6.23	45.70	13.63
China	16.62	130.70	12.72
Italy	8.75	71.30	12.27
Argentina	4.38	46.50	9.42
Mexico	4.05	68.90	5.87
Brazil	1.05	26.70	3.93
Canada	3.30	104.80	3.14
United Arab Emirates	1.43	62.90	2.27
Thailand	0.98	46.60	2.10
Netherlands	0.78	38.10	2.06
United States	10.01	690.10	1.45
Dominican Republic	0.91	N/A	N/A
Puerto Rico	0.74	N/A	N/A
Natural Gas Imports by Region			
Asia Pacific	207.26	590.6	35.09
Europe and Eurasia	90.67	1101.1	8.23
South and Central America	10.94	154.5	7.08
North America	17.35	863.8	2.01
Middle East	4.60	403.1	1.14
Africa	N/A	109.8	N/A
Total world	330.83	3,222.9	10.26

Source: BP, "Statistical Review of World Energy," June 2012.

Note: Dependence above 100% implies an increase in stocks of gas for 2011.

Tables 3.2 and 3.3 provide a useful snapshot of the world LNG exports and imports, but it is also important to see how the industry has evolved and to gain some insight into its future prospects. Table 3.4 shows the major LNG exporters and importers 10 years previously, in 2001, with a major participant being defined as an exporter or importer of LNG exceeding 5 billion cubic meters (bcm) of equivalent gas for the year. From 2001 to 2011, world LNG trade rose from 143 to 331 bcm, increasing by a factor of 2.3. When we focus on exporters, we see that Indonesia led the world in 2001 but that its LNG exports actually fell slightly by 2011, reflecting the very significant drawdown in Indonesian resources. The change in Algerian exports shows a similar story.

Table 3.4 Major Exporters and Importers of LNG in 2001

Major Exporters		Major Importers	
Country	Quantity (bcm)	Country	Quantity (bcm)
Indonesia	31.80	Japan	74.07
Algeria	25.54	South Korea	21.83
Malaysia	20.91	France	10.45
Qatar	16.54	Spain	9.84
Australia	10.20	Taiwan	6.30
Brunei	9.00	Italy	5.25
Nigeria	7.83		
Oman	7.43		
United Arab Emirates	7.08		
World LNG trade	142.95		

Source: BP, "Statistical Review of World Energy," June 2002.
Note: Qualification as a major exporter or importer is LNG exceeding 5 bcm for the year.

For LNG, the important current story is the rise of Qatar to preeminence as its exports soared from 16.54 to 102.60 bcm over the decade. Qatar draws its natural gas principally from the conventional gas reservoir that constitutes both the South Pars Field and the North

Field that straddle the Persian Gulf from the shoreline of Qatar to that of Iran (see Plate 8). But the development of Qatari LNG has been a decades-long struggle. For example, during the Iran–Iraq war, both nations attacked oil tankers in the Persian Gulf, and shippers had little interest in sending LNG tankers to load Qatari LNG. The eventual ascent of Qatari LNG was due to persistence as well as financing from Japan, which became a principal customer for Qatari LNG.[7] Australia occupied the fifth position as an LNG exporter in 2001 and ranked fourth in 2011, but over the decade, it expanded its exports by a factor of 2.5. Australia deserves special mention as an LNG exporter because it possesses major shale resources and is very actively expanding its LNG export capacity, as discussed more fully in Chapter 7, "The Other Contending Nations." Nigeria also dramatically expanded its LNG exports over the decade, more than tripling its volume and moving from seventh to fifth position.

Also interesting are countries that exported little or no LNG in 2001 but that have become significant players in world exports. Russia only began exporting LNG in 2009 and now is the world's eighth largest exporter, with plans to become the world's dominant exporter. For example, Russia has already sent an LNG tanker through the Arctic Northern Sea Route to test its feasibility, and it is accelerating the development of its LNG facilities in the far eastern island of Sakhalin. Trinidad and Tobago was a minor exporter in 2001, exporting 3.65 bcm; it expanded exports by a factor of more than five over the decade to become the world's sixth largest exporter in 2011. The import side shows more stability, but still with some dramatic changes. South Korea, Japan, and Taiwan already depended heavily on LNG imports in 2001, and they remain intensive importers. France, Spain, and the United Kingdom still depend very significantly on LNG imports. However, India and China have had the most dramatic changes. Neither nation imported LNG in 2001, yet they have become very major importers, and they occupied the fifth and sixth positions for total LNG imports in 2011.

These developments in the trade of LNG have also been accompanied by a maturation of the technology for liquefying and distributing natural gas. For example, the size of LNG trains has increased by a factor of almost 10 over the past 50 years, and in the past 25 years, the cost of building a liquefaction plant has fallen by 50%.

The LNG Infrastructure Today

We have seen that the LNG business has matured. A number of nations have come to depend on LNG exports as a major source of revenue; Qatar is most notable in this regard. Some nations, especially Japan, South Korea, and Taiwan, depend almost totally on LNG imports for their natural gas needs.

Table 3.5 gives further detail about the worldwide distribution of LNG liquefaction capacity, with 18 countries contributing to the total liquefaction capacity of 340 bcm per year. Currently, as Table 3.6 shows, 23 countries possess regasification facilities, with world regasification capacity exceeding world liquefaction capacity by a factor of 2.5. Clearly, much of the world's regasification capacity is idle each year, but these facilities still serve as standby facilities to help compensate for inadequate domestic resources. The two lists of 18 countries in Table 3.5 and 23 countries in Table 3.6 are virtually unique—only the United States possesses both liquefaction and regasification capacities. Of the 40 countries with capacity to participate in the LNG market, almost all are poised either to export or import LNG, not both.

Table 3.5 World LNG Liquefaction Terminals

Country	Number of Trains	Total Capacity (bcm per Year)
Algeria	14	27.5
Australia	6	26.9
Brunei	3	9.8

Country	Number of Trains	Total Capacity (bcm per Year)
Egypt	4	16.6
Equatorial Guinea	2	5.0
Indonesia	12	36.8
Libya	2	0.8
Malaysia	6	30.9
Nigeria	4	29.5
Norway	2	5.8
Oman	2	14.6
Peru	2	6.1
Qatar	18	94.1
Russia	2	13.0
Trinidad and Tobago	4	20.5
United Arab Emirates	3	7.6
United States	3	1.9
Yemen	2	9.1
World total	86	340

Source: International Energy Agency, "Natural Gas Information, 2011," 2012, p. II.60.

Table 3.6 World LNG Regasification Terminals

Country	Number of Vaporizers	Total Capacity (bcm per Year)
Argentina	6	3.2
Belgium	11	9.5
Brazil	4	7.9
Canada	8	10.6
Chile	6	6.0
China	7	13.4
Dominican Republic	2	2.4
Dubai	–	3.2
France	30	25.1
Greece	6	5.3

Country	Number of Vaporizers	Total Capacity (bcm per Year)
India	24	16.8
Italy	9	11.9
Japan	235	264.2
Korea	78	110.0
Kuwait	–	7.5
Mexico	11	19.1
Portugal	5	5.5
Puerto Rico	2	4.0
Spain	43	63.3
Taiwan	22	33.8
Turkey	12	12.9
United Kingdom	35	53.9
United States	87	157.9
World total	643	847

Source: International Energy Agency, "Natural Gas Information, 2011," 2012, p. II.58.

Table 3.7 shows new liquefaction plants under construction, and Table 3.8 lists countries building new import capacity. Only five countries are now building liquefaction capacity, with Australia being the dominant participant, constructing more than 70% of total new world capacity. Taken together, these projects will expand world liquefaction capacity by almost one-third. On the import side, as shown in Table 3.8, there are currently 28 regasification projects under construction, scattered across 15 nations, with China, India, and France accounting for 40% of the capacity under construction. Total world regasification capacity will increase by 14%. Comparing the export capacity under construction from Table 3.7 with the import capacity being built per Table 3.8 shows that regasification capacity will continue to exceed liquefaction capability.

Table 3.7 Liquefaction Plants Under Construction

Country	Number of Projects	Total Capacity (bcm per Year)
Algeria	2	12.7
Angola	1	7.2
Australia	14	70.7
Indonesia	1	2.8
Papua New Guinea	2	9.1
World total	20	102.4

Source: International Gas Union, "World LNG Report 2011," June 2012, p. 55.

Table 3.8 LNG Regasification Plants Under Construction

Country	Number of Projects	Total Capacity (bcm per Year)
Argentina	1	5.1
China	6	18.9
France	1	13.0
India	5	15.0
Indonesia	1	4.1
Israel	1	2.5
Italy	1	3.7
Japan	3	8.8
Korea	1	9.4
Malaysia	1	5.5
Mexico	1	5.1
Poland	1	5.0
Portugal	1	2.8
Singapore	2	8.3
Spain	2	11.5
World total	28	118.7

Source: International Gas Union, "World LNG Report 2011," June 2012, p. 58.

As we have seen, the United States is a minor player in the world LNG trade, being quite predominately an LNG importer. Table 3.9 shows the position of the United States in world LNG trade. It has a single liquefaction plant in Kenai, Alaska, through which it makes modest exports to Japan. The 13 existing regasification plants in the United States are concentrated in the Gulf Coast region, especially in Texas and Louisiana, but Georgia, Maryland, and Massachusetts also host regasification plants. These regasification plants feed the extensive natural gas pipeline network of the continental United States. The regasification plant in Puerto Rico serves only the island and does not connect to the rest of the U.S. system.

Table 3.9 LNG Export and Import Facilities of the United States

Existing LNG Terminals		
Export	**Import**	
Kenai, AK	Everett, MA	Freeport, TX
	Cove Point, MD	Sabine, LA
	Elba Island, GA	Hackberry, LA
	Lake Charles, LA	Sabine Pas, TX
	Gulf of Mexico	Pascagoula, MS
	Offshore Boston (2)	Peñuelas, PR
Approved LNG Terminals		
Export (Under Construction)	**Import (Not Under Construction)**	
Sabine, LA	Freeport, TX	
	Port Lavaca, TX	
	Baltimore, MD	
LNG Terminals Proposed to the Federal Energy Regulatory Commission		
Export		**Import**
Freeport, TX	Hackberry, LA	Robbinston, ME
Corpus Christi, TX	Cove Point, MD	Astoria, OR
Coos Bay, OR		Corpus Christi, TX
Lake Charles, LA	Astoria, OR	
	Lavaca Bay, TX	

Sources: Federal Energy Regulatory Commission, "North American LNG Import/Export Terminals: Existing," December 5, 2012; Federal Energy Regulatory Commission, "North American LNG Import/Export Terminals: Approved," December 5, 2012; and Federal Energy Regulatory Commission, "North American LNG Import/Export Terminals: Proposed/Potential," December 5, 2012, available at http://ferc.gov/industries/gas/indus-act/lng.asp.

To be able to build an LNG plant requires a permit from the Federal Energy Regulatory Commission (FERC). There is one LNG liquefaction plant currently under construction in Sabine, Louisiana. Interestingly, this plant was built originally as a regasification plant, but it is now being converted to a liquefaction plant, with an eye to exports. Three regasification plants are permitted but are not yet under construction. Almost certainly these will never be built as regasification plants, but there is interest in converting them to liquefaction plants. There are eight proposed, but not approved, liquefaction plants, and three regasification plants in the same situation. Almost certainly, these regasification plants will never be built either. Finally, some of the existing regasification plants may eventually be converted to liquefaction plants.

The statistics from Table 3.9 on the LNG plants of the United States tell the compelling story of the shale gas revolution in the United States as well as any simple example can. Consider this quotation from the 2005 edition of the "Annual Energy Outlook," published each year by the U.S. Energy Information Administration (USEIA): "In the reference case [the most likely case], the United States is expected to become increasingly dependent on LNG, with imports projected to increase from 0.4 trillion cubic feet in 2003 to 6.4 trillion cubic feet in 2025."[8] By contrast, the 2012 edition of the same publication estimated that the United States will be exporting 25.5 bcm of natural gas by 2020.[9] Just one year later, the same USEIA publication changed the date for beginning exports from 2020 to 2016, and it predicted exports of 7.4 bcm for 2020. However, the prospect of the United States exporting gas is currently quite controversial and has become a highly politicized dispute.

The Potential for Exports of U.S. Natural Gas

The shale gas revolution in the United States has presented the nation with the problem of natural gas in quantities that far exceed what has been necessary for its use historically. However, worthy additional uses abound. First, natural gas as a fuel for electrical power generation could be expanded. Second, natural gas is an important feedstock for industry, particularly for pharmaceuticals and fertilizer, and many companies want to expand its use for this purpose. Compared to prices in many nations, natural gas has become quite inexpensive in the United States, and many manufacturers beyond the pharmaceutical and fertilizer industries hunger for inexpensive natural gas as a source of competitive advantage compared to producers in other nations. Third, natural gas is becoming an attractive fuel for vehicles, especially for companies that run large fleets. Fourth, owners of natural gas are anxious to begin exporting natural gas as LNG. Of course, these four applications of the new natural gas bounty all compete for the same resource.

As a source fuel for electrical power generation, natural gas is much cheaper than coal, and it is about 50% to 60% less polluting.[10] (This claim abstracts from the environmental costs of securing natural gas or coal, which Chapter 4, "Environmental Costs and Benefits," addresses.) Before the Arab Oil Boycott of 1973–1974, oil was widely used to generate electricity, and coal use was declining. Natural gas generated nearly 30% of electrical power, but it was used mainly in Texas, Louisiana, and Oklahoma due to federal price controls. After the Carter administration banned the use of natural gas for electrical power generation, the use of coal increased into the late 1980s, until those restrictions were abandoned piecemeal from 1987 to 1989. Coal's share of power generation approached its peak of 80% of all fossil-fuel electrical generation in 1989, but it has been declining since then. By the end of 2012, natural gas and coal were at parity, each producing about 32% of total U.S. electricity, with gas expected to surpass coal imminently.[11]

Ironically, as the U.S. use of natural gas for power generation has grown quickly, Europe has been using less natural gas and more coal for power generation. This is apparently due to the European Union

Emission Trading Scheme for emission allowances that helps to make coal cheaper than natural gas. Some major European utilities are closing their natural-gas-fired plants.[12] By contrast, in the United States, the total cost of electrical generation is cheapest when fueled by natural gas, so the United States is building almost only gas-fired generating capacity.[13] Between 2011 and 2015, the United States is expected to have built 258 new gas-fired plants.[14] Around the world, however, coal continues to grow as a fuel for electrical power generation. Globally traded coal used in power generation doubled during the first decade of this century, and most observers expect this trend to persist and generate continuing harm to the environment.[15] If other nations can replicate the success of the U.S. shale gas industry, they may be able to avert this fate.

In the industrial sector, natural gas provides 35% of total energy, mostly focused on manufacturing in the chemical, food, paper, metals and minerals, and petroleum and coal products industries.[16] Manufacturing mainly uses natural gas for heating, but it also serves as a primary feedstock for the production of ammonia and hydrogen. In addition, some natural gas is converted to ethane and propane, which serve as feedstock for manufacturing various chemical products, including a variety of plastics.[17]

Cheap natural gas in the United States is helping to revitalize the rust belt: "Plunging prices have turned the U.S. into one of the most profitable places in the world to make chemicals and fertilizer, industries that use gas as both a feedstock and an energy source. And they have slashed costs for makers of energy-intensive products such as aluminum, steel, and glass."[18] Price is critical, as natural gas accounts for about 70% of the cost of producing fertilizer and 25% of the cost for many plastics. Dow Chemical is building a multibillion-dollar plant in Freeport, Texas, to convert natural gas into plastics. Royal Dutch Shell plans a similar plant near Pittsburgh. Chevron and Formosa Plastics have similar large-scale investment plans.[19] From 1998 to 2004, producers closed many U.S. fertilizer plants and sent some of their equipment overseas. New plants are now being constructed.[20] The new low prices for natural gas are so beneficial to the economy that the *Financial Times* opines that low energy costs will add 1% growth to U.S. gross domestic product (GDP) over the next decade and that shale gas will fuel a general economic boom in the United States.[21]

Natural gas can be used as a vehicle fuel as LNG or as *compressed natural gas* (CNG). In May 2012 there were 1,047 CNG fueling stations and 53 LNG stations in the United States, many privately owned by large vehicle fleet operators. This compares to more than 150,000 stations that sell gasoline.[22] There is a movement to build out a more adequate natural gas refueling infrastructure, particularly along interstate highway corridors, but it is clearly a nascent project with an uncertain future. The service station companies Pilot and Flying J are adding LNG tanks at more than 100 truck stops, with the aim of providing coast-to-coast refueling stops by the end of 2013. The first movers to natural gas for transportation are large fleets, with Waste Management, AT&T, Frito Lay, and United Parcel Service already operating fleets powered by natural gas. Navistar, Cummins, and GM are all offering trucks powered by natural gas.[23] The potential cost savings are huge, as trucks powered by natural gas cost about 40% less per mile to operate.

All these important uses for natural gas—generating electricity, fueling industry, powering vehicles—are critically important and are sharp competitors to the idea of exporting LNG. Not surprisingly, there are strong advocates for using U.S. natural gas domestically and for banning exports. Partially due to this opposition, the FERC has been slow to approve proposals for liquefaction facilities. Opponents of LNG exports argue that gas is more valuable to the United States when used as a raw material for its own economy in the construction of finished products than when it is shipped abroad as a raw material to be used in the creation of value-added projects by another nation. For example, the *Financial Times* carried an article making the case for domestic use: "At issue is whether the US wants to export its energy wealth in the form of an unfinished commodity or as products such as petrochemicals or steel, to which American workers have added value."[24]

Defenders of the idea of LNG exports criticize their opponents as nativists, mercantilists, and opponents of free trade. They also point to other benefits. If the Unites States were to export LNG, then it might be used to displace coal in power generation, leading to reduced greenhouse emissions. U.S. exports could potentially have a geopolitical benefit, helping stimulate a worldwide market for LNG and increasing the diversity of suppliers for key U.S. allies that depend heavily on imported LNG, namely Japan. Opponents of LNG exports argue that exporting gas will cause the domestic price to rise, canceling out the cost advantage that would help the U.S. economy grow and stimulate employment. For them, the key to the value of natural gas in its domestic use is its cheap price compared to the price that gas commands in other nations. In addition, exporting LNG means more domestic gas production, with more pressure on the U.S. environment.

A number of studies have explored the feasibility, costs, and benefits of allowing LNG exports from the United States. They generally tend to find that the effect on domestic costs will not be large, and they tend to favor allowing LNG exports. But of course, these reports also generate their own rebuttals.[25] Most important among these studies is one commissioned by the Department of Energy. This report, "Macroeconomic Impacts of LNG Exports from the United States," reached a number of conclusions regarding allowing LNG exports:

- Allowing LNG exports would create net economic benefits.

- These benefits would outweigh reduced capital and wage income to U.S. consumers.

- Allowing LNG exports would cause a modest rise in domestic natural gas prices.

- A successful LNG export industry would depend on continuing rich domestic shale gas production and low U.S. prices.
- World market conditions might make LNG exports uncompetitive.
- Allowing LNG exports would create some winners and losers in the U.S. economy.
- Allowing exports would not affect overall U.S. employment levels.[26]

Most of the reports on the feasibility and advisability of allowing LNG exports consider the real possibility that world market conditions might not allow the U.S. export industry to flourish. For example, if other nations can replicate the U.S. shale revolution, exporting U.S. LNG might not be profitable.[27] Presently, it appears that many nations are stepping away from nuclear power generation, which increases the demand for natural gas significantly. However, this is a very tentative movement that already exhibits considerable backsliding. If the world continues to rely on nuclear power, then there will be less demand for U.S. LNG exports. In addition, the potential for worldwide expansion of the LNG market depends on how successful the world is in bringing solar, wind, and other renewable sources of energy online.

The key economic argument against U.S. LNG exports is an economic one: Liquefying and transporting natural gas from the United States is too expensive. For example, the report commissioned by the Department of Energy used a number of scenarios to analyze the prospects for LNG exports. In the "reference [most likely] case," the report found that "global natural gas demand is met by global supplies without U.S. LNG exports. This outcome also implies that U.S. LNG exports under a U.S. reference scenario would not be lower cost than existing or planned sources of LNG in other regions of the world and thus do not displace them."[28]

LNG Pricing and Markets

From its tentative beginnings in the 1960s, the LNG business has grown remarkably, even though the LNG production chain requires tremendous capital investment that must all be in place before any portion can be deployed. There must be a source of gas, a liquefaction plant, a vessel to ship the gas, and a regasification plant that can accept the shipped LNG and feed it into a distribution network. Because of these complex system requirements, early LNG projects were possible only on a long-term-contract basis. A deal would be made to build the liquefaction and regasification plants and to build an LNG carrier dedicated to servicing the two plants. This was clearly necessary, especially in the early days of the LNG industry, because it would make little economic sense to build any single component—a ship or a plant, for example—on speculation and merely hope that the other necessary elements of the value chain would somehow fall into place.

As a result of the logic of this value chain, the LNG industry has long been dominated by long-term contracts. Often the country needing the gas has been a developed country, while the country that can provide the gas has lacked a well-developed economy and capital infrastructure. For example, we have seen that Japan depends entirely on importing LNG to meet its need for natural gas and that Qatar has become the world's leading LNG exporter. To get the Qatari LNG business off the ground, Mobil Oil provided considerable expertise, the Japanese trading firm Mitsui Bussan contributed key financing, and the Japanese utility Chubu Electric committed to long-term purchases of the produced LNG.[29]

For many LNG projects, the LNG buyer commits to purchasing a given quantity of LNG annually for a period of decades. For example, in its first LNG project with Qatar, Chubu Electric committed to buying 2 million tonnes per year from 1997 to 2021.[30] Pricing of the gas over such a long period is difficult, and largely for this reason, it became standard to index the price of delivered LNG to the price of oil. In a period of volatile and generally escalating oil prices, this method of pricing has become quite contentious. Figure 3.1 shows the basis of that contention. From the mid-1990s until the mid-2000s, the relative prices of crude oil and natural gas were fairly stable, making a linkage between crude oil and LNG prices fairly sensible. But in recent years, the relative value of oil has risen by a factor of almost four. Of course, the price of natural gas per unit of energy dramatically increases when the price of LNG is linked to that of oil.

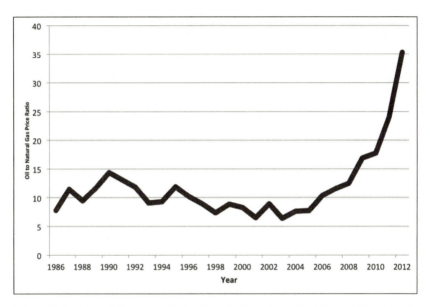

Figure 3.1 Ratio of the Price of One Barrel of Crude Oil to 1,000 Cubic Feet of Natural Gas, 1986–2012

Source: BP, "Statistical Review of World Energy," June 2012.

Many purchasers of natural gas would like to move away from long-term oil-indexed contracts to the opportunity to transact in the spot market—a market for the more-or-less immediate delivery of LNG, which would make the LNG market somewhat like the stock market. As recently as 1995, the spot LNG market was virtually nonexistent. By 2011, the percentage of world LNG trade traded on a spot market basis was 25%. Similarly, in 1995, there were almost no spot cargoes of LNG, but by 2011, there were more than 1,000, and there were about 20 countries exporting spot cargoes and 25 nations importing spot LNG.[31] Expressed in similar terms: From 2000 to 2011, the short-term world LNG trade increased dramatically, from about 8 bcm to over 80 bcm, and the short-term trade as a portion of all LNG trade increased from about 3% to 28%.[32]

Figure 3.2 shows the grounds for the economic urgency with which many natural gas importing nations would like to move to a spot market pricing basis and why they would like to see a robust trade in LNG. As the figure shows, the price of natural gas in LNG-dependent Japan is much higher than in the United States. European prices, where much natural gas is acquired from the Russian Federation under long-term oil-linked contracts, exhibit a significant, but less dramatic, gap in prices, as Table 3.10 indicates. The United States enjoys the world's cheapest natural gas, while Japan suffers the highest price. There has been some success in abandoning oil-linked pricing and moving to a spot market basis. Kansai Electric Power of Japan, Tokyo Gas, Osaka Gas, and Chubu Electric have all succeeded in initiating contracts based on spot market prices. Similarly Gazprom, the giant Russian gas production and trading firm, has been forced to de-link its gas prices from oil in some instances, much to the benefit of utilities in Germany, Italy, France, and Poland.[33]

Table 3.10 World LNG, Estimated March 2013 Landed Prices ($ per Million Btu)

Lake Charles, Louisiana	$3.01
Cove Point, Maryland	3.34
United Kingdom	9.94
Spain	15.25
Rio de Janeiro	16.84
India	15.70
China	19.35
Japan	19.75
Korea	17.75

Source: Federal Energy Regulatory Commission, Market Oversight, www.ferc.gov/oversight.

Note: Btu = British thermal unit.

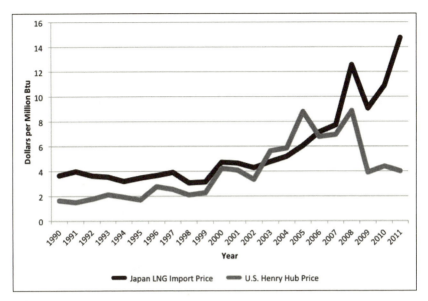

Figure 3.2 Natural Gas Prices, Japan and the United States, 1990–2011

Source: BP, "Statistical Review of World Energy," June 2012.

Of course, natural gas at the wellhead is a very different product from natural gas delivered to a Japanese home or industrial site. Some have argued that even very large price differentials, such as those in Figure 3.2, cannot be closed because of the costs involved. In the interesting article, "The Math Doesn't Add Up on the US's Ambitions to Export Natural Gas," Steve LeVine reasons as shown in Table 3.11.[34] He takes the December 2017 futures price of U.S. natural gas as the basic input price, because 2017 is the date he estimates LNG liquefaction facilities can be operational and up-to-scale in the United States. As LeVine notes, the $4–$5 price differential appears quite attractive, but other suppliers, notably Qatar, could still shrink their profit margins to undercut U.S. pricing. So while the gap between U.S. and Asian prices might be enormous, the costs of getting U.S. gas to Asian users closes much of that differential, making the prospects for LNG exports look much more tenuous. This is especially true if one considers the long lead times, the multibillion-dollar costs of liquefaction plants, the presence of even lower-cost natural gas suppliers in the market, the high variability of prices along the supply chain,[35] and the possibility of other nations enjoying their own shale gas revolutions.[36]

Table 3.11 Costs for Liquefying and Transporting U.S. Natural Gas to Asia

Item	Cost per 1,000 Cubic Feet
Wellhead cost (futures price for December 2017)	$4.90
Transport to liquefaction facility	1.00
Liquefaction cost	2.14
Shipment to Asia	2.87
Regasification	0.88
Transport to end user	1.50
Total delivered cost	**13.29**
Current U.S. price	3.63
Current Asian long-term contract price	18.00

Source: Steve LeVine, "The Math Doesn't Add Up on the US's Ambitions to Export Natural Gas," December 7, 2012, available at http://qz.com/35142.

Notes

1. Bill White, "The Cold Facts about a Hot Commodity: LNG," oildrum.com, October 4, 2012.

2. Jamie Goode, "Mercaptans and Other Volatile Sulfur Compounds in Wine," wineanorak.com, 2006. Available at www.wineanorak.com/mercaptansinwine.htm.

3. International Energy Agency, "Gas: Medium-Term Market Report 2012," 2012, p. 117.

4. Bob Shively, John Ferrare, and Belinda Petty, *Understanding Today's Global LNG Business*, Laporte, CO: Enerdynamics Corp., 2010, p. 27.

5. Much of this discussion of LNG draws from this excellent article by Bill White, "The Cold Facts about a Hot Commodity: LNG," oildrum.com, October 4, 2012.

6. International Energy Agency, "Gas: Medium-Term Market Report 2012," 2012, pp. 126–127.

7. Kohei Hashimoto, Jareer Elass, and Stacy Eller, "Liquefied Natural Gas from Qatar: The Qatargas Project," Stanford University and James A. Baker Institute, December 2004.

8. USEIA, "Annual Energy Outlook 2005: With Projections to 2025," February 2005, p. 49.

9. USEIA, "Annual Energy Outlook 2012," June 2012, p. 62.

10. ExxonMobil, "Outlook for Energy 2013," December 2012, p. 32.

11. Realclearenergy.com, "Natural Gas about to Pass Coal in Power Generation," July 16, 2012; and Tom Fowler, "Exxon Declares Gas King," *Wall Street Journal*, December 8, 2011.

12. Peter C. Glover, "Irony of Ironies: Europe Switches to Coal as US Gas Glut Reduces Emissions," *Energy Tribune*, July 12, 2012.

13. Realclearenergy.org, "Levelized Costs of New Electric Generation," August 27, 2012.

14. Rebecca Smith, "Cheap Natural Gas Unplugs U.S. Nuclear-Power Revival," *Wall Street Journal*, March 15, 2012.

15. Richard K. Morse, "Cleaning Up Coal," Foreignaffairs.com, July/August 2012.

16. Massachusetts Institute of Technology, "The Future of Natural Gas," 2010, p. 101.

17. Massachusetts Institute of Technology, "The Future of Natural Gas," 2010, p. 110.

18. Ben Casselman and Russell Gold, "Cheap Natural Gas Gives New Hope to the Rust Belt," *Wall Street Journal*, October 23, 2012.

19. Daniel Gilbert, "Chemical Makers Ride Gas Boom," *Wall Street Journal*, April 18, 2012.

20. Ben Casselman and Russell Gold, "Cheap Natural Gas Gives New Hope to the Rust Belt," *Wall Street Journal*, October 23, 2012. See also Daniel Yergin, "The Real Stimulus: Low-Cost Natural Gas," *Wall Street Journal*, October 22, 2012.

21. Philip K. Verleger, Jr., "The Coming US Boom and How Shale Gas Will Fuel It," *Financial Times*, April 23, 2012.

22. USEIA, "Annual Energy Outlook 2012," June 2012, p. 36.

23. Rebecca Smith, "Will Truckers Ditch Diesel?" *Wall Street Journal*, May 23, 2012. See also Jason Lange, "Shale Energy Boom Dangles Prospect of Leap in Economic Growth," Reuters.com, May 24, 2012; Ken Silverstein, "Natural Gas

Vehicles Driven to Outpace Oil," *Forbes*, March 18, 2012; and "Natural Gas Vehicles: Long Road Ahead," EnergyBiz.com, March 7, 2012.

24. Gregory Meyer, "LNG: U.S. Weighs the Cost of Gas Exports to Economy," *Financial Times*, July 17, 2012.

25. See Charles Ebinger, Kevin Massy, and Govinda Avasarala, "Liquid Markets: Assessing the Case for U.S. Exports of Liquefied Natural Gas," Brookings Institution, May 2012; Kenneth B. Medlock, III, "U.S. LNG Exports: Truth and Consequence," Rice University Baker Institute for Public Policy, August 10, 2012; Michael Levi, "A Strategy for U.S. Natural Gas Exports," Hamilton Project, June 2012; and Industrial Energy Consumers of America, "Re: Hamilton Project: 'A Strategy for U.S. Natural Gas Exports' by Michael Levi," July 16, 2012.

26. NERA Economic Consulting, "Macroeconomic Impacts of LNG Exports from the United States," December 2012.

27. Clifford Krauss, "Exports of American Natural Gas May Fall Short of High Hopes," *New York Times*, January 4, 2013.

28. NERA Economic Consulting, "Macroeconomic Impacts of LNG Exports from the United States," December 2012, p. 37.

29. Kohei Hashimoto, Jareer Elass, and Stacy Eller, "Liquefied Natural Gas from Qatar: The Qatargas Project," Stanford University and James A. Baker Institute, December 2004, p. 5.

30. Kohei Hashimoto, Jareer Elass, and Stacy Eller, "Liquefied Natural Gas from Qatar: The Qatargas Project," Stanford University and James A. Baker Institute, December 2004, p. 25.

31. International Gas Union, "World LNG Report 2011," June 2012, pp. 16–17.

32. International Energy Agency, "World Energy Outlook 2012," OECD/IEA, 2012, p. 153.

33. Emiko Terazono, "Japan's LNG in Crucial Pricing Shift," *Financial Times*, December 18, 2012.

34. See Steve LeVine, "The Math Doesn't Add Up on the US's Ambitions to Export Natural Gas," December 7, 2012. Available at http://qz.com/35142.

35. From January 2011 through May 2012, the daily rate to lease an LNG tanker ranged from a low of $60,000 to as high as $150,000. International Energy Agency, "Gas: Medium-Term Market Report 2012," 2012, p. 106.

36. Another report reaches a somewhat similar conclusion about the viability of U.S. LNG exports. See Charles Ebinger, Kevin Massy, and Govinda Avasarala, "Liquid Markets: Assessing the Case for U.S. Exports of Liquefied Natural Gas," Brookings Institution, May 2012, especially Figure 11 on page 41 and the accompanying discussion.

4

Environmental Costs and Benefits

Without doubt, the new technologies of the natural gas revolution, particularly hydraulic fracturing, give rise to significant environmental challenges. First, any use of hydrocarbons is under serious attack due to longstanding and familiar issues of air and water pollution and other environmental pressures associated with their consumption. More recently, a developing understanding of the role of hydrocarbons in fomenting climate change has provided additional reasons to be concerned about the dependence of modern economies on coal, gas, and oil. Beyond these general problems associated with all hydrocarbons, unconventional hydrocarbons bring with them their own specific challenges, which are the focus of this chapter.

Water plays a central role in hydraulic fracturing, and water demand, use, and disposal all give rise to special environmental concerns not encountered in general hydrocarbon acquisition and consumption. Hydraulic fracturing may also have its own special impacts on air quality, as well. In addition, the act of hydraulic fracturing and the disposal of water used in the fracturing process have been shown to cause increased seismic activities. In short, hydraulic fracturing may cause, and water disposal definitely has caused, at least minor earthquakes, giving rise to greater fears of stimulating destructive earthquakes. We can think of all energy drilling as a type of heavy industry that gives rise to adverse effects at the earth's surface. But the location and widely distributed nature of the unconventional energy industry cause their own particular adverse effects on land and the social environment around the drilling activity.

The natural gas revolution also brings very clear environmental benefits. In many ways, the development of hydraulic fracturing, horizontal drilling, and the build out of the liquid natural gas (LNG) infrastructure are much less environmentally destructive than alternatives presently available. In addition, the energy revolution has brought undeniable benefits to local communities where drilling takes place. Finally, the rapid increase in the availability of hydrocarbons made possible by the energy revolution in the United States has already created many widespread benefits for people around the world, and all these benefits must also be weighed in the balance of any unbiased assessment of the environmental and social impact of the natural gas revolution. This chapter considers each of these issues in turn.

Water Supply

As the name suggests, hydraulic fracturing relies critically on fluid and pressure, and water is the absolutely key ingredient in making the technology work. As I have noted, shale gas wells in the United States generally require about 4 million gallons of water for the fracturing process. In more challenging geological environments, such as those that appear to be emerging in China, the water demands can be greater still. In most environments, different uses compete for available water supplies, with these demands ranging from drinking water, to irrigation for croplands, to water for golf courses. So the demand for water for fracturing must find its place in the scheme of supply and demand.

While 4 million gallons gives the impression of being a great deal of water, in some contexts it is not so large. Humans use a tremendous amount of water. Fracking a shale gas well requires 18,000 cubic meters of water, about the same amount required to water an 18-hole golf course for a month.[1] Considering the quite dry state of Texas, with its large shale gas industry, the total demand for water for hydraulic fracturing represents less than 1% of total water use. However, in some particularly dry areas, the portion of water used for fracturing can exceed 10%. Further, the demand for fracturing water more than doubled from 2008 to 2011, and it may well increase substantially in the years ahead.[2] In LaSalle County, Texas, located in the Eagle Ford Shale play, the percentage of water demand for fracking is predicted to reach 40% of total water usage, but statewide the total should not exceed 2%.[3] This area of Texas receives only about 20 inches of rainfall per year.

Water demand varies by area, of course, as does its cost. Like Texas, Colorado is another dry area, and according to industry estimates, water for fracking in Colorado was about 6.5 billion gallons for 2012. However, that figure is disputed, and others say it may be twice as much.[4] Whichever figure is correct, that is one-tenth to two-tenths of 1% of total usage in the state. For comparison, more water is used in Colorado for fracking than is used to make snow at the state's ski resorts, but both of these are very small proportions compared to the 86% used for irrigation and agriculture.[5] Table 4.1 shows the proportion of water devoted to shale gas production in four major plays in the United States. In all cases, shale gas production accounts for less than 1% of water usage in the area.

Table 4.1 Water Usage for Shale Gas in Major Gas Play Basins

Play	Proportion of Total Water Usage Devoted to Shale Gas
Barnett	0.4%
Fayetteville	0.1%
Haynesville	0.8%
Marcellus	<0.1%

Source: Massachusetts Institute of Technology, "The Future of Natural Gas," 2010, p. 44.

It is also important to consider the comparative demand for water for producing energy from other sources. Although the demand for fracking water appears to be quite high, not only is it relatively small compared to total demand, but also shale gas production uses less water than most other methods of energy production. A study by the Massachusetts Institute of Technology noted, "Indeed, the 'water intensity' of shale gas development, at around one gallon of water consumed for every million Btu of energy produced, is low compared to many other energy sources. By way of contrast, several thousand gallons of water per million Btu of energy produced can be used in the irrigation of corn grown for ethanol."[6] Table 4.2 shows the water required to produce 1 million Btu of energy for different fossil sources and methods, along with nuclear energy and biofuels. Of all these, shale gas is the least water intensive. By contrast, the production of ethanol requires more than 1,000 times as much water per unit of energy produced because of the irrigation demands of corn.

Table 4.2 Water Required for the Production of Energy by Different Sources and Methods

Energy Resource	Gallons of Water Used per 1 Million Btu of Energy Produced
Barnett Shale natural gas	1.47
Coal (no slurry transport)	2–8
Coal (with slurry transport)	13–32
Nuclear (uranium ready to use in a power plant)	8–14
Conventional oil	8–20
Syngas—coal gasification	11–26
Oil shale	22–56
Tar sands	27–68
Synfuel—Fischer–Tropsch (from coal)	41–60
Enhanced oil recovery	21–2,500
Biofuel (irrigated corn ethanol, irrigated soy biodiesel)	>2,500

Source: Howard Rogers, "Shale Gas: The Unfolding Story," *Oxford Review of Economic Policy*, 2011;27:117–143. See p. 131.

Note: Btu = British thermal unit.

The costs that drillers pay for fracking water vary tremendously. For example, the price depends on the overall supply and whether water can be delivered easily to the well pad or has to be moved by truck. In addition, the price depends on the competing uses of water and local peculiarities of the water market. For example, Texas landowners sell water to frackers for about a penny a gallon.[7] But the costs can be much more, as the *Wall Street Journal* reports: "In North Dakota's Bakken Shale, one of the current fracking hot spots, fresh water delivered to a drilling site costs between 10 and 14 cents per gallon, according to Continental Resources Inc., an Oklahoma City-based oil driller. Water alone can cost upward of $400,000 per fracturing attempt—and Continental plans more than 200 next year in North Dakota."[8]

Partially because water is so fundamental to life, its use and price are highly contested, but surely the market value of water matters in determining the wisest use of this vital resource. Colorado farmers paid $30 for an acre-foot of water in 2012, but oil and gas companies willingly paid $3,300 for the same amount.[9] An acre-foot is about 326,000 gallons, implying a cost per gallon of about 1 cent when the water is used for fracking, but one-hundredth of a cent when used for irrigation. While we might all agree that irrigating crops is an ultimately higher use for water, energy is also vital, and price signals do guide the rational in determining how to use any resource. A *Wall Street Journal* interview with a Texas cattle rancher, Darrell Brownlow, makes this point quite vividly. He said, "If the economically depressed region has to choose between the two, the choice should be simple." The article continues: "Mr. Brownlow, who has a Ph.D. in geochemistry, says it takes 407 million gallons to irrigate 640 acres and grow about $200,000 worth of corn on the arid land. The same amount of water, he says, could be used to frack enough wells to generate $2.5 billion worth of oil. 'No water, no frack, no wealth,' says Mr. Brownlow, who has leased his cattle ranch for oil exploration."[10]

The water used in fracking does not need to be as pure as drinking water, but there are limits to how impure the water can be. Water nearer the earth's surface tends to be less saline, with really deep water having a higher salt content. As Vikram Rao notes, "Water aquifers tend to get salty at greater depths. This is why most fresh water in the world is found at depths less than 300 meters, more often less than half that. Consequently, salt water bodies are quite prevalent in most places and have no use for human consumption or agriculture. Using salty water for fracking ensures no competition with other conventional uses."[11] In addition, gray water from effluent treatment plants could also be used, leading some to advocate fracking only with nonpotable water. Doing so can restrict the ecological impact of the demand for water and can improve the economics in some cases of fracking as well.

There is a strong, but still nascent, trend toward using nonpotable water for fracking, although the statistics vary considerably, as does the proportion of fracking conducted with nonpotable water in different areas. For example, the Susquehanna River Basin Commission, which monitors water usage in central Pennsylvania, says that 14% of water used for fracking was being recycled as of late 2012, and that this was an increase in two years from less than 1%.[12] However, another report says that in the Marcellus Shale, which includes most of Pennsylvania, about 70% of fracking water is recycled.[13] While water is relatively plentiful in the moist northeastern United States, the case is quite otherwise in Texas, where only about 20% of fracking water used in Texas in 2011 was recycled or brackish, perhaps suggesting that the 70% figure for the Marcellus Shale is overstated.[14] Economics and local conditions largely determine the recycling rate. For example, because of the local geology, disposal of used fracking water via pumping into injection wells is difficult in the Marcellus region, promoting a high rate of recycling. The cost of acquiring water is also a determining factor.

Both the economics and environmental concerns are driving improved sourcing of fracking water. Some drillers are implementing technologies that allow the use of nonpotable water for hydraulic fracturing and that also require no subsequent treatment.[15] Instead of requiring water, Shell has successfully used a foam of carbon dioxide to frack a well in Egypt.[16] Supplying nonpotable water can also be a source of revenue for municipalities. Near Denver, Colorado, the small town of Aurora is providing 2.4 billion gallons of effluent water over a five-year period for $9.5 million—water that would have been useless otherwise.[17] As the fracking industry develops, contention for water and pressures to reduce the environmental impact of water demand will be relentless and more pointed in some areas than others. While the United States is fortunate in being relatively amply supplied with water, even in such areas as Texas, Colorado, and North Dakota, the case is quite otherwise elsewhere. China has 20% of the world's population but only 6% of the world's water.[18] Further, some gas-rich areas of China are particularly dry, including the Songliao, Bohai, Ordos, Tarim, and Junggar Basins.[19]

Fracking Fluid

As noted in Chapter 2, "They Call It a Revolution," water is far and away the chief ingredient in hydraulic fracturing fluid, but there are many other ingredients. Table 4.3 shows the typical composition of fracking fluid by volume, primarily listing the various ingredients by their function but generally not showing the specific chemicals that perform those functions. The industry has long regarded the composition of fracking fluid as a trade secret and has struggled to keep its recipes private. However, environmental concerns have been effective in slowly prying this information from the industry.

Table 4.3 Typical Ingredients in Hydraulic Fracturing Fluid, by Volume

Ingredient	Percentage Volume
Water and sand	99.510%
Other	0.490
Acid	0.123
Friction reducer	0.088
Surfactant	0.085
Potassium chloride	0.060
Gelling agent	0.056
Scale inhibitor	0.043
pH adjusting agent	0.011
Breaker	0.010
Cross-linker	0.007
Iron control	0.004
Corrosion inhibitor	0.002
Biocide	0.001

Source: U.S. Department of Energy, "Modern Shale Gas Development in the United States: A Primer," April 2009, p. 62.

Increasing federal and state regulations has played an important role in the process of requiring increasing disclosure of the fracking fluid ingredients. Table 4.4 shows some of the typical compounds used in fracturing fluid, their purpose in the fracking process, and some of the most familiar uses of those items. While many of these are common household items and even ingestible by humans, many are quite nasty indeed and need to be handled with great caution. One certainly would not want many of these ingredients in one's drinking water.

Table 4.4 Some Key Chemicals Used in Hydraulic Fracturing Fluid

Additive Type	Compound	Purpose	More Familiar Uses
Diluted acid	Hydrochloric acid	Dissolves minerals and initiates cracks in shale	Swimming pool chemical
Biocide	Glutaraldehyde	Eliminates bacteria in water to reduce corrosion	Disinfectant, equipment sterilization
Friction reducer	Polyacrylamide	Minimizes friction between fluid and pipe	Water treatment, soil conditioner
	Mineral oil		Makeup remover, laxatives, candy
Gel	Guar gum or hydroxyethyl cellulose	Thickens water to suspend sand	Cosmetics, toothpaste, sauces, baked goods, ice cream
Iron control	Citric acid	Prevents precipitation of metal oxides	Food additive, food flavoring
Oxygen scavenger	Ammonium bisulfite	Removes oxygen from water to inhibit corrosion of pipe	Cosmetics, food, and beverage processing; water treatment
Proppant	Silica, quartz sand	Holds fractures open to allow gas to escape	Drinking water filtration, concrete, brick mortar
Scale inhibitor	Ethylene glycol	Prevents scale deposit on pipe	Automotive antifreeze, household cleansers, de-icing agent
Surfactant	Isopropanol	Increases viscosity of fluid	Glass cleaner, antiperspirant, hair-coloring agent

Source: Adapted from U.S. Department of Energy, "Modern Shale Gas Development in the United States: A Primer," April 2009, Exhibit 36, p. 63. See this source for a more complete listing.

Hydraulic Fracturing and Aquifers

Assuming that a driller has secured an ample supply of water to drive the fracking process, the next important issue is the effect of fracking on underground aquifers. As discussed in Chapter 2, the main ingredient of fracking fluid by volume is water, but the mix must also contain proppants to hold the shale fissures open. In addition, fracking fluid has historically contained some quite hazardous chemicals. Even though water accounts for 99% or so of the mix, 1% of 4 million gallons is quite a load of potentially harmful ingredients. Perhaps the greatest danger of fracking is the contamination of aquifers on which populations depend for their drinking water.

Plate 1 shows the typical drilling setup that provides the context for hydraulic fracturing. The well is drilled from the surface down through an aquifer and into the shale. The entire length of the well must be capable of resisting pressure so that fracturing fluid goes only where the driller intends. There are two main ways this process can go wrong and lead to aquifer contamination. If the well casing fails where it transits the aquifer, fracking fluid could be pumped through the point of failure and directly into the aquifer. Such a result is potentially disastrous if the fracking fluid contains toxic chemicals. The entire process of fracking depends on pumping the fracking fluid into the shale to break it up. While the aquifer generally lies many hundreds of feet above the shale bed in the typical situation, there is still the fear that the fracking fluid initially forced into the shale could migrate upward and into the aquifer. In addition, the whole purpose of the fracking operation is to free the gas from the shale that entraps it. This also raises the prospect that the methane could migrate into the aquifer instead of going up the well to be captured as the driller intends. The following finding sums up the situation quite well: A U.S. Department of Energy committee found that shale formations containing gas and oil are separated from aquifers by thousands of feet of impermeable rock, making contamination of water supplies by hydraulic fracturing nearly impossible.[20] Table 4.5 shows the typical separation between shale gas deposits and aquifers for several key shale plays. The considerable distances of rock do not take account of a defective well casing passing through an aquifer, however. In that case, the well's pipe containing the fracking fluid is in direct contact with the water in the aquifer.

Table 4.5 Separation Distance Between Gas Shales and Shallow Freshwater Aquifers in Major U.S. Gas Plays

Shale Play	Depth to Shale (Feet)	Depth to Aquifer (Feet)
Barnett	6,500–8,500	1,200
Fayetteville	1,000–7,000	500
Marcellus	4,000–8,500	850
Woodford	6,000–11,000	400
Haynesville	10,500–13,500	400

Source: Massachusetts Institute of Technology, "The Future of Natural Gas," 2010, p. 40.

The emotion surrounding the pollution of aquifers is intense, and the evidence on the occurrence of actual pollution is quite mixed. Perhaps the strongest emotional case against fracking was contained in the 2010 documentary film *Gasland*, written and directed by Josh Fox, which won a Sundance Film Festival Special Jury Prize. The most dramatic scenes of the film show water from a kitchen tap in Weld County, Colorado, being ignited with a cigarette lighter. The film very clearly charges that the methane being burned entered the water supply because of fracking. The specific charges in the film have been widely criticized, and it is not too strong to say that some of the most outrageous putative examples in the film have been debunked.

When methane enters a home's water supply, it is critical to determine the provenance of the gas. Chapter 2 distinguished thermogenic and biogenic methane, which have different chemical signatures, allowing tests to determine the type of gas. Fracking normally aims to obtain gas from thousands of feet below the surface of the earth, so it targets thermogenic gas. Biogenic gas, produced by plant and animal decay at low temperature, commonly lies near the surface. As Chapter 2 also noted, humans have long used this source of gas because it was so readily available, and such a natural seep of biogenic gas may have played a key role at the Oracle at Delphi. Similarly, the Eternal Flame Falls of Chestnut Ridge Park in New York has a burning seep of biogenic methane behind a waterfall, and it has been burning from early times, long before anyone ever heard of hydraulic fracturing.[21]

Colorado's Oil & Gas Conservation Commission investigated the claims of methane contamination and issued its "Statement on the Documentary *Gasland*," which definitely acknowledges some cases of water contamination from oil and gas drilling but also contains the following passages:

> The Colorado Oil and Gas Conservation Commission (COGCC) would like to correct several errors in the film's portrayal of the Colorado incidents. ...The occurrence of methane in the coals of the Laramie Formation has been well documented in numerous publications by the Colorado Geological Survey, the United States Geological Survey, and the Rocky Mountain Association of Geologists dating back more than 30 years. For example, a 1976 publication by the Colorado Division of Water Resources states that the aquifer contains "troublesome amounts of...methane." A 1983 publication by the United States Geological Survey similarly states that "[m]ethane-rich gas commonly occurs in ground water in the Denver Basin, southern Weld County, Colorado." And a 2001 report by the Colorado Geological Survey discusses the methane potential of this formation and cites approximately 30 publications on this subject....
>
> *Gasland* features three Weld County landowners, Mike Markham, Renee McClure, and Aimee Ellsworth, whose water wells were allegedly contaminated by oil and gas development. The COGCC investigated complaints from all three landowners in 2008 and 2009, and we issued written reports summarizing our findings on each. We concluded that Aimee Ellsworth's well contained a mixture of biogenic and thermogenic methane that was in part attributable to oil and gas

development, and Mrs. Ellsworth and an operator reached a settlement in that case.

However, using the same investigative techniques, we concluded that Mike Markham's and Renee McClure's wells contained biogenic gas that was not related to oil and gas activity. Unfortunately, *Gasland* does not mention our McClure finding and dismisses our Markham finding out of hand.[22]

Gasland also leveled similar charges of methane pollution of aquifers by fracking in Dimock, Pennsylvania, located in the heart of the Marcellus Shale. Segments of the film also showed flaming water taps in Dimock, and Pennsylvania's state regulators fined Cabot Oil & Gas Corporation for allowing gas to escape into the aquifer there. The Environmental Protection Agency (EPA) subsequently tested water there and found no health risks from any such contamination.[23] Events in Texas followed a similar trajectory. In 2010, the EPA director for the Texas region advocated "crucifying" (the actual word used) a few oil companies and charged Range Resources Corporation with contaminating at least two wells in the Barnett Shale with both methane and benzene. In April 2012, "the EPA finally withdrew the order, having been able to produce no evidence whatever that Range Resources was in any way responsible."[24] "The EPA is also facing scrutiny from the gas industry and Wyoming's governor over an investigation of possible water contamination related to fracking near Pavillion, Wyoming. In December [2011], the EPA released draft findings that groundwater there contained unsafe levels of benzene, a carcinogen, and other chemicals 'consistent with gas production and hydraulic fracturing fluids.' But state officials and others disputed the findings, and the EPA has agreed to take more water samples and postpone a peer review of the findings."[25] A study by scientists at Duke University in 2011 found contaminated drinking water from methane in gas wells in Pennsylvania, leading Pennsylvania's top official at the Department of Environmental Protection to accuse the researchers of biased and shoddy science. But in further study conducted in 2012, the same team of researchers found no such contamination.[26]

All these examples of charges followed by later recantations or subsequent inability to confirm the original findings emphasize the difficulty of making a truly informed judgment about the real dangers that fracking poses for ground water. This is not to imply that there are not problems. As already noted, Colorado regulators did confirm some cases of contamination. But there are numerous other instances of problems as well. The Groundwater Protection Council found 10 documented instances of groundwater contamination. These occurred in Texas from 1993 to 2008 and stemmed from faulty drilling or well completion.[27] Other instances of contamination abound: In Pennsylvania during 2011, at least 65 wells drilled in the Marcellus Shale were cited for faulty cement casings around wells.[28] In 2011, oil companies drilling in North Dakota reported more than 100 accidental releases of oil, drilling wastewater, or other fluids. State regulators say that many more went unreported.[29] ProPublica.com charges that discharges from injection wells "have repeatedly leaked, sending dangerous chemicals and waste gurgling to the surface or, on occasion, seeping into shallow aquifers that store a significant portion of the nation's drinking water."[30]

If a well casing leaks near an aquifer, some contamination will occur. There is no doubt that some well casings are bound to fail. The sheer number of wells makes that almost inescapable. To take an extreme example, Weld County in Colorado had 17,388 active oil and gas wells as of late 2011, more than almost any other county in the United States.[31] Across the country, with many tens of thousands of wells being drilled, it strains credulity to believe that there will not be some instances of pollution. But the true severity of the problem is difficult to assess. The U.S. Geological Survey study of 127 water wells in the Fayetteville Shale area of Arkansas found no groundwater contamination from natural gas drilling and concluded: "None of the data that we have looked at as part of this study suggests that any groundwater contamination is resulting from natural gas production activities."[32] Further, the trend seems to be toward much better performance on the part of industry. For example, a 2012 study from the State University of New York at Buffalo concluded that fracking was getting safer and should not lead to any major environmental problems.[33] Also, "The safety profile of hydraulic fracturing has improved dramatically in Pennsylvania since 2008. Environmental violations as a percentage of wells drilled dropped by more than half over the course of the years examined."[34]

For its part, the energy industry has exacerbated public concern over many of its policies and practices, at least until recently. It has long been known that fracking fluid often contains some quite toxic ingredients. Drillers have wanted to keep their recipes for fracking fluid private, insisting that the specific makeup of their fluid constitutes a valuable trade secret. The Energy Policy Act of 2005 enshrined a rule that was particularly galling to environmentalists—the so-called "Halliburton loophole." The Safe Drinking Water Act of 1974 gave the EPA the principal enforcement responsibility, including regulating the underground injection of chemicals, but allows the EPA to share this role with state agencies. The 2005 Energy Act excluded from this purview "the underground injection of fluids or propping agents (other than diesel fuels) pursuant to hydraulic fracturing operations related to oil, gas, or geothermal production activities."[35]

Nonetheless, a suite of other regulations and state laws, along with a slowly developing industry recognition of the issue, have prompted considerably better disclosure of the chemical ingredients. As of early 2012, Texas drillers were required to disclose the chemicals in their hydraulic fluid. Ohio has started requiring drillers to identify the chemicals in their fracking fluid by the unique Chemical Abstracts Service number. But in some respects, secrecy continues to prevail, and standards vary considerably by state. Colorado, Wyoming, and Montana are regarded as having the strongest requirements for disclosure, but West Virginia requires only a list of additives, without information on their proportions. The U.S. Securities and Exchange Commission is also demanding greater disclosure, based on the risks that investors may face with different procedures.[36] But the bigger news is the strong movement toward less toxic ingredients in the hydraulic fracking cocktail. To emphasize the safety of today's ingredients, Colorado Governor John Hickenlooper actually drank a glass of fracking fluid.[37]

"Produced Water"

"Produced water" is a euphemism for the portion of fracking fluid that returns to the surface after the fracking operation. This can be up to 75% of the initial volume of the fracking fluid, although generally a substantially smaller portion returns to the wellhead.[38] In addition to the chemicals that were sent down into the well as part of the original fracking fluid, the flowback water often picks up a considerably increased saline content because the fracking fluid dissolves naturally occurring salts in the shale bed. Also, shale beds frequently contain naturally occurring radioactive material (NORM), and the flowback water can be tainted with radiation. This flowback water creates another environmental consideration that the industry must address. Often the driller impounds the flowback water in a makeshift reservoir near the drilling pad, pending more permanent disposal. There have been numerous instances of flowback water entering the environment, including streams and rivers, and some drillers have acted quite irresponsibly in this matter. For example, in the Marcellus region of Pennsylvania, prior to and into 2011, some produced water was being sent to some wastewater treatment sites not capable of removing all the contaminants, such as barium and strontium.[39] Regulation and industry behavior have improved quite considerably. There are three main responsible ways to treat flowback water: Recycle the fracking fluid for the next fracking operation, as discussed above, pass the flowback through an appropriate water treatment plant, or pump the fluid into an approved injection well.[40]

Not every water treatment plant can adequately clean the toxins found in produced water, so treating flowback sometimes requires special treatment plants. Sometimes these suitable treatment plants are distant from the well sites, requiring that the contaminated water be trucked considerable distances. This process is costly and has its own environmental burdens, of course, stimulating the drive to find alternatives to water, to increase the rate of recycling, and to find better methodologies for treating the water. For example, some companies are developing mobile treatment units to treat the produced water on site. Several companies are quite actively trying to reduce water demand or to increase the reusage rate, for example. The company Gasfrac uses propane rather than water to frack gas wells. In the Eagle Ford Shale in Texas, some frackers are buying treated sewage water to use as fracking water.[41]

In many respects, the best way to dispose of the produced water is to inject it into disposal wells, according to the U.S. Department of Energy:

> Underground injection has traditionally been the primary disposal option for oil and gas produced water. In most settings, this may be the best option for shale gas produced water. This process uses salt water disposal wells to place the water thousands of feet underground in porous rock formations that are separated from treatable groundwater by multiple layers of impermeable rock thousands of feet thick.[42]

The EPA has primary responsibility for regulating injection wells, but it shares this responsibility with state regulatory agencies. There are five classes of injection wells, with Class II wells being the ones primarily used for disposing of fracking water.[43] Often these disposal wells are wells created previously in oil production. There are approximately 144,000 Class II wells operating in the United States, and more than 2 billion gallons are injected into these wells daily.[44] While the EPA has the responsibility to regulate these wells and assure the public that they are safe and pose no threat to water supplies, there have been some charges that leakage from injection wells does occur.[45]

Injection wells also have another problem. It now seems clear that the great weights of water injected into some wells have caused earthquakes, all of which have been quite minor to date. This problem came to great public notice in May 2011, due to events near Blackpool, England. There, the company Cuadrilla Resources drilled a test well that apparently set off two small earthquakes. The company acknowledged the possibility and voluntarily suspended drilling operations, a decision that was quickly reinforced by regulatory demands, even though "the two quakes were barely perceptible to humans."[46] Further investigation determined that the two quakes were of magnitude 1.5 and 2.3.[47] The British regulatory authorities have apparently judged these earthquakes to be of limited significance and have permitted the resumption of drilling.[48]

England is not alone in having this experience. In fact, scientists have long known that injection wells can cause small earthquakes, although determining that an injection well is the cause of any particular quake is extremely difficult. Nonetheless, there seems to be a clear increase in seismic activity in areas with injection wells, and this has accelerated with the current rapid development of shale gas. These kinds of quakes have been occurring in Alabama, Arkansas, California, Colorado, Illinois, Louisiana, Mississippi, Nebraska, Nevada, New Mexico, Ohio, Oklahoma, Texas, and British Columbia. In its overview of this problem, the National Research Council concluded:

> Since the 1920s we have recognized that pumping fluids into or out of the Earth has the potential to cause seismic events that can be felt. Seismic events in Basel, Switzerland between 2006 and 2008 were felt by local residents and were related to geothermal energy development. A string of small seismic events in Arkansas, Ohio, Oklahoma, and Texas in the past several years has been related to waste water disposal associated with oil and gas production.[49]

While environmentalists have been quick to capitalize on this additional problem with hydraulic fracturing and the disposal of fracking water, there is another important dimension to this story. Currently, there is a strong movement for addressing the problem of climate change by carbon capture and storage (CCS). However, the chief method of CCS requires the use of the same kind of injection wells and involves the same problems of induced seismicity, but at a more serious level, as the National Research Council also found: "CCS, due to the large net volumes of injected fluids, may have potential for inducing larger seismic events."[50]

Air Quality and the Industry's Carbon Footprint

When both natural gas and coal are delivered to a power plant, there is no doubt that burning natural gas has a much lower environmental impact in general, and a lower carbon footprint in particular, than does coal. However, any complete analysis would have to consider all the environmental impacts and would have to make the appropriate tradeoffs between water usage and disposal, carbon footprint, disturbances at the earth's surface, and so on. Even making a complete comparison of just the relative carbon footprints is daunting, although there is a very general belief that shale gas has a significantly lower overall carbon footprint than does coal. But even this general conclusion is contested. While a thorough study of this issue is beyond the scope of this book, one problem area deserves specific mention.

In the production of natural gas by any method, some methane invariably escapes into the atmosphere. Methane is a particularly potent greenhouse gas, having an effect that is approximately 20 times as large as carbon dioxide per unit volume if unburned methane is released into the atmosphere.[51] Some methane is released into the atmosphere at the wellhead, just because it is impossible to capture all the gas from the very start of production. Also, any leaks in any system of pipes can allow methane to escape as well.

The shifting economics of energy prices have also played a role. With natural gas prices at very low levels, it has become uneconomical to produce gas in certain plays. Further, natural gas is often associated with oil, which has a very high price today. Some drillers pursue oil and also incidentally produce gas, with no way to capture the gas and get it to market in an economical manner. The worst practice in this situation is "venting," simply releasing the unburned gas into the atmosphere. If the gas is first burned and the residue is then released into the air, a practice called *flaring*, the greenhouse effect is much reduced, but it is still quite significant. This problem of flaring has been quite extreme in the Bakken Shale of North Dakota. This area rather suddenly started producing large quantities of both gas and oil from associated deposits, but the area lies distant from the energy transmission infrastructure, making the capture and transport of natural gas uneconomical, but the production of oil is still very attractive. As a result, there has been a serious reliance on flaring in this area.

The *New York Times* reported in 2011 that about 30% of the Bakken gas that was being produced was flared and that this amounted to 100 million cubic feet of gas per day—enough energy to heat 500,000 homes for a day.[52] Besides the lost energy, of course, the flared gas has a significant greenhouse impact. The state is rushing to build out its pipeline network, but flaring was still a significant practice at the end of 2012. Flaring is also a worldwide problem and continues as a common practice in Russia, Iraq, Venezuela, Nigeria, and Kazakhstan.[53] According to a World Bank study, the gas lost to flaring worldwide is worth $50 billion per year.[54]

In assessing the impact of the natural gas revolution on air quality and climate change, it is key to determine the amount of gas being lost directly into the atmosphere or into the air after being flared. This topic has generated a continuing controversy that shows no promise of early resolution, and it certainly cannot be resolved here. The range of estimates for the amount of gas that is escaping is quite large, roughly in the range of 2.4% to 9% of the amount of gas actually produced. But various contestants in this debate persistently attack their opponents' methodology. Some regard the overall impact of shale gas as being worse than the use of coal for climate change. Rather than rehearse these ever-shifting and inconclusive arguments here, I refer the reader to this very robust, if inconclusive, literature.[55]

Physical Effects at the Earth's Surface

Oil and gas production is a heavy industry by any definition, but unlike a manufacturing facility, energy production has a widely distributed geographical effect, and this is particularly true for shale gas production, with its many wells. We have already considered the various effects associated with obtaining, using, and disposing of the large quantities of flowback fluids. Here we turn to factors that one might more obviously consider disturbances associated with drilling and moving equipment to and from the drilling area. First, the creation of a drilling site requires the clearing of land for a well pad, the area where the drilling equipment will be located. It also requires an impoundment pond for the produced water, storage tanks, and so on. In an area that is to be developed for shale gas production, wells are spaced 40 to 160 acres apart. Ideally, multiple wells would be drilled from a single well pad, but this is not always the practice.[56] A typical well pad might require 7 acres, although the actual space requirement varies.

Preparation and use of the well pad requires access, which implies the construction of roads to the well pad site. When the road is built, it carries considerable truck traffic. A single well could require as many as 1,000 truckloads merely to carry away the produced water for processing, for example. But all the drilling operations require considerable traffic. In addition, operations at the well site are noisy, a problem that is particularly irritating when the well pad is located near a residence, a circumstance that often occurs when a rural landowner leases mineral rights.

No one can rightly think that the energy industry is free from disturbing the physical world, and that pertains whether we are thinking of the conventional fossil energy industry, a sea of solar panels, or a field of windmills. The differences are a matter of quantity, type, and aesthetics. Most of the conventional fossil energy industry has taken place away from the general view of the public, but its effects occasionally explode into public consciousness when there is a large and visible effect. But the natural gas revolution differs from the conventional means of obtaining oil, coal, and gas by being widely distributed geographically, impinging on new physical environments that are closer to people's homes, and degrading areas treasured by all of us. In this sense, the unconventional fossil energy industry is similar to solar farms and wind farms—they are near us and in our view, making it more difficult to ignore the environmental and aesthetic costs of obtaining the energy on which our high level of consumption and its associated energy intensity depend.

The Social Dimension

The natural gas revolution has brought drilling to new areas, including many areas prized for their natural beauty and associated with an enduring nostalgia for rural life. This has been particularly true for the rural areas of the Marcellus Shale, in the heavily wooded and farming areas of Pennsylvania and New York. The social upheavals involved have been poignantly described in Seamus McGraw's book, *The End of Country* (2011). And the human drama that has affected many in the Marcellus region has been repeated in somewhat different terms in many other areas of the United States.

There can be no doubt that the dislocations described by many authors are real. For example, some property owners have leased their mineral rights only to become quickly distressed and disappointed by the sudden presence of a bustling industrial process right at their doorsteps. For some, the anticipated financial rewards have failed to materialize when their property proved to contain only minimal gas. For others, the payoffs have been quite handsome and have let quite a few people keep family homesteads and farms that they otherwise would have lost because they are uneconomical enterprises. Natural gas development has generated winners and losers in other ways as well. Many property owners have prospered and been well compensated for the upheavals that the new industry has brought to their areas. But local residents of the same area who own no property must endure a much greater level of activity and social disruption, with no compensating lease payments. However, in many instances, the boom times that gas drilling bring enrich employment opportunities for many and stimulate economic activity for a variety of local businesses as well.

Some of the results have been quite surprising and far-reaching. The desire to cash in on the fracking boom has led to local disputes between those who hope to benefit and others who prefer to retain the status quo. Even for those who lease, there are sometimes unpleasant surprises beyond lease payments that never quite materialize in the great amounts initially anticipated. There is some concern that allowing fracking on one's land can impair the ability to mortgage the property due to fear of contamination.[57] Around the world, many nations are now rushing to develop their own technical abilities to frack, and the changes are so vast that they promise to alter geopolitical power balances, as the next three chapters explore. On a more human scale, the fracking boom can also cause completely unanticipated effects for small players very far removed from the new drilling rigs. This has certainly been the case for the impoverished guar bean farmers of Rajasthan, who suddenly have become important economic players as the source of a previously insignificant bean of somewhat limited appeal as a foodstuff.[58]

The ultimate decisions on the social benefits or detriments of the natural gas revolution for areas of heavy activity largely depend on how one views economic growth in general. Many view the greater prosperity that their areas suddenly enjoy as a virtually unalloyed benefit, while others see the entire movement as clearly disastrous. This is the kind of issue that cannot be definitively resolved because much depends on personal perspective and the anticipated benefits or costs. Without question, when the frackers come to small towns, things are going to change, and these environmental and social effects continue to generate their own growing literature.[59]

Conclusion: From Coal to Natural Gas or from Natural Gas to Coal?

More than any other environmental or social development emerging from the natural gas revolution, there is one that encapsulates the scale and importance of the developments now sweeping the world. In the view of many, the United States has been the recalcitrant spoiler among developed nations in the race to save the world from climate change. Refusing to participate fully in the Kyoto Protocol and tardy in switching to renewables and other clean energy resources, the United States has been roundly excoriated by many other nations. By contrast, Europe has been portrayed as leading the charge to save the planet, with the famed German *Energiewende* (energy transition) being the favored poster child of proper energy behavior.

Something very unexpected and profound is now occurring that throws these value judgments into serious doubt. Against all expectation, the carbon emissions of the United States are falling, as Figure 4.1 shows. Meanwhile, carbon dioxide emissions in Europe are rising.

This stunning about-face is essentially a product of the natural gas revolution.[60]

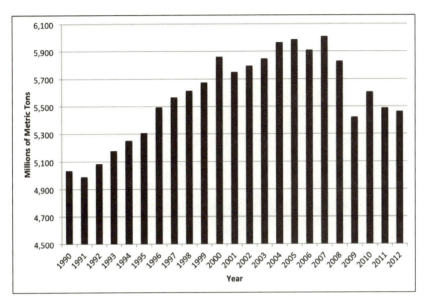

Figure 4.1 U. S. Carbon Dioxide Emissions from Energy Consumption, 1990–2012 (Millions of Metric Tons)

Source: U.S. Energy Information Administration (USEIA), "Monthly Energy Review," Table 12.1, "Carbon Dioxide Emissions from Energy Consumption by Source." Available at www.eia.gov/totalenergy/data/monthly/pdf/sec12_3.pdf.

Partially because natural gas in the United States has become so abundant and plentiful, coal-fired power plants are being shuttered across the United States and being replaced with natural gas combined cycle (NGCC) power plants, which are much more efficient than coal-powered plants. In 2005, the average gas-powered plant in the United States required 7,920 Btu to generate a kilowatt-hour of electricity, compared to the average coal plant which required 10,410 Btu for the same output of electricity. However, the most advanced NGCC plants require only 6,333 Btu versus the most efficient of the coal plants which require 7,754 Btu. Closing an average coal-powered plant and replacing its generating capacity with today's efficient NGCC plants results in an energy savings of 39%, with an attendant reduction in carbon dioxide emissions.[61] Further, the

United States is making this transition at a rapid rate, especially across the eastern half of the United States. By 2020, 15% or more of coal-generating capacity will close in many states in the upper Midwest, Southeast, and New England states, with almost every other state closing 5% to 15% of coal-fired generating capacity.[62]

Meanwhile, in radical contrast, the Europeans are closing gas-fired plants and building coal-powered plants. As the *Financial Times* reported in late 2012, "Europe has strict policies to promote forms of low-carbon energy but demand for coal, the dirtiest fuel for making electricity, has grown this year as that for less-polluting gas has shrunk. The reason is simple: price."[63] Europe has yet to get any significant natural gas from hydraulic fracturing and remains heavily reliant on relatively expensive gas imported largely from Russia. Both Germany and the Netherlands are building substantial new coal capacity. Europe is importing much of the coal for these plants from the United States; European coal imports from the United States increased 29% in just the year 2012.[64] Across the English Channel, British utilities are running their gas-powered plants at 37% of capacity but burning coal at coal-fired plants at 80% to 90% capacity.[65]

In what has been called the "irony of ironies,"[66] the environmentally heedless, hydrocarbon-dependent United States enjoys cheap natural gas and falling carbon dioxide emissions, while the virtuous and environmentally conscious Europeans are shunning hydraulic fracturing, closing gas-powered plants, and building coal-fired electrical capacity. This has to be reckoned as a stunning and completely unanticipated environmental consequence of the natural gas revolution, and one that should at least stem certitude, smugness, and sanctimony over the ultimate environmental virtue or vice of the natural gas revolution.

Notes

1. Sion Morgan, "Shale Gas Extraction Could Be 'Catastrophic,' AMs Told," Walesonline.com, March 7, 2013.

2. Kate Galbraith, "As Fracking Increases, So Do Fears about Water Supply," *New York Times*, March 7, 2013.

3. Kate Galbraith, "Unlocking the Secrets Behind Hydraulic Fracturing," *New York Times*, January 14, 2012.

4. Jack Healy, "For Farms in the West, Oil Wells Are Thirsty Rivals," *New York Times*, September 5, 2012.

5. Jack Healy, "For Farms in the West, Oil Wells Are Thirsty Rivals," *New York Times*, September 5, 2012.

6. Massachusetts Institute of Technology, "The Future of Natural Gas," 2010, p. 44.

7. Kate Galbraith, "As Fracking Increases, So Do Fears about Water Supply," *New York Times*, March 7, 2013.

8. Alison Sider, Russell Gold, and Ben Lefebvre, "Drillers Begin Reusing 'Frack Water,'" *Wall Street Journal*, November 18, 2012.

9. Jack Healy, "For Farms in the West, Oil Wells Are Thirsty Rivals," *New York Times*, September 5, 2012.

10. Russell Gold and Ana Campoy, "Oil's Growing Thirst for Water," *Wall Street Journal*, December 6, 2011.

11. Vikram Rao, "Sustainable Shale Gas Production Is Feasible," Naturalgaseurope.com, August 30, 2012.

12. Alison Sider, Russell Gold, and Ben Lefebvre, "Drillers Begin Reusing 'Frack Water,'" *Wall Street Journal*, November 18, 2012.

13. Naturalgasasia.com, "Halliburton's New Technology Enables Reuse of Produced Water," March 7, 2013.

14. Kate Galbraith, "As Fracking Increases, So Do Fears about Water Supply," *New York Times*, March 7, 2013.

15. Naturalgasasia.com, "Halliburton's New Technology Enables Reuse of Produced Water," March 7, 2013.

16. Naturalgasasia.com, "Shell Fracking with Foam," August 15, 2012.

17. Jack Healy, "For Farms in the West, Oil Wells Are Thirsty Rivals," *New York Times*, September 5, 2012.

18. Naturalgaseurope.com, "Balancing Water Risks Will Be Key to Releasing China's Shale Gas Potential," December 24, 2012.

19. Naturalgaseurope.com, "Balancing Water Risks Will Be Key to Releasing China's Shale Gas Potential," December 24, 2012.

20. George P. Mitchell and Mark D. Zoback, "The Duty to Fracture Responsibly," Naturalgasamericas.com, February 20, 2012.

21. See U.S. Geological Survey, "Dissolved Methane in New York Groundwater," September 2012. Available at http://pubs.usgs.gov/of/2012/1162/. This document discusses the widespread occurrence of methane in ground water.

22. State of Colorado Oil & Gas Conservation Commission, "Statement on the Documentary *Gasland*," no date. See also Matt Ridley, "The Shale Gas Shock," The Global Warming Policy Foundation, GWPF Report 2, 2011.

23. The following three articles address the Dimock experience: Daniel Gilbert and Russell Gold, "EPA Backpedals on Fracking Contamination," *Wall Street Journal*, March 30, 2012; Kenneth P. Green, "EPA Exonerates Fracking in Pennsylvania," Aei-ideas.org, July 25, 2012; and Mike Soraghan, "EPA's Dimock Results Cloud Pa.'s Pollution Case," E&E Reporter, May 30, 2012.

24. John Steele Gordon, "Crucifying the Oil and Gas Industry," *Commentary*, April 27, 2012.

25. Daniel Gilbert and Russell Gold, "EPA Backpedals on Fracking Contamination," *Wall Street Journal*, March 30, 2012.

26. Kevin Begos, "Marcellus Shale Study Claims Gas Drilling Did Not Contaminate Drinking Water Wells," Huffingtonpost.com, July 10, 2012.

27. Kate Galbraith, "Proposed Rules on Fracking Gain Cautious Praise," *New York Times*, December 8, 2012.

28. Eliza Griswold, "Situation Normal All Fracked Up," *New York Times*, November 17, 2011.

29. Nicholas Kusnetz, "North Dakota's Oil Boom Brings Damage Along with Prosperity," ProPublica.com, June 7, 2012.

30. Abrahm Lustgarten, "Injection Wells: The Poison Beneath Us," ProPublica.com, June 26, 2012.

31. Kirk Johnson, "Drilling in Fast-Growing Areas Ushers in New Era of Tension," *New York Times*, October 24, 2011.

32. Naturalgaseurope.com, "No Contamination Found in Sampled Shale Gas Exploration Wells," January 10, 2013.

33. Jon Entine, "Fracking Safety Improves Dramatically, Says Independent Study," Forbes.com, May 15, 2012.

34. Jon Entine, "Fracking Safety Improves Dramatically, Says Independent Study," Forbes.com, May 15, 2012.

35. A *New York Times* editorial introduced the "loophole" appellation: "The Halliburton Loophole," November 3, 2009. For a discussion of the legal issues involved, see Susan L. Sakmar, "The Global Shale Gas Initiative: Will the United States Be the Role Model for the Development of Shale Gas Around the World?" University of San Francisco Law Research Paper No. 2011-27, 2011.

36. Kate Galbraith, "Unlocking the Secrets Behind Hydraulic Fracturing," *New York Times*, January 14, 2012. See also "Fight Escalates Over Chemical Secrecy in Hydraulic Fracturing," Naturalgaseurope.com, July 2, 2012; and Deborah Solomon, "SEC Bears Down on Fracking," *Wall Street Journal*, August 25, 2011.

37. Ben Wolfgang, "I Drank Fracking Fluid, Says Colorado Gov. John Hickenlooper," *Washington Times*, February 12, 2013.

38. Chris Mooney, "The Truth about Fracking," *Scientific American*, November 2011, pp. 80–85.

39. Robbie Brown, "Gas Drillers Asked to Change Method of Waste Disposal," *New York Times*, April 19, 2011.

40. KPMG, "Watered-Down: Minimizing Water Risks in Shale Gas and Oil Drilling," 2012. Available at www.kpmginstitutes.com.

41. Kate Galbraith, "As Fracking Increases, So Do Fears about Water Supply," *New York Times*, March 7, 2013.

42. U.S. Department of Energy, "Modern Shale Gas Development in the United States: A Primer," April 2009, p. 68.

43. For an overview of the different types of wells, their safety, and their regulation, see U.S. Department of Energy, "Modern Shale Gas Development in the United States: A Primer," April 2009, pp. 32 ff.

44. Environmental Protection Agency, "Class II Wells: Oil and Gas Related Injection Wells (Class II)." Available at http://water.epa.gov/type/groundwater/uic/class2/.

45. See Abrahm Lustgarten, "Injection Wells: The Poison Beneath Us," ProPublica.com, June 26, 2012.

46. David Jolly, "U.K. Company Suspends Controversial Drilling Procedure," *New York Times*, June 1, 2011.

47. Henry Fountain, "Add Quakes to Rumblings Over Gas Rush," *New York Times*, December 12, 2011.

48. Alex Morales, "U.K. Plans to Allow Shale Gas Drilling to Resume This Year," Businessweek.com, October 16, 2012.

49. National Research Council, "Induced Seismicity Potential in Energy Technologies," June 15, 2012.

50. National Research Council, "Induced Seismicity Potential in Energy Technologies," June 15, 2012. See p. 1 of the included Executive Summary and p. 2 of the full document.

51. See Mary Lashley Barcella, Samantha Gross, and Surya Rajan, "Mismeasuring Methane: Estimating Greenhouse Gas Emissions from Upstream Natural Gas Development," IHS CERA, August 2011; and John M. Broder, "U.S. Caps Emissions in Drilling for Fuel," *New York Times*, April 18, 2012.

52. Clifford Krauss, "In North Dakota, Flames of Wasted Natural Gas Light the Prairie," *New York Times*, September 26, 2011.

53. Ken Silverstein, "The Other F-Word of Shale Drilling," *Forbes*, September 27, 2012.

54. Joe Gurowsky, "Gas Flaring Back in the Spotlight," Foreign Policy Association, November 9, 2012. Available at http://foreignpolicyblogs.com.

55. See Mary Lashley Barcella, Samantha Gross, and Surya Rajan, "Mismeasuring Methane: Estimating Greenhouse Gas Emissions from Upstream Natural Gas Development," IHS CERA, August 2011; Lawrence M. Cathles III, Larry Brown, Milton Taam, and Andrew Hunter, "A Commentary on 'The Greenhouse-Gas Footprint of Natural Gas in Shale Formations,' by R. W. Howarth, R. Santoro, and Anthony Ingraffea," *Climatic Change*, 2012;113:525–535; L. M. Cathles, "Assessing the Greenhouse Impact of Natural Gas," working paper, June 6, 2012; Lawrence M. Cathles, Larry Brown, Andrew Hunter, and Milton Taam, "Press Release: Response to Howarth et al's Reply," February 29, 2012; Bill Chameides, "Natural Gas: A Bridge to a Low-Carbon Future or Not?" Huffingtonpost.com, July 20, 2012; Robert W. Howarth, Renee Santoro, and Anthony Ingraffea, "Methane and the Greenhouse-Gas Footprint of Natural Gas from Shale Formations," *Climatic Change*, 2011;106:679–690; Michael Levi, "Yellow Flags on a New Methane Study," Council on Foreign Relations, cfr.org, February 13, 2012; Abrahm Lustgarten, "More Reasons to Question Whether Gas Is Cleaner Than Coal," ProPublica.com, April 12, 2011. Available at www.propublica.org/article/more-reasons-to-question-whether-gas-is-cleaner-than-coal. Accessed April 27, 2011; Naturalgaseurope.com, "'The Entire Natural Gas System' Is Driving Methane Emissions: MIT Study," December 6, 2012; Vikram Rao, *Shale Gas: The Promise and the Peril*, Research Triangle Park, NC: RTI Press, 2012; Jeff Tollefson, "Methane Leaks Erode Green Credentials of Natural Gas," *Nature*, January 2, 2013; Bryan Walsh, "Natural Gas and the Invisible Spill: How Much Methane Is Reaching the Atmosphere?" *Time*, April 10, 2012; and Tom Zeller, Jr., "Studies Say Natural Gas Has Its Own Environmental Problems," *New York Times*, April 11, 2011.

56. U.S. Department of Energy, "Modern Shale Gas Development in the United States: A Primer," April 2009, p. 21.

57. See Kurt Cobb, "How the Fracking Mess Is about to Make the Mortgage Mess Worse," *Energy Bulletin*, May 20, 2012; and Elisabeth N. Radow, "Homeowners and Gas Drilling Leases: Boon or Bust?" *NYSBA Journal*, November/December 2011, pp. 10–21.

58. Gardiner Harris, "In Tiny Bean, India's Dirt-Poor Farmers Strike Gas-Drilling Gold," *New York Times*, July 16, 2012; Naturalgaseurope.com, "The Impact of Soaring Guar Gum Prices," June 21, 2012; and Braden Reddall, "Frackers in Frantic Search for Guar Bean Substitutes," Reuters.com, August 13, 2012.

59. For some recent commentary on these social aspects, see Michael Barone, "North Dakota Boom Shows Importance of Free Markets," Investors.com, July 20, 2012; Ellen Cantarow, "How Rural America Got Fracked," Europeanenergyreview.eu, June 4, 2012; "Booming North Dakota by the Numbers," *Economist*, March 16, 2013; Eenews.net, "Ballot Measure to Ban Fracking Floated in Colorado Town," June 1, 2012; Mary Esch, "For NY Farmers, Fracking Means Salvation—Or Ruin," Associated Press, May 22, 2012; Daniel Gilbert and Kris Maher, "Shale Gas Fuels Legal Boom," *Wall Street Journal*, October 31, 2011; Jeff Goodell, "The Big Fracking Bubble: The Scam Behind Aubrey McClendon's Gas Boom," *Rolling Stone*, May 5, 2012; Eliza Griswold, "Situation Normal All Fracked Up," *New York Times*, November 17, 2011; Jack Healy, "For Farms in the West, Oil Wells Are Thirsty Rivals," *New York Times*, September 5, 2012; "With Ban on Drilling Practice, Town Lands in Thick of Dispute," *New York Times*, November 25, 2012; Jon Hurdle, "New York Town Is Sued Over Ban on Fracking Discussion," *New York Times*, February 12, 2013; "Utica Shale May Be Its Own Energy Game-Changer," Energy.aol.com, October 7, 2011; Bill McKibben, "Why Not Frack?" *New York Review of Books*, March 8, 2012; Steven Mufson, "In North Dakota, the Gritty Side of an Oil Boom," *Washington Post*, July 18, 2012; Mireya Navarro, "New York Sues Over a Drilling Rules Plan," *New York Times*, May 31, 2011; "Report Outlines Rewards and Risks of Upstate Natural Gas Drilling," *New York Times*, September 7, 2011; Vikram Rao, *Shale Gas: The Promise and the Peril*, Research Triangle Park, NC: RTI Press, 2012; Katharine Q. Seelye, "Pennsylvania Hunting and Fracking Vie for State Lands," *New York Times*, November 11, 2011; Mike Soraghan, "Wyoming Official Pins Pavillion Pollution Complaints on Greed," *E&E Reporter*, June 6, 2012; and Sabrina Tavernise, "Pennsylvania Set to Allow Local Taxes on Shale Gas," *New York Times*, February 7, 2012.

60. Institute for Energy Research, "U.S. Energy-Related Carbon Dioxide Emissions Are Declining," July 20, 2012.

61. David K. Bellman, "Power Plant Efficiency Outlook," Working Document of the NPC Global Oil & Gas Study, Topic Paper #4, May 8, 2007. See Table 1, p. 7.

62. Charles Ebinger, Kevin Massy, and Govinda Avasarala, "Liquid Markets: Assessing the Case for U.S. Exports of Liquefied Natural Gas," Brookings Institution, May 2012. See Figure 4.

63. Sylvia Pfeifer, "Cost Advantage Fuels Demand for Coal," *Financial Times*, October 3, 2012.

64. Guy Chazan and Gerrit Wiesmann, "Shale Gas Boom Sparks EU Coal Revival," *Financial Times*, February 3, 2013.

65. Sylvia Pfeifer, "Cost Advantage Fuels Demand for Coal," *Financial Times*, October 3, 2012.

66. Peter C. Glover, "Irony of Ironies: Europe Switches to Coal as US Gas Glut Reduces Emissions," *Energy Tribune*, July 12, 2012. See also Robert Bryce, "Ban Natural Gas! No, Ban Coal!" National Review Online, June 11, 2012. Available at http://www.nationalreview.com; Fiona Harvey, "Coal Resurgence Threatens Climate Change Targets," *Guardian*, October 29, 2012; Institute for Energy Research, "U.S. Energy-Related Carbon Dioxide Emissions Are Declining," July 20, 2012; Terry Macalister, "King Coal Nears the End of the Line," *Guardian*, March 7, 2013; Richard K. Morse, "Cleaning Up Coal," Foreignaffairs.com, July/August 2012; and Wolf Richter, "Natural Gas Is Pushing Coal Over the Cliff," *Business Insider*, August 21, 2012.

5

The United States and China[*]

The United States and China are the world's two largest consumers of energy and possess the world's two largest economies. For its part, the United States brandishes the world's most capable military, including the most formidable navy. Compared to the United States, China has a very rapidly accelerating economy, which provides the resources to fuel its burgeoning military capability. These features make these two nations the most important countries in the world for understanding the relationship between geopolitics and energy in general, as well as for comprehending the effects that the natural gas revolution will have on world energy and geopolitics.

Energy in the United States and China

Ever since the Industrial Revolution, economic productivity has depended on exploiting energy derived from nonorganic sources—energy other than that derived from muscle power and plant life. At any given moment, technology is fixed, and economic productivity

---

[*] This chapter draws from a number of other sources, including three of my recent articles: "Geopolitical Threats to World Energy Markets," *Journal of Social, Political, and Economic Studies*, Summer 2011, 36, pp. 154–196; "Geopolitics and World Energy Markets," in Betty and Russell Simkins (eds.), *Energy Finance: Analysis and Valuation, Risk Management, and the Future of Energy*, Hoboken, NJ: John Wiley & Sons, Inc., 2013, pp. 19–48; and "The Natural Gas Revolution and the World's Largest Economies," *Journal of Social, Political, and Economic Studies*, Winter 2012, 37, pp. 415–467.

remains closely tied to the techniques available to use energy, especially hydrocarbons, nuclear, and hydropower. This claim does not belie important differences in how nations and economies exploit energy resources, as even the richest and most industrialized economies differ significantly in how effectively they turn energy into economic product. Table 5.1 presents data on the world's 10 largest economies, their consumption of energy, and their energy use relative to their economic product. The United States has the world's largest economy by far—twice as large as China's. Of course, China's economy has been expanding much more rapidly than the U.S. economy, and almost everyone expects China's rapid growth to continue.

Although the United States has a gross domestic product (GDP) slightly more than twice as large as China's, China has recently overtaken the United States in total energy consumed. This implies that the United States is much more efficient in using energy, at least as measured by GDP produced per unit of energy. As Table 5.1 shows, the United States generates $21.46 of GDP per gallon of oil equivalent, while China is only able to produce $9.10 for the same amount of energy. Of course, there are many reasons for these differences besides pure industrial or economic efficiency. China has many millions of people who consume energy yet produce almost no measured GDP. Further, the United States effectively outsources much of its energy consumption to China because China operates many energy-intensive industries and sends finished products back to the United States. As a result, China expends energy on behalf of the United States as the real consumer of the goods produced with that energy. Figure 5.1 compares the United States and China both in terms of energy consumption and growth of GDP.

Table 5.1 The World's Large Economies: Energy Consumption and Energy Efficiency

GDP Rank	Rank Among 10 Economies		Country	Energy Consumption (Million Gallons of Oil Equivalent)	2011 USD GDP ($Trillions)	USD GDP (per Gallon of Oil Equivalent)
	Energy Consumption	Energy Efficiency				
1	2	7	United States	698,604	14.991	21.46
2	1	9	China	804,474	7.318	9.10
3	5	3	Japan	147,029	5.867	39.90
4	6	4	Germany	94,325	3.601	38.18
5	8	5	France	74,777	2.773	37.08
6	7	6	Brazil	82,165	2.477	30.15
7	9	2	United Kingdom	61,016	2.445	40.07
8	10	1	Italy	51,873	2.194	42.30
9	3	10	Russian Federation	211,062	1.858	8.80
10	4	8	India	172,119	1,848	10.74
			Ten largest economies	2,397,443	45.372	18.93
			Total world	3,778,736	68.656	18.17
			Ten largest economies as a percentage of the world	63.445652	66.09	

Abbreviations: GDP = gross domestic product; USD = United States dollar.

Sources: Energy-related information was drawn from BP, "Statistical Review of World Energy," June 2012. GDP data were provided by the World Bank, available at http://data.worldbank.org/indicator/NY.GDP.MKTP.CD, accessed March 29, 2013.

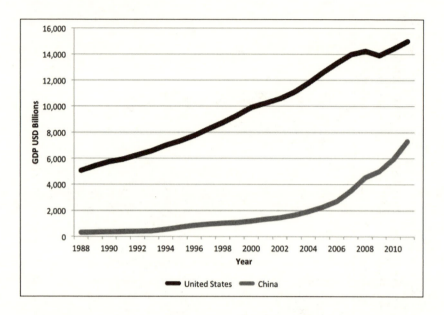

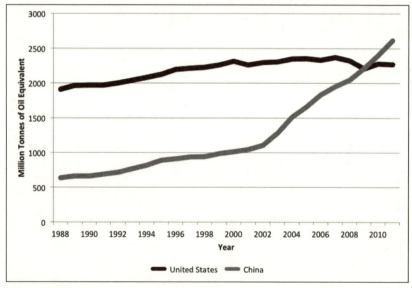

Figure 5.1 The United States and China, GDP and energy consumption, 1988–2011.

Sources: Energy-related information was drawn from BP, "Statistical Review of World Energy," June 2012. GDP data were provided by the World Bank, available at http://data.worldbank.org/indicator/NY.GDP.MKTP.CD, accessed March 29, 2013.

Table 5.1 also includes GDP and energy consumption for the other eight largest economies of the world. While the United States is twice as productive in using energy as China, Italy is almost twice as productive as the United States. The seven most highly developed economies are much more energy-efficient than are Russia, China, and India. In general, more highly developed economies tend to be more energy-efficient, and the smaller the energy sector is as a proportion of the total economy, the greater the energy efficiency tends to be. As Table 5.1 shows, the 10 largest economies account for just about two-thirds of the world's GDP and energy consumption, implying that these largest economies are just slightly more energy-efficient than the world as a whole. More specifically, the 10 largest economies produce $18.93 of GDP for each gallon of oil, compared to the world's $18.17.

Table 5.2 shows the primary sources of energy for both China and the United States, expressed in the common units of million tonnes of oil equivalent (MTOE). Both countries rely very heavily on hydrocarbons in their energy mix, with China deriving 92.6% of all energy from hydrocarbons compared to the 86.4% reliance in the United States. However, among the hydrocarbons, China and the United States differ quite significantly in the sources on which they depend most heavily. Most notably, 70% of all energy in China comes from coal, compared to only 22% in the United States. However, the United States is twice as reliant on oil as is China, and the United States obtains 28% of its energy from natural gas, compared to China's less than 5%.

Table 5.2 Primary Sources of Energy, 2011

Million Tonnes of Oil Equivalent

Country	Oil	Natural Gas	Coal	Nuclear	Hydroelectric	Renewable	Total	All Hydrocarbon
China	461.8	117.6	1,839.4	19.5	157.0	17.7	2,613.2	2,418.9
US	833.6	626.0	501.9	188.2	74.3	45.3	2,269.3	1,961.5
Percentage from Each Source								
China	17.7	4.5	70.4	0.7	6.0	0.7	100.0	92.6
US	36.7	27.6	22.1	8.3	3.3	2.0	100.0	86.4

Source: BP, "Statistical Review of World Energy," June 2012.

Both the United States and China are essentially self-reliant for coal, and the United States has become a significant coal exporter, largely because it has been reducing its domestic consumption of coal for some time. China's heavy reliance on coal, especially for electrical power generation, bears a large responsibility for the country's staggering pollution problem, which it must solve, to some extent, by migrating to other energy sources. In part, China's heavy use of coal remains as a legacy of the Communist era, with its weak ability to secure convertible currencies to finance imports. In addition, China's previous poor economic and technological development shifted its energy reliance toward coal. As China continues to mature economically, its transportation sector will grow relative to other parts of its economy, so transportation fuels will become a larger part of China's energy mix. China can reduce its dependence on coal by developing its domestic gas resources and using gas to replace coal in generating electrical power.

China's Shale Gas Resources

Table 5.3 compares the natural gas resources of the United States and China, drawing on estimates of proved reserves and technically recoverable resources provided by BP and the U.S. Energy Information Administration (USEIA). In terms of proved reserves, the United States has twice as much natural gas as China. However, if we consider technically recoverable shale gas resources, China's natural gas resource base is 50% larger. ven China's huge gas resources, its almost desperate need for all the energy it can acquire and its special need for cleaner energy, China is understandably moving aggressively to acquiring more natural gas. However, China must overcome a number of very significant stumbling blocks to convert those technically recoverable gas resources into usable energy.

Table 5.3 Estimates of Proved and Technically Recoverable Gas Resources (Billions of Cubic Meters)

	BP	U.S. Energy Information Administration	
Country	Proved Reserves	Proved Reserves	Technically Recoverable Shale Gas Resources
United States	8,500	7,716	24,409
China	3,100	3,030	36,104

Sources: BP, "Statistical Review of World Energy," June 2012; and USEIA, "World Shale Gas Resources: An Initial Assessment of 14 Regions Outside the United States," April 2011, p. 4.

The United States has a good understanding of its gas resources; in contrast, the understanding of China's gas resources remains very poor. The United States has had an active program of oil and gas drilling for about 150 years, and it has long been the home of the most sophisticated energy technology. China's geology remains comparatively poorly understood, and energy technology there remains behind the world standard. China recognizes that it is behind the curve in gas technology and has initiated very aggressive steps to acquire the knowledge it needs. Anyone who has observed the transformations in China over the past 30 years must understand how quickly China may ascend the learning curve and transform its standing in the world in economic performance and technological competence. Plate 9 shows the major shale gas basins of China. They range from the Tarim Basin in the Taklimakan Desert in China's extreme west, to the Bohai Basin on the littoral of the East China Sea, to the Sichuan Basin in the south. Advances in the knowledge of China's geology will likely lead to the discovery of other important basins. Even without those future discoveries, we know that China already possesses very large gas resources.

China is currently operating its 12th Five-Year Plan to cover 2011–2015, and it has initiated a Shale Gas Development Plan for 2011–2015. The plan for shale gas prominently declares shale gas to be a mineral distinct from other hydrocarbons; this distinction frees shale gas from the grip of China's extant big three state-owned energy firms: China National Petroleum Corporation (CNPC), China Petroleum and Chemical Corporation (Sinopec), and China National Offshore Oil Corporation (CNOOC).[1] China's ambitious plans call for the rapid production of shale gas, reaching 6.5 billion cubic meters (bcm) by 2015 and 100 bcm by 2020. As Table 5.4 shows, China consumed 117.6 MTOE of natural gas in 2011, which is approximately equivalent in energy value to 165 bcm. In sum, China wants to produce enough shale gas by 2020 to equal two-thirds of its current consumption. However, *China Daily* reports that as of 2013, China is producing essentially zero shale gas.[2]

Table 5.4 United States and China, Hydrocarbon Consumption, Production, and Import Reliance (Million Tons of Oil Equivalent)

	Oil	Natural Gas	Coal
China			
Consumption	461.8	117.6	1,839.4
Production	203.6	92.3	1,956.0
Implied imports	258.2	25.3	N/A
Import reliance (%)	55.9	21.5	N/A
United States			
Consumption	833.6	626.0	501.9
Production	352.3	592.3	556.8
Implied imports	481.3	33.7	N/A
Import reliance (%)	57.7	5.4	N/A

Source: BP, "Statistical Review of World Energy," June 2012.

The first major impediment that China faces in exploiting its shale reserves is securing improved assessment and acquisition technology. To that end, China is investing in U.S. and other companies with the necessary expertise. However, the *Wall Street Journal* points out that China suffers from a "legal vacuum for shale gas development,"[3] which impedes the acquisition of the needed technology, and China's legendary lack of respect for intellectual property rights constitutes yet another legal and technological stumbling block to cooperation with Western firms possessing the requisite energy knowledge and exploration techniques.

Even with the right technology in place, China faces some brutal facts of geology and water limitations. Compared to the United States, much of China's shale gas appears to be located farther below ground and to exist in a more complex geological setting that will make its acquisition more difficult.[4] Compared to the United States, China also suffers from a paucity of water resources. As we have seen, the water demands of hydraulic fracturing have caused contention in the United States, but the problems are almost certain to be worse in China. The World Economic Forum estimates that China is extracting 25% more ground water per year than nature can replace.[5] This is a countrywide estimate, but the problems are even worse in some areas of natural gas deposits.

The Tarim Basin shown on the left of Plate 9 provides a compelling example of the difficulties. The Tarim Basin is essentially the area of the Taklamakan Desert. In the days of the active trade along the Silk Road, various routes ran either north or south of the Taklamakan, with very few brave souls daring to cross the desert directly. According to some contested etymology, the name means something like "the place from which no one returns," "if you go in, you won't come out," or "Desert of Death." If these appellations are insufficient to convey the basic idea, the travails experienced by Sven Hedin, Aurel Stein, and other early Western tomb robbers of Chinese Turkestan are even more compelling.[6] Of course, the need for energy has driven successful exploitation in even more hostile regions, so the terrain and climate are probably not insurmountable.

Not only is water scarce in some Chinese shale basins, the deeper shale formations demand substantially more water per well than wells in the United States typically require. Wells in the United States average about 4 million gallons per well.[7] Some estimates put the amount of water necessary for a Chinese well at 100% greater or even more.

When gas finally reaches the wellhead, transportation becomes an immediate issue. The United States already possesses about 300,000 miles of gas pipelines, constituting an amazingly dense network that blankets the entire country. By comparison, China has yet to develop any comparable infrastructure, and some of the basins are far from the existing modest network that China does possess. All these technological problems—complex geology, deeper shale strata, scarce water, poor pipeline infrastructure—conspire to raise the cost of drilling a shale well in China compared to in the United States. One estimate shows the typical cost in the United States as being about $3 million and estimates that the cost of a comparable well in China is $5 to $12 million.[8] The cost factor can be quite serious. Even in the United States, with a cheaper cost per well, many wells appear to be uneconomical with prices for natural gas lying in the $3 to $4 per million British thermal unit (Btu) region.

Only time will tell whether China can exploit its shale resources in an economical manner, but China certainly has the economic need for greatly expanded and much cleaner energy resources. Further, the national ambitions that China appears to hold also demand much more energy than China currently commands. However, recent world history suggests that companies and countries are sufficiently willing to do whatever it takes to secure the energy that their ambitions require.

Energy Imports for China and the United States

Every nation requires adequate energy supplies to sustain its economic viability and provide for its national security, but these concerns are especially intense for two nations with the world's largest economies and greatest geopolitical pretensions. Both the United States and China rely very heavily on hydrocarbons in their energy mix—86.4% and 92.6%, respectively, as Table 5.2 illustrates. Both the United States and China are essentially self-reliant in coal production, so import issues concern mainly oil and natural gas, and neither nation produces enough oil or natural gas to meet its current needs.

Up through World War II, the United States generally provided a tremendous amount of oil to the world. However, this oil was obtained by exploiting the most easily available resources, which led ultimately to a decline in U.S. oil production and a period of heavy reliance on imported oil that continues to the present. Both China and the United States import slightly more than half their oil, but the United States relies on oil in its energy mix twice as much as China does. Nonetheless, oil imports are critical for both nations, as oil continues to play a vital role in transportation. Energy sources are somewhat fungible, and previous chapters have shown that natural gas will probably play an increasing role in transportation.

While natural gas is already important in the hydrocarbon energy mix, and while it will become even more important still, oil remains the most critical form of energy because of its energy density and wide range of uses. Thus, both the United States and China will remain highly dependent on securing adequate oil resources for some time. While there is much talk of energy independence for the United States and no such happy prospect in the offing for China, both nations currently depend very heavily on hydrocarbon energy, much of which both nations import. Table 5.4 compares the import demands of both nations, with the almost equal reliance of both nations on imported oil in terms of their energy mix. If we summarize the overall situation for hydrocarbon imports in the common terms of MTOE, we find that the United States currently imports 514 MTOE in oil and gas, while China imports only 283.5; China meets the balance of its energy consumption with its massive domestic coal consumption.

As shown in the bottom panel of Table 5.4, the United States imports one-third more natural gas than China—33.7 MTOE for the United States versus 25.3 for China. The United States also imports almost twice as much oil—481.3 MTOE for the United States compared to China's 258.2. In total, the United States imports 26.3% of its hydrocarbon needs from other nations, while China depends on other countries for only 11.7%. These figures appear to expose an important vulnerability for the United States as being highly dependent on other nations for its energy.

Table 5.5 shows the principal sources for oil and natural gas imports for China and the United States, indicating the percentages derived from each geographical area for oil or method of importation for natural gas. As the table indicates, China draws 60% of its oil imports from the distant Middle East and West Africa, with another 14% coming almost totally by seaborne trade from the Asia Pacific region and from Latin America. This nearly 75% reliance on oil imports shipped by sea renders China extremely dependent on secure sea lanes, particularly those in the Indian Ocean and the South China Sea. In contrast to China's reliance on long-distance seaborne oil imports, the United States secures over half of its oil imports from Canada, Mexico, and Central and South America, with almost all imports from Mexico and Canada coming via pipeline. Thus, this entire oil import region in the Western Hemisphere either utilizes pipeline delivery or lies well within the close control of the U.S. Navy. The United States secures an additional 16% of its oil from West Africa, via fairly secure sea lanes across the Atlantic Ocean, leaving the United States still reliant on the Middle East for 22% of its imported oil.

Table 5.5 China and United States, Net Oil and Gas Imports, 2011 (Percentage from Each Source)

Net Oil Imports by Source (Percentages)		
Source	**China**	**United States**
Canada	0.4	28.8
Mexico	0.6	7.5
South and Central America	7.2	16.1
Former Soviet Union	16.4	8.1
Middle East	46.4	21.9

Net Oil Imports by Source (Percentages)		
Source	China	United States
West Africa	14.2	15.6
Asia Pacific	8.2	-2.4
Rest of world	6.7	4.4
Total	100.0	100.0
Net Natural Gas Imports by Method (Percentages)		
Method	China	United States
Pipeline	40.2	85.6
LNG (liquid natural gas)	59.8	14.4

Source: BP, "Statistical Review of World Energy," June 2012.

In the case of natural gas, 86% of U.S. gas imports enter the country via pipeline, as shown in the bottom panel of Table 5.5. The United States imports most of its liquid natural gas (LNG) from nearby Trinidad and Tobago or from distant Qatar. However, all expectations suggest that within a year or two, the United States should not need any LNG imports. As we saw in Chapter 3, "Liquid Natural Gas and the World Gas Revolution," the United States is actually building LNG export facilities and canceling the construction of import facilities.

In 2011, China received 60% of its imported natural gas via seaborne LNG tankers. Until recently, China imported all its gas via LNG and had no international gas pipeline connections. However, a pipeline from gas-rich Turkmenistan to China started operating at the end of 2010. The pipeline takes gas from the fields of eastern Turkmenistan and ships the gas via pipeline through Uzbekistan and Kazakhstan, skirting Kyrgyzstan's northern border and reaching Horgos in the Xinjiang region of China. By 2013, this pipeline was performing well, and additional parallel pipelines were under construction, with plans to more than double deliveries from 30 to 65 bcm per year. Another gas pipeline from Kazakhstan to China is also contemplated.[9] These pipelines will ameliorate China's dependence on seaborne gas, although the ultimate effects of these pipeline deliveries depend on the growth of China's economy and China's ability to tap its own natural gas resources. China currently pursues a quite aggressive "all of the above" strategy for securing energy supplies, including natural gas. So China's demand for natural gas could grow so quickly over the next several decades that it still needs to rely on LNG imports. After all, China not only has to fuel its burgeoning economy, but it desperately needs to displace coal-powered electrical power generation to reduce pollution; a greater reliance on natural gas may be the way China chooses to do this, at least until renewable energy technologies mature.

For both China and the United States, all energy imports from the Middle East must negotiate the formidable chokepoints of the Bab el-Mandab at the exit of the Red Sea or the Strait of Hormuz at the mouth of the Persian Gulf, as shown in Plate 10. Once clear of this area, ships bound for the United States have already reached the open sea and can sail down the coast of Africa, around the Cape of Good Hope, and across the Atlantic. China must negotiate more contested waters in the Indian Ocean, along the coast of Iran, along the shore of India, then through the Strait of Malacca (Plate 11), into the South China Sea, and finally north to the major cities of China. (Alternative routes to avoid the Strait of Malacca and to transit the Sunda Strait, Lombok Strait, or Makassar Strait are feasible, but they add days and expense to the transit.) A contemplated pipeline across the Malay Peninsula would be an expensive and cumbersome option to avoiding the Strait of Malacca. In addition, much of the South China Sea is disputed by a variety of nations, including China, Taiwan, Japan, the Philippines, and Vietnam, as Plate 12 shows. Some of these contentious areas are the Paracel Islands, the Spratly Islands, the Senkaku/Diaoyu Islands, and the Scarborough Shoal. The claimant nations are not so much interested in their claims to the actual islands as much as they hope to control rich resources in the area, especially hydrocarbons.

The Geopolitical Dimension of Energy Imports

Following the collapse of the Soviet Union, the United States emerged as the world's sole superpower. For a brief time, it towered far above all other nations in prestige and military power, even though it was apparently intent on dissipating its strengths in a continuing orgy of debt and ultimately pointless wars in Iraq and Afghanistan. During this period, China embarked upon one of the world's most amazing economic and social transformations, enjoying a string of successes that have encouraged the greatest aspirations for world prestige and perhaps even engendered a presumption to supplant the United States in global preeminence.

Not surprisingly, then, one of the most important debates in current geopolitics concerns the future of China and the United States and the great fear that a struggle for geopolitical pride of place may occur. Some analysts see only the peaceful economic rise of China in the offing, while others foresee a China increasingly aiming to establish a dominant position. One of the most forceful and articulate expressions of this second point of view is Aaron Friedberg's *A Contest for Supremacy: China, America, and the Struggle for Mastery in Asia*.[10] Similarly, Robert D. Kaplan has sounded a warning about Chinese aspirations, particularly related to sea power, in his book *Monsoon: The Indian Ocean and the Future of American Power*, as well as in a number of other writings.[11]

Others see little potential for conflict and portray a China bent almost exclusively on its economic and social future. For example, Piers Brendon concludes: "So China's priority is to tackle these problems. It aims to build a rich and great society, dedicated to peace, progress, harmony, sustainable development, and international cooperation."[12] Another key position shows a keen awareness of China's ambitions but counsels that there will be an unavoidable backlash against rising Chinese power as other nations coalesce around the

United States to balance against a rising and too-aggressive China. This is the position of Edward Luttwak in his recent book, *The Rise of China vs. the Logic of Strategy*: "It is the straightforward assumption that China's economic and military growth will persist at a rapid pace, and that China's global influence will also increase in step, that generates the now widespread expectation that China is bound to emerge as the world's predominant power in the foreseeable future, eclipsing the United States. Yet that must be the least likely of outcomes, because it would collide with the very logic of strategy in a world of diverse states, each jealous of its autonomy."[13] A thorough exploration of these great issues of geopolitics lies far beyond the scope of this book. However, in any geopolitical contest between the United States and China, securing energy to match national aspirations will be key, and those energy needs presently largely depend, and will continue to depend, upon sea lanes.[14]

As Table 5.4 shows, the heavy reliance of the United States on importing hydrocarbons seems to reveal an important vulnerability compared to China. This appearance is quite misleading, however, as the security of energy transport depends ultimately on the ability to protect those vital deliveries. In terms of current military power, there is little comparison between U.S. military might and that possessed by other nations. While only combat ultimately reveals true military strength, and analysts use diverse peacetime measures of strength, one that is particularly relevant for energy is naval strength and the ability to deploy sea power to control the key sea lanes on which world energy transport has long depended. A simple but very demonstrative measure of that sea power is the strength of each nation's fleet of aircraft carriers. But even that apparently simple and clear measure betrays different understandings of what really counts as an aircraft carrier.

Globalsecurity.org reckons that there are 32 aircraft carriers worldwide, with the United States possessing 20 of them. Another also quite inclusive listing counts 30 aircraft carriers, including all quasi-aircraft carriers displacing at least 20,000 tons, but this measure excludes three others below that size. Table 5.6 lists 27 aircraft carriers, including 12 possessed by the United States. These 12 are the largest in the world by far, accounting for two-thirds of total world aircraft carrier displacement and deck space. In addition, they are nuclear-powered and more sophisticated than any other aircraft carriers. In addition, the United States is laying down the new and improved Gerald R. Ford class of carriers. By any measure, the United States has about two-thirds of total world capacity and a large multiple of any single nation's capacity.[15]

Table 5.6 Aircraft Carriers of the World

Country	Carrier Class	Number	Displacement	Total Displacement
United States	Ford	2	102,000	204,000
United States	Nimitz	10	102,000	1,020,000
China	Liaoning	1	65,000	65,000
Russia	Kunetzov	1	65,000	65,000
United Kingdom	Queen Elizabeth	2	65,000	130,000
India	Vikramaditya	1	45,000	45,000
France	DeGaulle	1	40,600	40,600
India	Vikrant	1	40,000	40,000
Brazil	Sao Paulo	1	33,600	33,600
Japan	22DDH	2	30,000	60,000
India	Viraat	1	28,700	28,700
Italy	Cavour	1	26,000	26,000
United Kingdom	Invincible	1	20,300	20,300
Japan	Hyuga	2	20,000	40,000

Source: "World-Wide Aircraft Carriers (Including Large Deck Amphibs/Sea Control)," available at www.freewebs.com/jeffhead/worldwideaircraftcarriers/, accessed March 29, 2013.

As Table 5.6 shows, China possesses one aircraft carrier, which some have characterized as a "starter carrier,"[16] and it is a very recent acquisition, beginning its sea trials only in August 2011. Further, it is quite low in quality. The ship was originally begun by Ukraine, but China purchased it in an incomplete state in 1998 and has been refitting and upgrading it since then. By itself, the carrier has little value, as the Chinese navy must build a suitable sustaining fleet and master fleet operations, as well as vastly upgrade the skill of its pilots in operations at sea, before the carrier could possibly be ready for battle. Even then, the displacement of the U.S. fleet of carriers will outweigh China's by a factor of more than 20 and will have a capacity of even much greater preponderance. Nonetheless, the choice to spend on initiating a carrier program certainly suggests that China is positioning itself for a greater world presence. There is more to naval strength than aircraft carriers, of course, although these are the largest and most prestigious ships of any of today's navies. In terms of total naval capabilities, one recent study finds a 10:1 advantage in overall naval strength for the United States over China presently, with the United States enjoying greater relative power than that commanded by Great Britain in 1900 and exceeded only by the United States itself in 1990 after the collapse of the Soviet Union.[17]

While the United States may currently enjoy a position of overwhelming military superiority, that may not hold for the future. Whatever China's geopolitical intentions and aspirations, it certainly behaves increasingly like a nation determined to build the capacity to protect its own energy supplies and to secure its ability to project military power. Again, this book cannot offer a detailed examination of the future of geopolitical ascendancy, but two aspects of China's evolution are particularly noteworthy: the "string-of-pearls" and "sea-denial" strategies.

The *string-of-pearls strategy* involves China's acquisition of a "necklace" of places of accommodation for its military, especially its navy, that would stretch along the littoral of the Indian Ocean, connecting the South China Sea with the oil-rich Persian Gulf on which its lifeline of energy imports depends. Whether China actively seeks such a strategic position is a matter of considerable debate. In support of the idea of a string-of-pearls strategy, there can be no doubt that China is actively helping friendly nations to build or upgrade their port facilities in a manner that would make accommodating the Chinese navy easier. For example, China is helping Pakistan build a port facility in Gwadar on the western end of the Pakistani coast, cooperating with Sri Lanka on a fueling station, constructing a container facility in Bangladesh, and so on. Without doubt, China is very active along the coast of the Indian Ocean. But, of course, Chinese energies have spilled out all across the world, including Africa, South America, and the Caribbean. Whatever its ultimate intentions, China's behavior in the Indian Ocean is consonant with a nation pursuing its commercial interests as well as geopolitical ascendancy.[18]

According to many naval analysts, China realizes that it cannot confront the United States in a direct way at sea. Instead, it may be pursuing a *sea-denial strategy*, in which it develops asymmetric military resources that would threaten U.S. ships sufficiently to hold them well off the east coast of Asia, giving China freedom of operation closer to the East-Asian shore. Technologies to accomplish this might include anti-ship ballistic missiles, sophisticated mines, interference with satellite communications, and so on. The goal would not be to defeat the United States at sea directly but to make operations close to the coast of Asia too risky for valuable U.S. assets such as aircraft carriers. Achieving such a goal would give China freedom of operation inside its first island chain, a geographical area that incorporates Taiwan, for example. Such an effective sea-denial or anti-access strategy would clearly help to ensure China's free flow of energy through the South China Sea as well.[19]

At first glance, such geopolitical concerns may seem distant, or even fanciful. However, military planners and the highest levels of U.S. government are starting to be concerned about China's growing military capabilities. The official 2010 "Quadrennial Defense Review Report," published by the U.S. Department of Defense, contains the following passage:

The Air Force and Navy together are developing a new joint air–sea battle concept for defeating adversaries across the range of military operations, including adversaries equipped with sophisticated anti-access and area denial capabilities. The concept will address how air and naval forces will integrate capabilities across all operational domains—air, sea, land, space, and cyberspace—to counter growing challenges to U.S. freedom of action. As it matures, the concept will also help guide the development of future capabilities needed for effective power projection operations.[20]

Similarly, the United States launched a so-called "Asian pivot" in diplomacy in 2012. It would require a willful blindness not to see the growing importance of Chinese military strength in the thinking of the U.S. government in these changes in policy. The shale revolution will play an important role in the future of energy security for both China and the United States.

The Shale Gas Revolution and the Future of Energy Geopolitics

According to many analysts, the United States stands on the brink of achieving the holy grail of "energy independence." Of course, others regard this prospect as fanciful. Assume, however, that the United States does manage to become hydrocarbon-independent in that it produces sufficient MTOE of coal, gas, and oil to equal its hydrocarbon consumption. This would not mean that the United States would be import- and export-free. The mix of the three hydrocarbons produced by the United States will almost certainly not be the mix that consumption requires. So the United States might export natural gas while still needing to import oil, for example. Further, if we consider the actual import and export behavior of many nations, we see that they frequently import and export the same hydrocarbon. This is certainly true of the United States, which imports natural gas from Canada and exports it to Mexico. These reflections lead to the conclusion that even in the happiest circumstance of energy independence, the United States will not be free of international trade in hydrocarbons. Further, many allies will certainly not be energy-independent, and the United States will need its sea power to maintain free sea lanes for the energy on which those allies will depend. Further, the United States will have ongoing geopolitical commitments unrelated to energy that will require a strong navy.

Increasingly strong domestic energy production in the United States will mean that the Persian Gulf will become less important to the narrow geopolitical interests of the United States, but the Middle East will still be one of the most important energy regions in the world. If the United States strives to maintain its current geopolitical position, it will still require a level of international commitment and force projection that resemble the current situation. Thus, for the United States, energy independence will not lead to energy autarky; the United States will continue to be deeply committed to active involvement with the world energy market.

China is far from developing its shale resources to a degree that they can make an important impact on China's energy consumption needs. Similarly, China's ability to project military power abroad is also quite limited. However, given China's recent history of developing more rapidly than anyone expects, one might now reasonably anticipate a very rapid change in those circumstances over the next one or two decades. Further, China has been very active in developing energy deliveries from continental Asia, most notably in the case of Turkmen pipeline gas deliveries, and it will certainly continue to accelerate those developments. For example, Russia very much needs new markets and, as Chapter 6, "The World's Other Large Economies," discusses, Russia and China have significant plans for Chinese acquisition of Russian energy.

Nonetheless, China's anticipated growth trajectory almost certainly will depend on energy deliveries arriving by sea from distant origins, such as the Middle East and Africa. For this reason, as well as many others, China will continue to build its navy, seeking to have a credible "blue water" force. In the short run, China's navy is unlikely to be strong enough to confront the United States in a meaningful way. But as China's navy acquires strength, it will almost certainly help to maintain the freedom of the seas on which its energy lifeline depends. Whether China will seek to build sufficient military strength and choose to use it in a way that seeks to displace the United States from its currently leading position requires a crystal ball and a vision that lie beyond the gaze of this book.

Notes

1. Elliot Brennan, "The 'Fracking' Revolution Comes to China," *Diplomat*, March 21, 2013.

2. Joseph Boris, "Resourceful Thinking," *China Daily*, February 8, 2013. See also Naturalgasasia.com, "China's First Shale Gas Next Year," October 5, 2012.

3. Kevin Jianjun Tu, "China's Problem with Shale," *Wall Street Journal*, October 24, 2012.

4. Naturalgasasia.com, "China Should Not Overdo Shale Gas Development," November 10, 2012.

5. Tim Daiss, "China's Nascent Shale Gas Industry Gains Momentum," *Energy Tribune*, July 10, 2012.

6. Peter Hopkirk tells the story of the western exploration of Chinese Turkestan in his wonderful book, *Foreign Devils on the Silk Road: The Search for the Lost Treasures of Central Asia*, London: John Murray Publishers, 2006.

7. Chen Aizhu, "China's Ragtag Shale Army a Long Way from Revolution," Reuters. com, March 11, 2013.

8. Chen Aizhu, "China's Ragtag Shale Army a Long Way from Revolution," Reuters. com, March 11, 2013.

9. See Robert W. Kolb, "The Natural Gas Revolution and Central Asia," *Journal of Social, Political, and Economic Studies*, Summer 2012, 37, pp. 141–180; and Vladimir Socor, "China to Increase Central Asian Gas Imports Through Multiple Pipelines," *Eurasia Daily Monitor*, August 9, 2012, 9, pp. 152.

10. Aaron L. Friedberg, *A Contest for Supremacy: China, America, and the Struggle for Mastery in Asia*, New York: W.W. Norton & Company, 2011. See also Aaron L. Friedberg and Robert S. Ross, "Here Be Dragons: Is China a Military Threat?" *National Interest*, September/October 2009, pp. 19–34.

11. Robert D. Kaplan, *Monsoon: The Indian Ocean and the Future of American Power*, New York: Random House, 2010. Kaplan explores related issues in "Center Stage for the 21st Century: Power Plays in the Indian Ocean," *Foreign Affairs*, March/April 2009; "Geography Strikes Back," *Wall Street Journal*, September 7, 2012; "Lost at Sea," *New York Times*, September 21, 2007; "South Asia's Geography of Conflict," Center for a New American Security, August 2010; "The Geography of Chinese Power," *Foreign Affairs*, May/June 2010, pp. 22–41; "The Revenge of Geography," *Foreign Policy*, May/June 2009, pp. 96–105; and "The Geopolitics of Shale," Stratfor.com, December 20, 2012.

12. Piers Brendon, "China Also Rises," *National Interest*, November/December 2010, pp. 6–13. See p. 13.

13. Edward N. Luttwak, *The Rise of China vs. the Logic of Strategy*, Cambridge, MA: Belknap Press, 2012. See p. 4.

14. These issues of energy and geopolitics have generated a substantial cottage industry of analytics and research. See, for example, Pablo Bustelo, "China and Oil in the Asian Pacific Region: Rising Demand for Oil," *New England Journal of Public Policy*, 2007, 21, pp. 171–201. See also Robert E. Ebel, "Energy and Geopolitics in China: Mixing Oil and Politics," Center for Strategic & International Studies, November 2009; James Fishelson, "From the Silk Road to Chevron: The Geopolitics of Oil Pipelines in Central Asia," School of Russian and Asian Studies, December 12, 2007; P. K. Gautam, "Mapping Chinese Oil and Gas Pipelines and Sea Routes," *Strategic Analysis*, July 2011, 35, pp. 595–612; Mikkal E. Herberg, "Pipeline Politics in Asia: Energy Nationalism and Energy Markets," National Bureau of Asian Research, NBR Special Report #23, September 2010, pp. 1–6; Bo Kong, "The Geopolitics of the Myanmar–China Oil and Gas Pipelines," National Bureau of Asian Research, NBR Special Report #23, September 2010, pp. 55–66; Tatsuo Masuda, "Security of Energy Supply and the Geopolitics of Oil and Gas Pipelines," *European Review of Energy Markets*, December 2007, 2, pp. 1–32; Kenneth B. Medlock, Amy Myers Jaffe, and Peter R. Hartley, "Shale Gas and U.S. National Security," James A. Baker III Institute for Public Policy, Rice University, July 2011; Carlos Pascual, "The Geopolitics of Energy: From Security to Survival," Brookings Institution, Research Paper, January 2008; Minxin Pei, "China's Achilles' Heel," *Diplomat*, February 8, 2012; Alan Riley, "The New Geopolitics Shale Could Bring," Naturalgaseurope.com, December 13, 2012; David Scott, "The Great Power 'Great Game' Between India and China: 'The Logic of Geography,'" *Geopolitics*, 2008, 13, pp. 1–26; and Frank A. Verrastro, Sarah O. Ladislaw, Matthew Frank, and Lisa A. Hyland, "The Geopolitics of Energy: Emerging Trends, Changing Landscapes, Uncertain Times," Center for Strategic & International Studies, October 2010.

15. See "World Wide Aircraft Carriers," GlobalSecurity.org, available at www.globalsecurity.org/military/world/carriers.htm; and "World-Wide Aircraft Carriers (Including Large Deck Amphibs/Sea Control)," available at www.freewebs.com/jeffhead/worldwideaircraftcarriers/. Table 5.6 omits three very small ships from consideration, with one each being owned by Spain, Italy, and Thailand. For information on the Gerald R. Ford class of carriers, see Ronald O'Rourke, "Navy Ford (CVN-78) Class Aircraft Carrier Program: Background and Issues for Congress," U.S. Congressional Research Service, March 13, 2013.

16. Andrew S. Erickson, Abraham M. Denmark, and Gabriel Collins, "Beijing's 'Starter Carrier' and Future Steps," *Naval War College Review*, Winter 2012, 65, pp. 15–55. See also Jane Perlez, "China Shows Off an Aircraft Carrier but Experts Are Skeptical," *New York Times*, September 25, 2012.

17. Brian Crisher and Mark Souva, "Power at Sea: A Naval Power Dataset, 1865–2011," Florida State University working paper, 2012.

18. For more on the "string-of-pearls" strategy, see Sergei DeSilva-Ranasinghe, "Why the Indian Ocean Matters," *Diplomat*, March 2, 2011; Aaron L. Friedberg, *A Contest for Supremacy: China, America, and the Struggle for Mastery in Asia*, New York: W.W. Norton & Company, 2011; James Holmes and Tashi Yoshihara, "Is China Planning String of Pearls?" *Diplomat*, February 21, 2011; IntelliBrief, "China: 'String of Pearls' Strategy," April 1, 2007; Robert D. Kaplan, "Center Stage for the 21st Century: Power Plays in the Indian Ocean," *Foreign Affairs*, March/April 2009, and *Monsoon: The Indian Ocean and the Future of American Power*, New York: Random House, 2010; Daniel J. Kostecka, "Places and Bases: The Chinese Navy's Emerging Support Network in the Indian Ocean," *Naval War College Review*, Winter 2011, 64, pp. 59–78; C. Raja Mohan, "Tanzanian Pearl," *Indian Express*, March 27, 2013; Harsh V. Pant, "Great Game in the Indian Ocean," *Japan Times*, June 14, 2011; Christopher J. Pehrson, "String of Pearls: Meeting the Challenge of China's Rising Power Across the Asian Littoral," Strategic Studies Institute, July 2006; David Scott, "The Great Power 'Great Game' Between India and China: The Logic of Geography,'" *Geopolitics*, 2008, 13, pp. 1–26; and Mandip Singh, "China Base a Threat to India Navy?" *Diplomat*, December 17, 2011.

19. For an introduction to the debate on China's presumed "sea-denial" strategy, see Eric S. Edelman, "Understanding America's Contested Primacy," Center for Strategic and Budgetary Assessments, 2010; Andrew S. Erickson, Abraham M. Denmark, and Gabriel Collins, "Beijing's 'Starter Carrier' and Future Steps," *Naval War College Review*, Winter 2012, 65, pp. 15–55; Aaron L. Friedberg, "China's Challenge at Sea," *New York Times*, September 4, 2011, and *A Contest for Supremacy: China, America, and the Struggle for Mastery in Asia*, New York: W.W. Norton & Company, 2011; Aaron L. Friedberg and Robert S. Ross, "Here Be Dragons: Is China a Military Threat?" *National Interest*, September/October 2009, pp. 19–34; Bill Gertz, "China's High-Tech Military Threat," *Commentary*, April 2012; Robert D. Kaplan, "Center Stage for the 21st Century: Power Plays in the Indian Ocean," *Foreign Affairs*, March/April 2009; "Lost at Sea," *New York Times*, September 21, 2007; and "The Geography of Chinese Power," *Foreign Affairs*, May/June 2010, pp. 22–41.

20. U.S. Department of Defense, "Quadrennial Defense Review Report," 2010. See p. 32.

6

The World's Other Large Economies[*]

This chapter continues the exploration of the natural gas revolution by focusing on the world's eight largest economies after the United States and China. These countries, which are quite diverse, include the four largest economies of the Eurozone: Germany, France, the United Kingdom, and Italy. The other four economies we discuss in this chapter are India, Japan, the Russian Federation, and Brazil. Differences among these countries are striking. For example, Russia takes pride of place as the world's largest energy exporter, while Japan depends most on energy imports among these economies. The group also includes a country very strongly committed to nuclear power, France, as well as Germany, with its strong commitment to renewable energy resources.

---

[*] This chapter draws from a number of other sources, including three of my recent articles: "Geopolitical Threats to World Energy Markets," *Journal of Social, Political, and Economic Studies*, Summer 2011, 36, pp. 154–196; "Geopolitics and World Energy Markets," in Betty and Russell Simkins (eds.), *Energy Finance: Analysis and Valuation, Risk Management, and the Future of Energy*, Hoboken, NJ: John Wiley & Sons, Inc., 2013, pp. 19–48; and "The Natural Gas Revolution and the World's Largest Economies," *Journal of Social, Political, and Economic Studies*, Winter 2012, 37, pp. 415–467.

Table 6.1 parallels Table 5.2, which reports on the sources of primary energy for China and the United States. As with China and the United States, most of these eight countries depend on hydrocarbons to a significant degree. Only Brazil, with its heavy reliance on hydroelectric power, and France, with its nuclear power generation, obtain less than 80% of their total energy from hydrocarbons. Further, these countries vary considerably in their mix of hydrocarbons. Russia obtains the smallest percentage from oil, 19.8% of total energy, and the highest percentage from gas, 55.7%, while Brazil obtains the least from gas, 9.0%, and the most from oil, 45.2%. Coal utilization provides only 3.7% of total energy but 52.9% of India's. All these different ways of obtaining energy across these nations imply very different participation rates in, and impacts from, the natural gas revolution, and this is true even before we consider the shale endowments possessed by each nation.

Table 6.1 Primary Sources of Energy, 2011

Million Tonnes of Oil Equivalent

Country	Oil	Natural Gas	Coal	Nuclear	Hydro-electric	Renewable	Total	All Hydrocarbon
Japan	201.4	95.0	117.7	36.9	19.2	7.4	477.6	414.1
Germany	111.5	65.3	77.6	24.4	4.4	23.2	306.4	254.4
France	82.9	36.3	9.0	100.0	10.3	4.3	242.9	128.3
Brazil	120.7	24.0	13.9	3.5	97.2	7.5	266.9	158.6
United Kingdom	71.6	72.2	30.8	15.6	1.3	6.6	198.1	88.1
Italy	71.1	64.2	15.4	0.0	10.1	7.7	168.5	89.4
Russian Federation	136.0	382.1	90.9	39.2	37.3	0.1	685.6	609.0
India	162.3	55.0	295.6	7.3	29.8	9.2	559.1	512.9
Percentage from Each Source								
Japan	42.2	19.9	24.6	7.7	4.0	1.5	100.0	86.7
Germany	36.4	21.3	25.3	8.0	1.4	7.6	100.0	83.0
France	34.1	14.9	3.7	41.2	4.2	1.8	100.0	52.8
Brazil	45.2	9.0	5.2	1.3	36.4	2.8	100.0	59.4
United Kingdom	36.1	36.4	15.5	1.3	0.7	3.3	100.0	88.1
Italy	42.2	38.1	9.1	0.0	6.0	4.6	100.0	89.4
Russian Federation	19.8	55.7	13.3	5.7	5.4	0.0	100.0	88.8
India	29.0	9.8	52.9	1.3	5.3	1.6	100.0	91.7

Source: BP, "Statistical Review of World Energy," June 2012.

Revolutions create uncertainty, and the natural gas revolution is no exception. For many nations of the world, we know relatively little about their shale resources, and our understanding of the size, location, and accessibility varies widely across different countries. One of the first systematic attempts to understand more of the world's resources was undertaken by the U.S. Energy Information Administration (USEIA) and published as "World Shale Gas Resources: An Initial Assessment of 14 Regions Outside the United States." This study omitted many regions and reflects varied levels of knowledge about different regions. Table 6.2 presents some of the key results of the study and includes data from the United States and China for comparison. Of the eight nations of this chapter's focus, the report does not present any conclusions regarding Japan, Russia, or Italy. The report's assessment of proved reserves closely matches the estimates provided by BP in its "Statistical Review." For the five nations in our group for which the report provided estimates of technically recoverable shale resources, the estimated total was 14,074 billion cubic meters (bcm). For the nations examined in the USEIA report, the total of technically recoverable shale resources exceeded proved reserves, but these shale resources are only technically recoverable. Even though these preliminary estimates are bound to be quite inaccurate, the 60,000 bcm of China and the United States taken together still dwarf the estimated total for these other nations.

Table 6.2 Estimates of Proved and Technically Recoverable Gas Resources (Billions of Cubic Meters)

	BP	USEIA	
Country	Proved Reserves	Proved Reserves	Technically Recoverable Shale Gas Resources
United States	8,500	7,716	24,409
China	3,100	3,030	36,104
Japan	N/A	N/R	N/R
Germany	100	176	227

	BP	USEIA	
Country	Proved Reserves	Proved Reserves	Technically Recoverable Shale Gas Resources
France	N/A	6	5,097
Brazil	500	365	6,400
United Kingdom	200	255	566
Italy	100	N/R	N/R
Russian Federation	44,600	N/R	N/R
India	1,200	1,073	1,784
Total	58,300	12,621	74,587
Total excluding Russia	13,700	12,621	74,587

Abbreviations: N/A = Not available or negligible; N/R = Not reported by USEIA in the study.

Sources: BP, "Statistical Review of World Energy," June 2012; and USEIA, "World Shale Gas Resources: An Initial Assessment of 14 Regions Outside the United States," April 2011, p. 4.

These eight nations differ quite substantially in their levels of consumption at the rates at which they are producing and consuming their proved reserves, as Table 6.3 shows. At its current rate of production, Germany has only a 10-year supply, and the United Kingdom has only a 4.4-year supply, indicating a production of almost 25% of its proved reserves per year. At the other end of the scale, Russia is producing at a rate that gives it a 74-year supply, even though it has prodigiously large production. Consumption differs radically across these countries as well. Germany has a population of approximately 81 million and consumes 72.5 bcm per year, for a rate of 895 cubic meters per person per year. By contrast, the Russian population is about 143 million, with a consumption of 425 bcm per year, or almost 2,972 cubic meters per person per year. Thus, the average Russian consumes 3.3 times as much gas as the average German, a difference that can be explained largely by the large gas subsidies in Russia. Of these eight nations, only Russia both produces more than it consumes and stands as a net exporter. Russia exports substantial amounts of gas via pipeline, along with modest liquid natural gas (LNG) exports. The other countries are all substantial net importers. Of these importing nations, France, Brazil, the United Kingdom, and Italy rely on a mix of pipeline and LNG flows, but Japan has only LNG import possibilities, as does India. Germany, by contrast, imports only via pipeline. All these important differences imply that we must examine the circumstances of each nation in detail if we are to see their different positions and possibilities in the natural gas revolution.

Table 6.3 Natural Gas Data for the World's Other Large Economies

Country	Natural Gas (Billions of Cubic Meters) Proved Reserves	Production	Consumption	Reserves/ Production	Net International Flows Pipe-line	LNG
Japan	N/A	N/A	28.5	N/A	0.0	107.0
Germany	100	10.0	72.5	10.0	84.0	0.0
France	N/A	N/A	40.3	N/A	32.3	14.6
Brazil	500	16.7	26.7	29.9	9.74	1.05
United Kingdom	200	45.2	80.2	4.4	11.8	25.3
Italy	100	7.7	71.3	13.0	60.8	8.8
Russian Federation	44,600	607.0	424.6	73.5	−176.9	−14.4
India	1,200	46.1	61.1	26.0	0.0	17.1
Total	46,700	732.7	805.2	63.7	15.6	158.3
Total excluding Russia	2,100	125.7	380.6	16.7	192.5	172.7
Total excluding Russia and India	900	79.6	319.5	11.3	192.5	155.6

Abbreviation: LNG = liquid natural gas.

Source: BP, "Statistical Review of World Energy," June 2012.

Japan

Japan has essentially zero domestic hydrocarbon resources. As a result, not only must it import all its natural gas, but it must also acquire all its oil and coal from abroad. In addition, as an island, it has no pipeline connections to other nations, so all its imports arrive by ship. In the case of natural gas, this implies that Japan imports all its supplies as LNG. Historically, and not surprisingly, Japan has been heavily reliant on nuclear power. In 2010, for example, Japan derived 13% of all its energy from nuclear power, compared to the 17% that came from natural gas. Following the March 2011 earthquake and accompanying tsunami that led to the nuclear disaster at Fukushima, Japan vowed to move toward permanently shuttering its nuclear facilities. There is some indication now that it may not do so, or at least not quickly.[1] However, if Japan does move away from nuclear power, it will become even more heavily reliant on hydrocarbon imports, including LNG. These circumstances might suggest that Japan has little to gain from the natural gas revolution, but that is very far from being the case. In fact, even though Japan does not participate directly in the natural gas revolution, being bereft of any domestic hydrocarbon resources, it stands to be a large beneficiary in two important respects: the price it must pay for its imports along with its reliability of supply.

Compared to all the other nations of the world, Japan typically pays a higher price for its natural gas. Part of the reason for this is quite clear, as it must ultimately pay the costs of liquefying gas and shipping it to Japan, often from quite distant sources. Figure 6.1 shows the natural gas cost difference between the United States and Japan, with prices expressed in dollars per million British thermal unit (Btu). In recent years, the difference has been very large, sometimes exceeding a factor of 4:1. For example, in summer 2012, the price of pipeline natural gas in the United States was under $3.00 per million Btu, while Japan was paying about $15.00 for LNG imports of the same quantity.

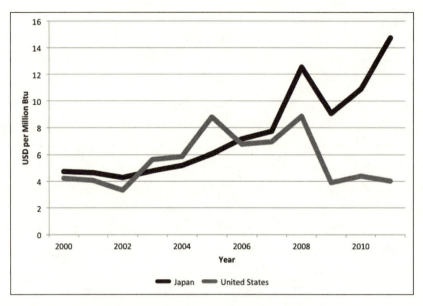

Figure 6.1 Natural gas prices in Japan and the United States.

Source: BP, "Statistical Review of World Energy," June 2012.

Over most of the recent decades, natural gas prices have been highly correlated with crude oil prices, but in recent years, that has changed substantially, with the relative price of gas per unit of energy being much lower than that of oil. Part of that increasing ratio of crude to gas prices has been due to the supply surge created by the natural gas revolution. Nonetheless, LNG prices have stayed quite high. One promise of the natural gas revolution is the development of a truly world market for natural gas, with many suppliers of LNG. The development of such a system would result in gas being priced based on its own supply and demand factors, with a spot price tied to current supply and demand rather than to decades-long contracts linked to oil prices. In short, a worldwide abundance of supply would create a natural gas market with many competing suppliers and would give Japan an opportunity to pay the world price of pipeline gas plus an LNG differential consisting of only transportation, liquefaction, and regasification costs.[2]

Far and away, Japan is the world's largest LNG importer, importing more than the next three major importers (South Korea, the United Kingdom, and Spain) combined.[3] In 2011, it imported 107 bcm of LNG from 19 different countries. Its five largest suppliers, in rank order, were Malaysia, Australia, Qatar, Indonesia, and Russia, together accounting for 72% of Japan's 2011 imports.[4] Clearly, Japan has a diversity of suppliers, but some of these sources are geopolitical rivals, and some are themselves dependent on long sea lanes through potentially hostile waters. In light of the natural gas revolution, Japan stands to secure supplies from a still greater variety of suppliers, some of whom are more reliable allies. For example, the recent decision to allow at least some LNG exports from the United States can only increase Japan's security of supply. In a geopolitically quiescent world, this increased security of supply has limited benefit, but it could become extremely important in less pleasant circumstances. Heightened import potential from sources like Australia and the United States increases Japan's energy security even without actually importing LNG from these friendly nations, but merely because it will have the potential to receive LNG supplies from the nation with the world's strongest navy, as well as from nations that must be regarded as friendly to Japan.[5] In fact, that has already happened to some extent, with Australia supplanting Malaysia as Japan's largest LNG supplier in 2012, a year in which Japan's LNG imports increased by 11%.[6]

The Eurozone Economies: Germany, France, and Italy

Germany, France, and Italy are the three largest economies in the Eurozone. The general prospects of these countries apply broadly, but not universally, to other countries that have embraced the European project. With respect to natural gas in the Eurozone, the dominating factor for these three nations is their low production, coupled with their very large reliance on natural gas that arrives via pipeline from Russia, as detailed in Table 6.4.

Table 6.4 Import Reliance by Germany, France, and Italy, 2011 (Billions of Cubic Meters)

	Source			Import Method			
	Western Europe	Russia	Other	Total Pipeline	LNG	Total Imports	Russian Dependency (%)
Germany	53.2	30.8	0.0	84.0	0.0	84.0	36.6
France	23.6	8.6	0.2	32.3	14.6	46.9	18.4
Italy	16.5	15.4	28.9	60.8	8.7	69.6	22.2
Total	**93.3**	**54.8**	**29.0**	**177.1**	**23.3**	**200.4**	**27.3**

Abbreviation: LNG = liquid natural gas.

Source: BP, "Statistical Review of World Energy," June 2012.

Germany imports only via pipeline, securing over half its imports from Western European nations (Denmark, the Netherlands, Norway, and the United Kingdom). The balance, 37%, of Germany's imports comes from Russia. France receives gas via pipeline and LNG, relying on Russia for 18% of its imports. Italy imports both via pipeline and LNG and has the most diversified sources of supply. In addition to receiving pipeline gas from Western Europe and Russia, Italy obtains pipeline gas from Algeria and Egypt. In addition, Italy receives LNG shipments from a variety of nations, with about 75% of its LNG coming from Qatar. This leaves Italy with a 22% dependence on Russia for its imports. For these three nations considered together, 27% of all imported gas comes from Russia via pipeline.

Thus, Western Europe has had a continuing reliance on the Soviet Union, and now the Russian Federation, for much of its supply of natural gas. In the Soviet era, supplies came from Russia and from its republics in central Asia, most notably Turkmenistan. The Soviets routed their pipelines from their captive republics into Russia and then through the Ukraine and on to markets in Western Europe. The breakup of the Soviet Union left this legacy pipeline network in place but under the control of a variety of fractious independent nations, resulting in disputes of supply and transport. For example, all pipelines from the newly independent nation of Turkmenistan went only north to Russia, leaving Turkmenistan with its very rich natural gas resources as a price and transportation hostage to Russia. Not surprisingly, Turkmenistan has struggled to develop other markets for its gas, including the recently opened pipeline to China.[7] Summarizing the transport issue, the main pipelines of the Soviet area were collected in Russia and then ran to the west through Ukraine. In the past five years, disputes between Russia and Ukraine resulted in Russia's shutting off supplies at least three times.[8] As a result, the Eurozone has a problem with security of supply, while Russia has a vulnerability in its capacity to deliver gas to its market in Western Europe. In response to this situation, countries of the Eurozone are trying to diversify their suppliers, while Russia aims to find alternative secure delivery routes to keep Western Europe tethered to its supplies.

Tables 6.2 and 6.3 indicate that Germany, France, and Italy have quite modest proved reserves relative to the size of their economies and their appetite for gas. But these resource estimates are almost surely very far below what will actually be proven to exist. Nonetheless, it is the best estimate available as of 2011–2012. Taken together, these three countries' estimated technically recoverable shale reserves are modest as well, even though France has an estimated 5.1 bcm of shale gas. However, none of these three nations has shown any significant interest in exploiting their shale sources. Italy probably has very little shale gas, and it was not actually covered by the USEIA's assessment. France apparently holds significant shale gas, but it has taken draconian measures to prohibit any exploitation of that gas. In 2011, France passed laws forbidding hydraulic fracturing and even exploration for shale gas.[9] To date, there has been no serious evidence that this decision might be reconsidered.

Like France, but without being so severe, Germany has been quite reluctant to move to exploit its shale reserves. As noted in Table 6.2, the estimate of Germany's shale gas was 227 bcm. However, a year later in 2012, Germany's Federal Institute for Geosciences and Natural Resources concluded that Germany's shale resources are actually as large as 2,300 bcm.[10] Further, France probably has Europe's largest shale resources. Germany has permitted only a few test wells, and all across Western Europe, there were only a few dozen test wells as of mid-2012.[11] Nonetheless, significant shale gas deposits are scattered across Western Europe, as Plate 13 shows. Even if Europe refuses to participate in the shale revolution now, those resources will remain available for future use.

Writing for *Forbes*, Matthew Hulbert summarized the European attitude quite well: "Simply put, shale gas isn't going to be a serious prospect on Charlemagne's turf any time soon. Europe needs global gas fundamentals to go its way elsewhere, or it risks ending up back at square one, bent over a Russian pipeline."[12] Hulbert refers, of course, to the potential that Russia might use Europe's gas dependency as a geopolitical weapon. While this is a potential problem for Europe, it must also be noted that Russia relies very heavily on European markets for its gas revenues, and those revenues are vital to the Russian government and even Russian society.

In some respects, the unwillingness of Western Europe to at least investigate the possibility of exploiting its domestic shale resources seems inexplicable, especially faced with the prospect of conflict with Russia. However, there are three strong factors that militate against the development of shale in France and Germany, as well as in some other Western European nations that possess gas. First, the population density of much of Northern Europe makes the exploitation of shale resources more difficult there than in the United States. For gas production, drilling pads and the other necessities, such as storage ponds for produced water, have to go somewhere, and the greater population density presents a strong impediment. Second, from a political perspective, the green parties of Europe are especially strong compared to similar lobbies in the United States, raising a genuinely higher hurdle. Third, there is the matter of the structure of property rights. In the United States, mineral rights are generally private property. In many instances, they are severable from surface rights, but mineral rights generally remain in private hands. And most often the owner of surface rights to land also owns the mineral rights beneath that land. In Europe, by contrast, governments generally own mineral rights. This implies that landowners have little to gain from the shale revolution. They suffer the prospect of merely bearing the costs of drilling operations at the surface, without receiving royalties or other benefits from the gas produced beneath their properties.

Even though it currently appears that Western Europe will not be a producer of shale gas in large quantities anytime soon, these nations, including Germany, France, and Italy, still stand to be significant beneficiaries of the worldwide shale revolution. The production of shale gas in the United States has already pushed down world prices and caused a number of suppliers to agree to renegotiate prices for their long-term contracts. Further, the buildout of the LNG infrastructure provides a viable alternative for nonlandlocked nations to diversify their imports away from excessive reliance on pipeline deliveries. As we noted, Germany imports no LNG, but it has perfectly adequate ports to receive LNG tankers. France and Italy both receive LNG, and they could easily expand their import capacity. Thus, the Eurozone is a substantial beneficiary of the natural gas revolution and is essentially a free rider: It stands to receive significant benefits from changes in the world gas situation, even without ever developing its own resources.

Russian Federation

Russia possesses the world's largest proved reserves and exports twice as much gas as the next largest exporting nation. In 2011, Russia exported more than 200 bcm of natural gas, almost all by pipeline. Other nations depend very heavily on those supplies, as we have seen for the large economies of Western Europe. In percentage terms, some other nations are even more dependent on gas they import from Russia. However, Russia itself depends on exporting hydrocarbons. Russian energy exports fund half of the federal budget and account for 20% of gross domestic product (GDP).[13]

To date, Russia has produced virtually no shale gas. While Russia was not included in the USEIA's initial assessment of world shale gas resources, there is every reason to believe that Russia possesses a gigantic shale gas endowment. Gazprom, the Russian state-owned natural gas company, estimates total shale gas as 5,000 to 20,000 bcm, implying that its unconventional resources might be about 2.5 times as vast as its world-leading conventional resources.[14] With so much gas, Russia might seem to be one of the largest likely winners from the shale revolution. Instead, it will probably be the greatest loser.

The shale revolution constitutes the main threat to Russia's dominant position in the world gas market, with its implications of permanently lower world prices, combined with the LNG buildout allowing greater choice of supplier by purchasing nations. In addition, Russia has long prospered from the prevailing pricing method for natural gas—long-term contracts with prices linked to oil. Every year, an increasing proportion of natural gas is traded on a spot market basis, and this move to spot market transactions and away from long-term oil-linked contracts has also been brought about largely by the "shale gale."

While Russia has the world's greatest reserves, it has lost the mantle of being the world's largest producer of natural gas, having just been surpassed by the United States. Further, much of Russia's easiest-to-access reserves have already been exploited, and Russia has been facing the need to make massive investments to acquire gas from new, distant, and more expensive fields. For example, Russia has been developing its massive Shtokman project. This field lies in the Arctic Circle, 350 miles from land and at a latitude that places it north of Murmansk and farther north than any land of Sweden, Norway, or Finland. As the project's website itself points out, the sea depth there is about 1,000 feet, wave heights exceed 75 feet, temperatures range down to –50 degrees Celsius, and icebergs as large as 4 million tons roam the sea.[15] Obviously, bringing gas from Shtokman to market was always going to be extremely expensive, but the project was thought to be viable with the United States as the primary target customer. However, in 2012, the United States produced more gas than Russia and advanced its own plans to be a net gas exporter. Not surprisingly, Russia put the Shtokman project on hold in August 2012.[16]

Russia is still advancing its Yamal Peninsula project. It too lies in the far north, almost 2,000 miles northeast of Moscow. But unlike the Shtokman project, at least it is on land and has pipeline connections that can join Russia's main pipeline network. This peninsula hosts more than 200 development sites and accounts for an enormous percentage of Russia's gas reserves. Given the harsh conditions and great distances, gas production there will be expensive as well, with production mainly slated to go into LNG. After an investment in excess of $40 billion, the project continues, but many wonder if Russia will be able to find an economically viable market for such expensive gas.[17]

Russia also confronts significant challenges in getting its pipeline gas to its principal customers. The main pipeline network of Eastern Europe was built during the Soviet era, with gas pipelines coming from the gas-rich fields of the republics of central Asia, most notably Turkmenistan, and running north into Russia to join the pipeline network there. These legacy pipelines pass largely through Ukraine, and then on to the main customers of Western Europe. This was unproblematic from a Soviet point of view when it controlled all these regions, but now Russia must deal with a variety of unruly independent states rather than republics that were within the steel grip of the Soviets.

On January 7, 2009, Russia shut off its gas supplies to the main European pipeline into the Ukraine, leaving gas shortfalls in 20 European countries during the coldest part of a very cold winter. After parsing the various claims, counterclaims, posturings, lies, and denials, the main reason seems to have been Russian displeasure at Ukraine's Orange Revolution combined with Ukraine's apparently appropriating some gas intended for the West.[18] There have been other cutoffs as well. For example, in early 2012, Europe was experiencing a particularly cold winter, with hundreds dying from the cold. Russia again reduced the flow of westward-bound gas into Ukraine, apparently mainly because of supply constraints, with Russians consuming much more gas than usual. But Russia also blamed Ukraine for taking more transit gas than it should. Whoever was to blame, people shivered across Europe.[19] There have been other supply disruptions as well, calling into question the reliability of Russia as a supplier of gas even in normal times. Of course, this heightens the concerns over the ways in which Russia might seek to use its gas supplies as a political lever in dealings with the Eurozone.

Further, Russia and its former dependencies, especially the Ukraine, seem to be locked in a continuing battle over gas. This largely explains why Russia has invested so massively in pipelines that link Russia directly to Western Europe, bypassing former portions of its empire, notably Ukraine. For example, Russia recently completed the Nord Stream pipeline that transits the Baltic Sea, linking Russia directly to Germany, as Plate 14 shows. Nord Stream began operations in 2010 and now supplies significant gas resources directly from Russia to Germany, and the route continues to be expanded with new parallel pipelines. The second went into operation in 2012, and Gazprom contemplates two additional lines. Further, a spur line from Germany now goes to the Czech Republic, and BP is interested in extending Nord Stream on to the United Kingdom.[20]

Russia is making similar investments with similar intentions in Southern Europe, and these maneuvers are related to Western Europe's awareness of concern over its energy dependence on Russia. This has led to something of a frenzied competition of pipeline planning and building. Russia essentially seeks to bypass Ukraine and possess its own routes to Europe to keep Europe as a tethered customer. Western Europe would like to secure a source of non-Russian gas from the Caspian region. Doing so would help free the Eurozone from Russia's geopolitical grip in the event of a crisis. Even if no crisis were ever to develop, such alternative supplies would help rein in Russia's gas pricing. Plate 15 shows three key pipelines of the "Southern Corridor." It might be accurate to call some of these "proposed pipeline routes." The Nabucco line would connect Western Europe to the Caspian region, with actual supplies coming from farther to the east, in Azerbaijan and potentially Turkmenistan. But not one length of the Nabucco pipeline has been laid to date. As of 2013, current planning has been focusing on more modest efforts to tap Caspian gas without Russian involvement.

Nabucco West, for example, is a more modest version of the full Nabucco plan shown in Plate 15, but there are other contenders as well, and the plans change frequently. One project is the Trans-Anatolian Pipeline Project (TANAP), which would transport Azeri gas from the Shah Deniz fields in the Caspian, into and across Turkey, and then up to Bulgaria or Greece to connect with pipelines there. The plan is to complete it by 2017, but as of mid-2013, no final route had been determined, and no pipe-laying had commenced. Similarly, a competing (or is it cooperating?) pipeline would be the Trans-Adriatic Pipeline (TAP). This proposed pipeline would start in Azerbaijan, transit Turkey, cross Albania, go under the Adriatic Sea to San Foca on the very heel of Italy, and then connect northward. The earliest projected start date for TAP deliveries is 2018. But again, no pipes are being laid. Further, it is not certain that there is sufficient gas coming from Azerbaijan to feed both pipelines. Plans are so deeply uncertain that any conclusion must await significant further developments.[21]

While the European Union dithers over its southern routes, the Russians are much more aggressive in at least moving toward action. The Blue Stream pipeline from Russia, across the Black Sea, to Turkey is already operational (see Plate 15). From a European point of view, the South Stream pipeline is much more direct, but it has the serious geopolitical flaw of providing Russian gas. For Russia, completing South Stream has two main virtues: It circumvents Ukraine, and building it might defeat plans for Nabucco, TANAP, and TAP, thereby keeping Western Europe dependent on Russian gas. If Russia builds South Stream, it may have excess export capacity, given its production problems, and it may also have a problem of insufficient demand, given the rapidly expanding gas production around the world. Further, the cost of South Stream appears to exceed €50 billion. Nonetheless, Russia formally started construction at the end of 2012, but actual construction work was slated to begin only in mid-2013 in Bulgaria, with work on the Black Sea section to begin in 2014.[22]

Further difficulties for Russia lie in its strange pricing behavior and the legal action its pricing has prompted from the European Union. Table 6.5 shows the prices paid by Russian gas importers in mid-2012. These price differentials clearly do not reflect the costs of production and transportation. Instead, they appear to be strongly motivated by political considerations, especially in the case of nearby Poland.[23] Also, the countries that are more distant tend to pay the least, probably because these nations have the best access to more competitively priced alternative sources. Even taking these factors into account, there seems to be little rationale. For example, Bulgaria is notoriously friendly toward Russia, given their shared Slavic ethnicity, but it pays one of the highest prices of all. In 2012, the European Union launched a formal proceeding to determine whether Gazprom was acting to monopolize the gas market and abusing its status as a dominant supplier to charge excessive prices. In pique, Vladimir

Putin opined that the European Union's gas laws were uncivilized,[24] yet the investigation continues.[25]

Table 6.5 Prices Paid in Mid-2012 for Russian Natural Gas

Importing Country	USD per 1,000 Cubic Meters
Poland	525.5
Czech Republic	503.1
Bulgaria	501.0
Greece	476.7
Serbia	457.3
Italy	440.0
Romania	431.8
Slovakia	429.0
Turkey	406.7
Austria	397.4
France	393.7
Hungary	390.8
Finland	384.8
Germany	379.3
Netherlands	371.4
United Kingdom	313.4

Abbreviations: USD = United States dollar.

Sources: Adnan Vatansever and David Koranyi, "Lowering the Price of Russian Gas: A Challenge for European Energy Security," Europeanenergyreview.eu, March 11, 2013; and Natalia Resnykaya, "Macedonians and the Poles Pay the Highest Prices to Gazprom in All of Europe," *Izvestia*, February 1, 2013, available at http://izvestia.ru/news/544100.

Perhaps the surest sign of Russian worry comes from Gazprom's assurances that it has no cause for concern about the shale revolution. Alexei Miller, CEO of Gazprom, dismissed the shale boom of the United States as a "soap bubble," assuring his listeners that it would "burst soon." He also opined that all the boreholes in the United States were empty.[26] From these assuredly empty holes, the United States somehow managed to produce more gas than all of Russia in 2012. For all the reasons explored in this section, Russia stands to be the nation that will lose the most from the shale revolution: It has lost or is losing its pricing power, its customers are much freer to buy from other suppliers, and its easiest-to-access gas supplies are waning. All the factors that are diminishing the importance of Russian gas are continuing, or even accelerating. Taken together, all these trends conspire to make Russia the country most likely to lose the most from the natural gas revolution.

United Kingdom

The United Kingdom has modest natural gas proved reserves that it produces and consumes at a prodigious rate. Table 6.2 shows that the United Kingdom has proved natural gas reserves of 200 bcm, but it produces 45.2 bcm from this reserve and consumes a total of 80.2 bcm, per Table 6.3. The technically recoverable shale resources are 566 bcm, or almost three times the proved reserves. These high ratios of production to reserves and of consumption to reserves leave the country in a somewhat delicate supply-and-demand balance, making its natural gas acquisition critical. In 2011, the United Kingdom had net natural gas imports via pipeline of 11.8 bcm and via LNG of 25.3 bcm. Britain's high rate of consumption relative to its reserves makes the future of gas supplies a genuinely open question.

Based on initial assessments of its gas resources, the United Kingdom appeared eager to exploit its shale resources. However, according to almost all parties involved, including the drilling company Cuadrilla Resources, hydraulic fracturing operations caused two small earthquakes near Blackpool in 2011. This led to a nationwide drilling suspension. At the end of 2012, U.K. regulators allowed operations to resume.[27] Further, the government decided in 2013 to foster gas drilling and to grant tax breaks as an incentive to spur production.[28]

This change of heart on shale gas was accompanied by a remarkable change in resource estimation. It now appears that Great Britain possesses phenomenally more gas than previously believed. In mid-2013, the British Geological Survey was poised to change the estimated shale resources of the United Kingdom to 36,000 to 48,000 bcm. This is a 75-fold increase in estimated shale resources compared to the 2011 estimate shown in Table 6.2. As one commentator notes, this would be "enough shale gas to heat every home in Britain for 1,500 years."[29] Of course, the economically recoverable gas would be only some fraction of this amount, but this still constitutes a remarkable change in the assessments of Great Britain's position in the natural gas revolution.

The uncertainty about the United Kingdom's future in gas is staggering. At more or less the same time that resource estimates were in such fluctuation, BP was still forecasting continuing import dependence for Western Europe, including the United Kingdom. Also at the same time, BP and other oil majors were committing to drill in the ocean about 50 miles west of the Shetland Islands. The field there has mainly oil, perhaps 8 billion barrels, but it also contains gas.[30]

There are other serious uncertainties coupled with these radically fluctuating resource estimates and indicators. Accessing shale resources involves problems in the United Kingdom that are similar to those on the continent, particularly high population density, governmental ownership of mineral rights, property owners' reluctance about drilling activities given the structure of property rights, and a vociferous environmental lobby. Thus, the United Kingdom's future as a producer of natural gas is just too difficult to predict with any confidence. There is even a chance that the United Kingdom will continue to depend on imports.

However, if the United Kingdom faces a future of imports, it at least enjoys an advantageous import situation. Via pipeline, the United Kingdom receives gas from the Netherlands and Norway, and it exports pipeline gas to Ireland and Belgium. Both the Netherlands and Norway have quite ample reserves relative to their consumption. The Netherlands consumes only about 1% of its proved reserves, while Norway consumes only a miniscule proportion of its proved reserves, leaving ample supplies for export. As a result, the United Kingdom is blessed with reliable pipeline partners. Further, given the United Kingdom's geographical position as an island on Europe's periphery, it is ideally placed to benefit from LNG deliveries in the emerging world market in natural gas.

India and Brazil

Table 6.6 presents key comparative information for India and Brazil and includes China as an additional reference point. These three countries comprise the "BICs" of the BRICs (*Brazil, Russia, India, and China*)—or, said another way, they comprise the BRICs with the one former superpower and current petro state omitted. The three countries are all quite different, yet they are similar in certain ways. China and India are supposedly rising geopolitical powers, while Brazil has more modest pretensions.

Table 6.6 A Comparison of India, Brazil, and China

Measure	India	Brazil	China
Population	1,220,800,359	201,009,622	1,349,585,838
GDP (USD)	1,847,976,748,681	2,476,652,189,880	7,318,499,269,769
Area (sq. km)	3,287,263	8,514,877	9,596,961
Energy consumption (million gallons of oil equivalent)	172,119	82,165	804,474
Energy consumption per capita (gallons of oil equivalent)	141	409	596
GDP per gallon of oil equivalent (USD)	10.74	30.15	9.10

Measure	India	Brazil	China
Percentage of energy from coal	52.9	5.2	70.4
Percentage of energy from oil	29.0	45.2	17.7
Percentage of energy from natural gas	9.8	9.0	4.5
Proved gas reserves (bcm)	1,073	365	3,030
Technically recoverable shale gas resources (bcm)	1,784	6,400	36,104

Abbreviations: bcm = billion cubic meters; GDP = gross domestic product; USD = United States dollar.

Sources: BP, "Statistical Review of World Energy," June 2012; U.S. Energy Information Administration, "World Shale Gas Resources: An Initial Assessment of 14 Regions Outside the United States," April 2011, p. 4; CIA, *World Factbook*, available at www.cia.gov/library/publications/the-world-factbook/index.html; and World Bank, "GDP (Current US$)," available at http://data.worldbank.org/indicator/NY.GDP.MKTP.CD.

All three countries have very large land masses. But China has 9.596 million square kilometers, and Brazil has 8.5 million square kilometers, giving both countries areas 2.5 to 3.0 times as large as India's (3.3 million square kilometers). China and India are the world's two most populous nations, each with a population more than six times as large as Brazil's. However, although Brazil's population is only one-sixth of India's, its GDP is one-third larger. China's GDP outstrips India's by a factor of almost four, although China's population is only 11% larger.

The three countries differ quite substantially with respect to their energy sources, consumption, and uses. With only a slightly larger population, China uses 4.7 times as much energy as India, and India uses more than twice as much energy as Brazil. Brazil and China are somewhat similar in their per capita energy consumption: 409 gallons of oil equivalent per year in Brazil, and 596 in China. But that contrasts with India's meager per capita 141 gallons of oil equivalent per year. India, although less efficient and less productive in so many ways, nonetheless maintains an edge in energy efficiency, producing $10.74 of GDP per gallon compared to China's $9.10. But both India and China are much less energy-efficient than Brazil, which squeezes $30.15 of GDP out of each equivalent unit of energy consumed. All three nations rely on coal for more than 50% of all energy, with China being the most heavily coal-dependent, and all three nations derive less than 10% of their energy from natural gas.

These countries also differ remarkably in terms of their apparent natural gas resources, at least according to contemporaneous estimates by the USEIA. The USEIA reports that China has 3,030 bcm of proved gas reserves, compared to India's 1,073 bcm and Brazil's meager 365 bcm. Table 6.7 shows the import situation for both India and Brazil. But the staggering difference falls in the estimate of technically recoverable shale gas: 36,104 bcm for China, compared to Brazil's 6,400 bcm and India's 1,784 bcm. This is a difference of more than 20 times between China and India, for a land mass that differs only by a factor of about three. With similar areas, China has more than five times the estimated shale resources of Brazil. Could the gas endowments of these three countries really be so radically different, or is the vast difference in estimates due to how little we presently know? Such reflections suggest that India and Brazil may have much more shale gas than currently known.

Table 6.7 Import Reliance by India and Brazil, 2011 (Billions of Cubic Meters)

	Pipeline	LNG	Total Imports	Consumption	Import Dependency (%)
India	0.0	17.1	17.1	61.1	28.0
Brazil	9.7	1.1	10.8	26.7	40.4

Abbreviation: LNG = liquid natural gas.

Source: BP, "Statistical Review of World Energy," June 2012.

Estimates of gas reserves, particularly technically recoverable reserves, depend on knowledge of geology. Where little is known of geology, estimated reserves must necessarily be lower. This seems to be part of the reason for this extremely large reported differential. While knowledge of China's gas reserves remains quite incomplete, India's resources are a relative mystery. In fact, India has just begun to try to understand the gas resources beneath its feet, having been very slow in studying its own shale prospects. The first actual discovery of Indian shale gas occurred only in the summer of 2011, and the summer of 2013 found India really just beginning its first serious efforts to understand its overall shale gas resources.[31]

Brazil has astoundingly large hydrocarbon resources that it has just recently begun to comprehend. The twenty-first century's largest discovery of hydrocarbon resources occurred in Brazil, in its fabled "pre-salt" offshore formations. Stretched along 500 miles of Brazil's coast, this formation consists of a thick salt cap that lies far below the ocean's surface. Beneath this layer of salt, at a depth of about 3 miles, lie very substantial deposits of oil and gas. Estimates of this resource are huge, and new information leads to constantly updated estimates, with many guesses now putting the total resource in excess of 70 billion barrels of oil equivalent, with perhaps 10 billion recoverable barrels.[32] On the heels of the pre-salt discovery has come news of discoveries of natural gas in the Parnaíba and Paraná basins. (See Plate 16: The map shows the Paraná basin, and the Parnaíba basin lies about 500 miles southeast of the Amazon delta, centered on the port city of Parnaíba.) These new estimates place Brazil's shale resources in the range of 12,000 bcm, only some of which would be recoverable.[33]

Until now, or at least pending development of its newly discovered resources, Brazil's stake in natural gas is relatively small, and its supply and demand situation is relatively simple. Focusing on hydrocarbon energy resources, Brazil derives only 16% of its energy from natural gas and an almost negligible amount from coal. Of its 26.7 bcm of consumption in 2011, it produced 16.7 bcm and imported the balance from Bolivia via pipeline, its only pipeline connection. About two-thirds of Brazil's LNG imports come from Qatar and 8% from Nigeria. The balance comes from a diversity of much smaller suppliers. While it has quite significant shale gas resources, Brazil has very ample supplies of oil, and these have been receiving the focus of its development efforts. In essence, Brazil presently remains a bystander to the natural gas revolution, largely due to its rich hydropower endowment and its focus on oil. But recent drought conditions reduced the production of hydropower, leading to greater gas imports to feed electricity generation. Partly in response to this condition, Brazil has begun turning to development of its natural gas.

India's economy has been growing at 7% to 8% in recent years, but it suffers from an energy infrastructure that is radically inadequate to its aspirations. In summer 2011, a general failure of India's power grid left almost 700 million people without power for days. To meet its development goals, India needs to enhance its general energy infrastructure, including the natural gas component. Without new discoveries, India faces the prospect of future energy constraints and continuing massive gas imports. India consumes slightly less than half as much natural gas as China and must import one-fourth of its annual consumption. In 2011, as Table 6.3 shows, India consumed 61 bcm, while producing 46 bcm and importing 17 bcm—all as LNG. Each year, India consumes about 4% of its proved reserve and holds technologically recoverable shale reserves estimated at 1,784 bcm or about 29 years of current consumption.

Surprisingly, for a major nation with a very large geographical area and very lengthy land borders, India currently imports no natural gas via pipeline. On the north, India has a border with a phalanx of small mountainous nations, the Himalayas, and China, with their own natural gas deficits. On India's western border, Pakistan consumes more natural gas than it produces and is unlikely to provide a stable energy partner for India in any event due to their political relationship. To the east, Bangladesh also consumes its entire small production of natural gas, and even Burma beyond has minimal resources. For any hope of securing natural gas pipeline imports, India must look farther to the west, to Turkmenistan and Iran, with their huge reserves, and there is much talk of pipelines coming to India from these distant lands.

Every week, there is further news about plans to develop the Turkmenistan–Afghanistan–Pakistan–India (TAPI) pipeline. (Plate 17 presents a general map of Central Asia, and Plate 18 traces the most important pipelines in the region.) To run from the Dauletabad fields in eastern Turkmenistan into India, the TAPI pipeline would have to traverse 1,000 miles and run through what can reasonably be described as a gauntlet. In Afghanistan, the line would pass near Herat, Helmand, and Kandahar, all of which have been in war news much more than energy news. In Pakistan, the pipeline would go through tribal areas that are hardly under full governmental control. As John Foster notes, "When construction will start is uncertain, because security in Afghanistan and the tribal areas of Pakistan remains a problem."[34] Beyond the technological challenges and the uncertain operating conditions prevailing in Afghanistan and Pakistan, the project would require a very bold consortium of investors. At best, it will be quite a few years before any gas arrives in India from the TAPI line, if it ever occurs.

Plate 18 also shows a potential pipeline from the rich gas fields of Iran's South Pars Field, extending all the way to Delhi. As of mid-2013, construction on this line appeared to be starting. It is expected to cost $7.5 billion and consist of a 900-kilometer portion in Iran and a 780-kilometer portion in Pakistan before reaching India. The United States has aggressively opposed the building of this line, first by maintaining that it violates the international sanctions against Iran that are currently in place. Under pressure from the United States, India backed out of the consortium in 2009. To complete the line just into the markets of Pakistan, it must run through the Balochistan tribal area of Pakistan, where security is a huge problem already. There is also a concern that the United States, if it is really serious about stopping the pipeline, could help exacerbate Balochi disruptions to the project.[35]

Conclusion

The eight countries that are the focus of this chapter are all major energy consumers because they must fuel their large economies. But their energy endowments and consumption show very marked differences. Also, they have moved at very different speeds in discovering and exploiting their shale gas resources.

For the Eurozone countries Germany, France, and Italy, domestic shale gas is unlikely to prove so large or so significant that it will imply a major change in these countries' energy futures. The United Kingdom has somewhat better overall prospects and seems more willing to undertake serious development. Japan stands alone among these countries as having essentially no hydrocarbon resources of its own in prospect, so it will remain virtually totally dependent on importing gas and oil. Russia's overwhelming endowment, on which it so heavily depends, appears less and less capable of sustaining Russia's pretensions to a place among the top rank of nations. Discoveries around the world, coupled with Russia's own production problems, make Russian gas less vital to the world every day.

India and Brazil stand out among these eight nations as wildcards in energy. Both have the extensive land masses that make hydrocarbon discoveries likely. Brazil has already made big initial discoveries, with resource estimates that are increasing almost constantly. Given Brazil's large hydropower resources, it appears virtually certain that Brazil can be totally energy-independent. India has a very serious energy situation, and knowledge of India's domestic gas is woefully inadequate. But that could quickly change with new discoveries. Even then, India's lack of pipeline and other energy infrastructure threaten its ability to effectively turn that anticipated resource into productive energy for homes and businesses.

Notes

1. Hiroko Tabuchi, "Japan Backs Off Goal to Phase Out Nuclear Power by 2040," *New York Times*, September 19, 2012.

2. For LNG pricing in the light of the natural gas revolution, see Javier Blas, "Japan Pushes Asia Gas Price Close to High," *Financial Times*, May 17, 2012; Alex Forbes, "The Exciting Future of LNG, and How It Will Transform the Global Gas Market," Europeanenergyreview.eu, February 2, 2012; Mari Iwata and Peter Landes, "Crisis in Japan Transforms Global Natural-Gas Market," *Wall Street Journal*, February 13, 2012; and Ken Koyama, "An Analysis on Asian Premium for LNG Price," Institute of Energy Economics, Japan, March 2012.

3. International Gas Union, "World LNG Report 2011," June 2012, p. 11, available at www.igu.org/igu-publications/LNG%20Report%202011.pdf.

4. BP, "Statistical Review of World Energy," June 2012, p. 28.

5. With respect to security of LNG supplies, see Steve LeVine, "LNG: Alaska Pitches Security, Diversity in Hunt for Gas Buyers," Energywire.com, April 11, 2012; Naturalgasasia.com, "U.S. Expected to Approve Expanded LNG Exports to Japan," July 29, 2012; Leslie Patti-Guzman, "LNG: Security of Gas Supply Will Matter in 2012," Naturalgaseurope.com, May 17, 2012; and Ken Silverstein, "LNG Export Ruling Heard Around the World," Energybiz.com, April 25, 2012.

6. Naturalgasasia.com, "Australia Becomes Japan's Biggest LNG Supplier," March 7, 2013.

7. See Robert W. Kolb, "The Natural Gas Revolution and Central Asia," *Journal of Social, Political, and Economic Studies*, Summer 2012, 37, pp. 141–180.

8. Elena Kropatcheva, "Playing Both Ends Against the Middle: Russia's Geopolitical Energy Games with the EU and Ukraine," *Geopolitics*, 2011, 16, pp. 553–573.

9. Yves de Saint Jacob, "France's 'Green Vote' Kills Shale Gas—and Targets Nuclear Power as Well," Europeanenergyreview.eu, July 21, 2011. See also Boris Martor and Raphael Chetrit, "French Parliament: Blind to the Bigger Energy Picture," Europeanenergyreview.eu, September 19, 2011.

10. Christian Wüst, "Fear of Fracking: Germany Balks on Natural Gas Bonanza," Spiegel Online International, www.spiegel.de/international/, October 5, 2012.

11. Benny Peiser, "Europe 'Dithering' over Joining Shale Gas Revolution," Publicserviceeurope.com, August 29, 2012.

12. Matthew Hulbert, "Why European Shale Is Totally 'Fracked,'" *Forbes*, July 12, 2012.

13. Matthew Hulbert, "Arctic Oil: Putin's Last Chance," Europeanenergyreview.eu, July 19, 2012.

14. Naturalgaseurope.com, "Russia Touts Unconventional Gas Promise," December 31, 2012.

15. See Shtokman Development AG, "Shtokman Gas and Condensate Field," available at www.shtokman.ru/en/project/gasfield/, accessed April 7, 2013.

16. Alan Riley, "Resetting Gazprom in the Golden Age of Gas," Europeanenergyreview.com, September 17, 2012.

17. See Adnan Vatansever and David Koranyi, "An Uphill Battle on Russian Gas Prices on the Horizon," Europeanenergyreview.eu, March 14, 2013. See also Naturalgaseurope.com, "Russia Activates the LNG Sector," January 20, 2013.

18. Vikram Rao, *Shale Gas: The Promise and the Peril*, Research Triangle Park, NC: RTI Press, 2012, p. 129.

19. Amanda Paul, "Gas Is Cut While Europe Freezes," *Today's Zaman*, February 12, 2012; and Andrew E. Kramer, "As Europe Shivers, Russia and Ukraine Point Fingers over Natural Gas Supply to the West," *New York Times*, February 3, 2012.

20. See Kostis Geropoulos, "Gazelle, Nord Stream Deal Final Blow to Ukraine," New Europe Online, Neurope.eu, January 21, 2013; Naturalgaseurope.com, "The Gazelle Gas Pipeline Has Connected the Czech Republic with Nord Stream," January 25, 2013; and Denis Pinchuk, "UPDATE 1-Gazprom Sees Deal to Build Pipeline to Britain in 2013," Reuters.com, November 14, 2012.

21. The following articles explore some of the issues involved in TANAP, TAP, and the various versions of Nabucco. Also, the website Naturalgaseurope.com provides a steady diet of the latest news on pipeline plans across the Southern Corridor: Naturalgaseurope.com, "First Out of the Gates: South Stream Starts Construction," December 13, 2012; Matthew Hulbert, "Gazprom Tightens Control Over European Supply," *Forbes*, November 26, 2012; Naturalgaseurope. com, "With US LNG Exports, the EU May Not Need Nabucco," October 8, 2012; Naturalgaseurope.com, "Final Exam: TAP Versus Nabucco West," February 4, 2013; and Naturalgaseurope.com, "Unprecedented Opportunity for NATO Allies' Natural Gas Diversification," January 17, 2013.

22. See Naturalgaseurope.com, "Full Cost of the South Stream Project to Exceed €50 Billion," February 1, 2013; Sofia News Agency, "Construction of Bulgarian South Stream Section Set for June 2013: Gazprom," Novinite.com, December 25, 2012; Naturalgaseurope.com, "First Out of the Gates: South Stream Starts Construction," December 13, 2012; and Naturalgaseurope.com, "South Stream Ready to Lay Pipes in 2014 South Stream," November 22, 2012.

23. Poland, which was paying the highest price of all in mid-2012, per Table 6.5, successfully negotiated a price reduction with Gazprom at the end of 2012. These data were originally published by Natalia Resnkaya, "Macedonians and the Poles Pay the Highest Prices to Gazprom in All of Europe," *Izvetsia*, February 1, 2013, available at http://izvestia.ru/news/544100.

24. Naturalgaseurope.com, "Putin Says EU Energy Law 'Uncivilised,'" December 21, 2012.

25. Jan Techau, "Russia's Geopolitical Gazprom Blunder," Naturalgaseurope. com, November 15, 2012; and Adnan Vatansever and David Koranyi, "Lowering the Price of Russian Gas: A Challenge for European Energy Security," Europeanenergyreview.eu, March 11, 2013.

26. David Francis, "How the U.S. Blew Up the Global Energy Market," *Fiscal Times*, April 5, 2013.

27. See Peter Fairley, "Fracking Quakes Shake the Shale Gas Industry," *Technology Review*, January 20, 2012; Henry Fountain, "Add Quakes to Rumblings Over Gas Rush," *New York Times*, December 12, 2011; Naturalgaseurope.com, "UK: Environment Agency Backs Fracking," May 8, 2012; and Sylvia Pfeifer and Andrew Bounds, "Shale Gas Fracking Blamed for Blackpool Quake," *Financial Times*, November 2, 2011.

28. Peter C. Glover, "UK Shale Gas Green-Lighted with Tax Breaks," Energytribune.com, March 28, 2013; and Louise Gray, "Shale Gas Could Heat All Homes for 100 Years," Telegraph.co.uk, April 5, 2013.

29. Peter C. Glover, "UK Shale Gas Green-Lighted with Tax Breaks," Energytribune.com, March 28, 2013.

30. Stanley Reed, "Oil Giants Invest Heavily in Exploration Near Shetlands," *New York Times*, March 28, 2013.

31. OGFJ Staff, "India's ONGC Finds First Shale Gas in Asia Near Durgapur," *Oil & Gas Financial Journal*, July 8, 2011.

32. Michael Place, "Brazilian Shale Bigger Than Pre-Salt, Says Regulator," *Business News America*, January 17, 2013.

33. Peter Millard, "Brazil Prepares to Surprise Drillers This Time with Gas," Bloomberg.com, February 8, 2013; Michael Place, "Brazilian Shale Bigger Than Pre-Salt, Says Regulator," *Business News America*, January 17, 2013; and Simon Romero, "New Fields May Propel Americas to Top of Oil Companies' Lists," *New York Times*, September 19, 2011.

34. John Foster, "Afghanistan, the TAPI Pipeline, and Energy Geopolitics," March, 23, 2010, available at www.ensec.org. See also Gawdat Bahgat, "The Geopolitics of Energy in Central Asia and the Caucasus," *Journal of Social, Political, and Economic Studies*, Summer 2009, 34, pp. 139–153; Marie Lall, "India's Gas Pipeline Efforts: An Analysis of the Problems That Have Prevented Success," National Bureau of Asian Research, NBR Special Report #23, September 2010, pp. 43–54; Naturalgaseurope.com, "Turkmenistan Signs Major Gas Deal with India, Pakistan," May 23, 2012; and Naturalgaseurope.com, "With Trans-Caspian on the Back-Burner, Turkmenistan Focuses on TAPI," February 20, 2012.

35. Jen Alic, "How Far Will the US Go to Derail Iran-Pakistan Pipeline," Oilprice. com, March 4, 2013.

7

The Other Contending Nations[*]

The two previous chapters explore the world's largest economies and their role in the natural gas revolution. We have seen that the effect on almost every one of them is significant, with some nations playing an active and pivotal role (most notably the United States), and other nations suffering (Russia) or enjoying (Japan) the effects of these sweeping changes. Many smaller nations also play an important role in the changes that are transforming world energy markets. First, some of these nations hold very large proved reserves. Only two of the ten largest economies in the world hold large proved reserves of natural gas—Russia with the largest and the United States with the fifth largest. Thus, this chapter rounds out our understanding of the future of natural gas by considering some of the key players in the gas market, based on their large proved reserves, notably those with reserves ranking second through fourth—Iran, Qatar, and Turkmenistan.

Second, some nations hold large reserves but have played essentially little or no role in the world gas market. Iraq has the world's twelfth largest reserves, but during its period of wars, sanctions, and political turmoil, its gas has been held off the world market. Perhaps it will soon reenter the community of nations in an active way, with implications for the gas market. Somewhat similarly, Saudi Arabia has

---

[*] This chapter draws from a number of other sources, including my recent article: "The Natural Gas Revolution and Central Asia," *Journal of Social, Political, and Economic Studies*, Summer 2012, 37, pp. 141–180.

the world's sixth largest reserves of natural gas, but these reserves will probably not be an important force in world markets, and it is important to understand why that is likely to be the case.

As a third factor, some nations with significant proved reserves have made little impact on world markets, but they are poised to do so soon. Australia's proved reserves rank in eleventh place, but Australia is very actively developing its massive shale resources and has ambitious plans to be a world supplier of liquid natural gas (LNG). Its proximity to energy-hungry Asian markets, coupled with its large export plans, will likely make it a potent force. Canada, with reserves placing it in eighteenth position, may also come to have a similar role.

Fourth, some countries have played essentially no important role in world gas markets and have been listed as having inconsequential proved reserves: Israel, Lebanon, Cyprus, Mozambique, and Tanzania. Recent discoveries of massive conventional reserves position each of these countries to become major exporters of natural gas in the decade ahead.

Finally, some countries also occupy or may soon hold an important position in the world of gas, some because they are key transit countries like Turkey and Ukraine. Others may become significant sources of gas for themselves and their region, such as Poland. This chapter considers all these countries, as well as a few others along the way.

Iran, Qatar, and Iraq

Iran, Qatar, and Iraq—arranged at the head of the Persian Gulf and along its eastern and western shores—possess tremendous conventional gas reserves, as the top panel of Table 7.1 shows. With total proved reserves for these countries of 61,725 billion cubic meters (bcm) and world reserves totaling 208,436 bcm, these three closely related countries hold 30% of total world reserves. Iran alone holds

16% of total world reserves. All told, the 10 countries listed in Table 7.1 account for almost 40%. But as the discussion of this section makes clear, the countries of greatest interest are the first three: Iran, Qatar, and Iraq.

Table 7.1 The Natural Gas of Iran, Qatar, and Iraq (Billions of Cubic Meters)

Reserves Rank	Country	Reserves	Production	Consumption	Production Minus Consumption
2	Iran	33,090	151.8	153.3	–1.5
3	Qatar	25,047	146.8	23.8	123.0
12	Iraq	3,588	1.9	N/A	N/A
Total: Iran, Qatar, Iraq		61,725	301	177	124.0
Other Arab States					
6	Saudi Arabia	8,150	99.2	99.2	0.00
7	United Arab Emirates	6,090	51.7	62.9	–11.2
16	Egypt	2,190	61.3	49.6	11.7
20	Kuwait	1,784	13.0	16.2	–3.2
25	Oman	950	26.5	N/A	N/A
29	Yemen	479	9.4	N/A	N/A
33	Bahrain	348	13.0	N/A	N/A
Total of other Arab states		19,991	274	228	–46

Abbreviation: N/A = Not available or negligible.
Source: BP, "Statistical Review of World Energy," June 2012.

Conventional reserves have been the source of all world supplies until very recently, and they will continue to meet the majority of the world's gas needs for some time. Consequently, they help form the base of the market. Each of these countries has had a quite different history recently. With proved reserves of natural gas placing it second only to Russia, Iran has quite significant production, but all that goes to meet domestic consumption, as the upper panel of Table 7.1

illustrates. Iran is actually even a slightly net deficit nation in natural gas. Iran has significant plans to change that position, but it faces continuing international sanctions, led by the United States, as it attempts to curtail Iran's nuclear development program. These sanctions aim at stifling Iran's gas production and impeding its international commerce. In the short run—while still under these somewhat effective international sanctions—Iran must find nearby trading partners willing to violate sanctions and capable of receiving gas via pipeline. In some cases, the pipeline must still be built to connect to its neighbors.

Iran has lengthy land borders with Iraq, Turkey, Turkmenistan, Afghanistan, and Pakistan, and it also adjoins Armenia and Azerbaijan. So all these countries are potential gas-trading partners. In fact, Iran acquires significant gas from Turkmenistan, which is therefore unlikely to be a customer for Iranian gas. However, Iran already does export gas to Turkey, Armenia, and Azerbaijan; the U.S. Energy Information Administration (USEIA) characterizes Iran as "a relatively minor and strictly regional exporter of natural gas."[1] These exports amount to less than 1% of world total export volumes and bring Iran only about $10.5 million per day, which is about one-twentieth of what Iran earns from exporting oil and condensates. Gas flows from Iran to Turkey via the Tabriz–Dogubayazit pipeline, with the flow amounting to about 30 million cubic meters per day. Turkey seems anxious to increase that flow, having signed a new import agreement in 2013.[2]

Iran exports gas to Iraq as well, with plans to increase this flow to 40 million cubic meters per day, largely to feed three electrical power plants. The pipeline for this gas will go from Iran, into Iraq, and on to Syria, although the Syrian outcome may well depend on political and military developments there.[3] While Iraq may be a current importer of Iranian gas, this condition will probably not persist in the long run, given Iraq's standing as the country with the twelfth largest proved reserves. As Table 7.1 shows, Iraq currently produces very little natural gas, with no reliable figures for its consumption.

However, if political conditions become stable, Iraq can certainly easily produce more than sufficient gas for its domestic needs and can become an exporter as well.

Iran and Pakistan are actively building a "peace pipeline" to allow delivery of gas to Pakistan, a major market with critical need for gas. The pipeline will run from Iran's South Pars Field and carry gas into southern Pakistan (see Plates 8 and 18). Much of the pipeline, especially on the Iranian side, is already built, and much is left to build in Pakistan. The cost of the portion in Pakistan should be about $1.5 billion, a problem for cash-strapped Pakistan, but China has offered Pakistan $500 million in financing to facilitate construction, which is supposed to be completed in 2014. In the view of the United States, this trade would fly in the face of the sanctions regime, but Pakistan seems determined to proceed. As one commentator notes: "The pipeline will go ahead largely because Pakistan's energy crisis dictates that it must."[4] Pakistan already suffers frequent electricity blackouts due to insufficient natural gas. One way the United States might have been able to impede the pipeline could have been to obstruct international financing, but China's loan may have solved that problem. However, the pipeline must run through the Balochistan region of Pakistan, an area of strong separatist activity. According to some reports, Saudi Arabia and the United States are trying to incite additional troubles in Balochistan to interfere with the pipeline's operation. Also, the pipeline was originally contemplated to extend into India, but under pressure and inducements from the United States, the Indian leg has been canceled.[5]

Qatar has been one of the most active participants in the worldwide gas market due to its very large production, which it ships mostly as LNG. Qatar and Iran are yoked together by the fact that they share the world's largest gas reservoir consisting of two parts, the North Field and South Pars Field, as Plate 8 illustrates. Together the areas form a lozenge shape that has its southwest edge along the northeast coast of Qatar and extends northeast, almost continuing the line of the Qatar peninsula pointing toward Iran. Qatar and Iran each have territorial waters that meet at the middle of the Persian Gulf. That boundary separates the Qatari portion of the field, the North Field, from the South Pars Field that belongs to Iran. From a geological perspective, these two fields constitute the same resource into which both Qatar and Iran can dip their "straws."

Qatar gained independence in 1971, a year that also saw its first major discoveries of natural gas. But production did not take off due to technical and financial difficulties, accompanied by the threat of terrorist action, particularly against LNG tankers. LNG production started to accelerate in the mid-1990s, largely with the help of financing from gas-needy Japan. Over the past decades, Qatar gas has moved from one success to the next.[6] In 1980, Qatar's proved reserves were only 2,800 bcm, but by 2011, they had grown to more than 25,000 bcm. Production in 1999 was only 22.1 bcm, but it expanded to 146.8 bcm by 2011. And domestic consumption increased 50-fold between 1965 and 2011. Now Qatar is the world's leading LNG exporter, exporting more than 100 bcm via LNG and an additional 20 bcm via pipeline. In 2011, Qatar exported LNG to 23 countries, with leading recipients being the United Kingdom, Japan, India, and South Korea, which together account for almost 60% of Qatari LNG sales.[7]

In spite of the claims by Qatari that they are unworried by potential new entrants as LNG exporters, the buildout of the world's LNG infrastructure may dislodge Qatar from its position in the catbird seat in the world's LNG market. For example, Poland has been able to successfully renegotiate its LNG import contract with Qatar, and Australia has already displaced Qatar as Japan's leading LNG supplier. Assuming that the shale revolution continues toward realizing its potential, a world price for LNG is likely to emerge, and it should be a price that reflects wellhead price plus a liquefaction and transportation differential. Such a development could present a serious problem for Qatar, a nation that depends very heavily on its LNG exports and uses that vast income to support one of the world's most generous and elaborate welfare systems, providing free education, free medical care, and low-cost housing to its citizens.[8] No doubt these benefits help keep the citizenry satisfied with Qatar's current somewhat benevolent autocracy. In sum, Qatar will continue to be a significant LNG supplier, but it may have to operate in a much more competitive environment and be satisfied with a much-reduced income flow from its gas exports.[9]

As a final consideration of the Persian Gulf and nearby Arab nations, the bottom panel of Table 7.1 shows key gas statistics for nearby Arab countries. These seven countries all possess major gas reserves, led by Saudi Arabia with the world's sixth largest reserves. However, these countries together play essentially no role in world gas trade, largely because of their remarkably high consumption of gas. Saudi Arabia, for example, has a quite high rate of consumption, and the United Arab Emirates is even a net importer. In many of these countries, generously subsidized gas prices contribute to excess consumption and help to frustrate export potential.

Central Asia and Turkey

Azerbaijan and the five "Stans" of central Asia—Turkmenistan, Tajikistan, Kazakhstan, Kyrgyzstan, and Uzbekistan—have all gone their separate ways since they escaped the grip of the Soviet empire. Bundling these six former Soviet republics with Turkey may seem strange at first glance, but Turkey has an important role as a potential transit corridor for getting the rich gas endowment of central Asia to the energy-importing countries of Western Europe. Table 7.2 provides basic information on the natural gas of these countries. Turkey, Tajikistan, and Kyrgyzstan have little in the way of gas resources. Tajikistan and Kyrgyzstan have small populations so do not consume very much gas, but Turkey, with its large population, has a fairly high level of consumption that it must satisfy through imports, at least some of which come from Iran, as we have seen. Of the four other countries, Turkmenistan dominates in terms of reserves, with 13 times as much gas as the nearest competitor, Kazakhstan, which has its own substantial endowment of oil. With smaller reserves, Uzbekistan actually produces more gas than Turkmenistan but consumes most of it domestically.[10] Azerbaijan has smaller production, but with its smaller consumption, Azerbaijan and Uzbekistan have similar amounts available for export. This means that Turkmenistan is the major potential exporter of the group, and we have seen in Chapter 5, "The United States and China," that Turkmenistan is already a major pipeline exporter of gas to China. Table 7.3 details the exports of natural gas from central Asia.

Table 7.2 The Natural Gas of Central Asia and Turkey (Billions of Cubic Meters)

Reserves Rank	Country	Reserves	Production	Consumption	Production Minus Consumption
4	Turkmenistan	24,319	59.5	25.0	34.5
19	Kazakhstan	1,881	19.3	9.2	10.1
21	Uzbekistan	1,602	57.0	49.1	7.9
22	Azerbaijan	1,271	14.8	8.2	6.6
N/A	Kyrgyzstan	N/A	N/A	N/A	N/A
N/A	Tajikistan	N/A	N/A	N/A	N/A
N/A	Turkey	N/A	N/A	45.7	N/A
Totals:		29,073	150.6	137.2	13.4

Abbreviation: N/A = Not available or negligible.

Source: BP, "Statistical Review of World Energy," June 2012.

Table 7.3 Gas Exports of Central Asian Nations (Billions of Cubic Meters per Year)

		From:			
		Kazakhstan	Uzbekistan	Turkmenistan	Totals
To:	Russia	11.45	7.15	10.14	28.74
	China	0	0	14.25	14.25
	Iran	0	0	10.20	10.20
Totals		11.45	7.15	34.59	53.19

Source: BP, "Statistical Review of World Energy," June 2012. Omitted from this table are very small exports among these central Asian countries.

With its fourth-in-the-world gas reserves, Turkmenistan could produce and export much more. It is clearly the potentially key gas player in this region and a potentially major player in the world gas market. But Turkmenistan is just largely that—a potentially key player—due mainly to its difficult geographical position as a landlocked country bordered mostly by other nations with rich gas resources and their own export ambitions (see Plate 17). Plate 19 shows the interior pipelines of Turkmenistan and their potential international connections.

Russia would like to keep Turkmen gas off international markets, or at least make Turkmen gas transit Russia. If Turkmenistan's only route for gas were through Russia, Russia could take up Turkmen gas at a steep discount, as it has previously. During Soviet days, all exported Turkmen gas went north to Russia because the Soviets built the pipelines and directed all central Asian pipelines into Russia before they headed to the west. After Turkmenistan gained its freedom, the only gas outlet for Turkmenistan was through the legacy pipelines to Russia, which was able to pay a very low price for Turkmen gas. Ever since gaining independence, Turkmenistan has been struggling to get its gas to world markets, and Russia has been trying to frustrate the same development. Turkmenistan's geographical position is a powerful ally to Russia's efforts.

Turkmenistan has had one very large success in its efforts to free its gas from Russia's grasp—a pipeline to China. This ambitious line was completed in 2010. It originates in Turkmenistan, ultimately reaching Horgos, China, in the Xinjiang region, after transiting Uzbekistan and Kazakhstan, where it skirts the northern border of Kyrgyzstan. This Central Asia–China dual pipeline is 1,150 miles long and was constructed in a virtually unbelievable 18 months.[11] The pipeline is scheduled to deliver 30 bcm per year for 30 years. So the 14.25 bcm delivered in 2011 per Table 7.3 should rise to 30 bcm for 2012 and subsequent years. But with its large reserves and small population, Turkmenistan remains hungry to reach other markets.

To the south of Turkmenistan lies Iran, with its even larger gas reserves. If Iran escapes from sanctions, it will likely become a major exporter, giving transit precedence to its own production. In the west, Turkmenistan borders the Caspian Sea. Turkmenistan has ambitions to move its gas across the Caspian, then through Azerbaijan, and then on, eventually, to Western Europe. Plate 20 shows the principal oil and gas pipelines leading from Baku on the Caspian westward. The dashed lines indicate planned or contemplated pipelines, while the heavy black line indicates the Baku–Tbilisi–Ceyhan (BTC) oil pipeline. If a pipeline went from Baku to Novorossiysk, it could connect to the Blue Stream pipeline across the Black Sea to Turkey, as shown in Plate 15. But this would do nothing for Europe's geopolitical vulnerability to Russian gas, nor would it help Turkmenistan escape Russian dominance, as the Blue Stream pipeline originates in Russia. By contrast, a pipeline running from Baku to Supsa could reach the Black Sea without transiting Russian territory. Similarly, a gas pipeline running along the route of the BTC oil pipeline could reach Erzurum and then connect to the yet-to-be-built pipelines of the Southern Corridor, as discussed in Chapter 6, "The World's Other Large Economies," and also shown in Plate 15.

Turkmenistan has sought to build a pipeline across the Caspian, but Russia has done everything possible to frustrate this, including raising environmental concerns, never mind that Russia exhibited no such green concerns when it built Nord Stream across the Baltic or

Blue Stream across the Black Sea. Russia also raises legal objections that turn on the arcane legal issue of whether the Caspian is a sea or a lake under international law.[12] But merely getting Turkmenistan's gas to the western shore of the Caspian is not a complete answer to the transit question. On the western shore lies Azerbaijan, with its own significant gas resources and export aspirations, so Azerbaijan stands as either a transit zone or as an impediment to Turkmen aspirations as well. For Turkmen gas to reach major markets to the southeast, like Pakistan and India, it must cross Afghanistan. Plans for the Turkmenistan–Afghanistan–Pakistan–India (TAPI) pipeline (see Plate 18) are advanced, but as discussed in Chapter 6, actually building such a line through such terrain—physical and political—will remain quite unlikely for the foreseeable future. In short, with the exception of its very significant success in getting its gas to China, Turkmenistan's aspirations as a major supplier of natural gas are held hostage by geography.

As shown in Table 7.2, Turkey has very little in the way of proved reserves of gas, and it imports almost all its natural gas.[13] Also, Turkey stands at the center of the world's greatest energy controversies, with its Black Sea coast, access to the Mediterranean, and position astride the land routes into Europe from Central Asia and the Persian Gulf region. It shows a strong tendency to cooperate with all. Turkey happily receives gas from Russia via the Blue Stream pipeline; it expresses willingness to work with Russia on its South Stream goals;[14] it stands ready to receive pipelines from Azerbaijan and points further east;[15] it has worked to improve its relations with Israel, given Israel's new standing as an incipient energy powerhouse[16] (see the section "The Eastern Mediterranean," later in the chapter); it already purchases gas from Iran; and it is happy to cooperate with Western Europe on its Southern Corridor ambitions. This cooperative stance does two main things for Turkey. First, it gives Turkey a wonderful diversification of suppliers. Second, it provides revenue in the form of transit fees for all the services that want to cross its territory.[17]

Turkey has been slow to access its shale gas resources, even though the USEIA estimates that the total resource is 425 bcm.[18] However, in recent months, Turkey has shown additional interest, but so far it has yet to become truly active in this arena.[19] But perhaps that stance is not a problem, given Turkey's wide diversity of potential suppliers and its ability to obtain gas on the world market.

The "Quiet Exporters"

I have dubbed four nations the "quiet exporters": Indonesia, Malaysia, Norway, and Canada, as shown in Table 7.4. They all hold substantial reserves that place them in the bottom half of the top 20 natural gas exports, with 33 to 97 bcm available for export each year. They are the quiet exporters because their positions are mostly stable, unlikely to change dramatically in the short run, and they are not major geopolitical forces. Norway has the largest amount of gas available for export, and it exports almost all of it via pipeline to countries farther south in Europe, with about half of its exports going to Germany and the United Kingdom (see Table 7.5). Canada exports gas by pipeline to the United States and receives small LNG shipments from Trinidad and Tobago as well as Qatar. (The exports to the United States go by pipeline in the western side of the continent, while LNG from Trinidad and Tobago arrives on Canada's Atlantic coast.) Malaysia and Indonesia export mainly via LNG to other Asian countries. Malaysia sends about two-thirds of its LNG to Japan, while Indonesia ships approximately one-third to Japan and one-third to South Korea. Between the two, they also supply small amounts to China, India, Taiwan, and Thailand.

Table 7.4 The "Quiet Exporters": Reserves, Production, and Consumption (Billions of Cubic Meters per Year)

Reserves Rank	Country	Reserves	Production	Consumption	Production Minus Consumption
14	Indonesia	2,965	75.6	37.9	37.67
15	Malaysia	2,435	61.8	28.5	33.28
17	Norway	2,070	101.4	4.0	97.40
18	Canada	1,983	160.5	104.8	55.66

Source: BP, "Statistical Review of World Energy," June 2012.

Table 7.5 The "Quiet Exporters": Net Exports (Billions of Cubic Meters per Year)

Country	Net Pipeline Exports	Net LNG Exports
Indonesia	8.7	29.2
Malaysia	0.3	33.3
Norway	92.8	4.0
Canada	61.4	–3.3

Abbreviation: LNG = liquid natural gas.

Source: BP, "Statistical Review of World Energy," June 2012.

Of these countries, Canada has the largest potential to become a "louder" exporter, with its large land mass and very large energy reserves that embrace not only gas but also oil in a variety of forms. For example, Canada has been involved in a continuing quest to export oil from its oil sands fields in Alberta, with the hope that the United States might eventually agree to construct the Keystone XL pipeline as part of a system that would ultimately bring Canadian oil from Alberta all the way to the Gulf of Mexico. As those plans continue in dispute, Canada has been contemplating sending its energy resources in Alberta on to British Columbia, where they could reach the open sea and Asia. In addition, the USEIA estimated Canadian technically recoverable shale gas resources as 10,987 bcm, which is almost half as large as the estimate for the United States.[20] Canada clearly has the resources and the technical capability to produce its shale gas and to become a major exporter, but that prospect lies some years in the future.

Poland and Ukraine

With Poland's northern border on the Baltic and Ukraine's southern border on the Black Sea, these two countries sit astride the route of any land-based pipeline that might bring Russian gas to Western Europe. Following World War II, the Soviets dominated both Poland and Ukraine, one as a satellite, and the other as a Soviet republic. In that period, Russia had no problem moving its gas through either area, given its power over both. During Soviet days, both Poland and Ukraine depended heavily on gas coming from Russia, and they continued to do so after independence and to the present day. Table 7.6 presents basic gas information for Poland and Ukraine and shows that both countries consume more than they produce.

Table 7.6 Poland and Ukraine: Reserves, Production, and Consumption (Billions of Cubic Meters)

Reserves Rank	Country	Reserves	Production	Consumption	Production Minus Consumption
38	Poland	121	4.3	15.4	–11.1
26	Ukraine	935	18.2	53.7	–35.5

Source: BP, "Statistical Review of World Energy," June 2012.

To meet its demand for gas consumption, Poland imported about 11 bcm in 2011, with 86% coming from Russia and 14% arriving from other European countries. The shortfall in production relative to consumption is much larger for Ukraine. It imported 40.5 bcm in 2011, all from Russia, leaving it totally dependent on Russian imports.

Since the dissolution of the Soviet Union, Russian–Polish relations have been none too warm, and Russian relationships with Ukraine have been very problematic, as we have seen, even resulting in cutoffs of Russian gas in winter. Both Poland and Ukraine show increasing interest in obtaining gas via LNG, but to date, those imports have been negligible to nonexistent.

Every day, Russia moves closer to freeing itself from needing to use gas routes across Poland and Ukraine to reach its lucrative Western markets. As we have noted, Nord Stream already operates and connects Russia directly to Germany across the Baltic. Similarly, Blue Stream crosses the Black Sea, creating a direct link from Russia to Turkey. Also, Russia is moving aggressively to construct South Stream, which it plans to be another southern route that avoids Ukraine altogether. When Russia no longer needs Poland or Ukraine as transit zones, they will obviously be in an even more vulnerable position with respect to their gas imports. In that context, one might expect the shale revolution to hold particular salience for both countries. Based on the assessment by the USEIA, Poland's technically recoverable shale reserves are 164 bcm and the Ukraine holds 1,104 bcm, enough for 10 and 21 years of current consumption, except that not all technically recoverable gas can actually be produced. Nonetheless, both countries hold significant shale resources compared to their consumption demands. Also, these estimates usually rise as exploration proceeds. In the case of Poland, for example, the Polish government now estimates shale reserves of 346 to 768 bcm.[21]

As shown in Table 6.5 (see Chapter 6), Poland has been paying the highest price in Europe for Russian gas imports, 68% higher than the United Kingdom, which pays the lowest. However, Poland recently won a price concession estimated at 10% to 20%, perhaps due to Russian concern over the European Union's legal attack on Russian pricing, as discussed in Chapter 6.[22] Perhaps more than any other country in Europe, Poland has striven to develop its shale resources, but its path has been far from trouble free.[23] At first, Poland moved aggressively to develop its shale and attracted ExxonMobil and Canada's Talisman Energy to explore. But then the government changed the tax regime, leaving both companies ready to abandon their efforts there.[24] Also, some of the test well results have been discouraging, and they have not been into production.[25] Finally, drillers have to obtain more than 30 different environmental permits to drill. The following summarizes the current state of shale development in Poland due to governmental policies: "Shale gas companies are also concerned that a planned new hydrocarbons law will not take into account an exceptionally capital intensive nature of unconventional projects. There are fears that proposed taxes will exceed the 40 percent level of the total tax burden and in effect slow the pace and scope of exploration works."[26] To date, Poland has not succeeded in obtaining any gas from shale. Nonetheless, even with its weak performance, it has gone farther down the road toward shale than any European country except the United Kingdom.

Ukraine probably has the worst energy relations with Russia of any country. In April 2013, Gazprom announced its commitment to export gas only by pipelines in which it holds a greater than 50% investment, and one Gazprom official has already said that the Ukrainian pipeline system will be "scrap metal" unless it is used by Russia.[27] Russia gives every indication of seriousness on this point, having already spent billions of dollars on pipelines whose main function is to avoid Ukrainian soil. Also, as noted before, Russia has shut off gas supplies to Ukraine more than once, leaving its citizens shivering in winter. In early 2013, the two countries were embroiled in a $7 billion dispute over gas deliveries. There is little sign that relations will improve anytime soon, and this dispute is largely geopolitical, as Russia wants to assert its dominance over this portion of its "near abroad."[28]

To escape the grasp of Russia, Ukraine aims to deploy a variety of strategies. First, it plans to develop its shale gas and hopes tvo be able to produce 6 to 11 bcm by 2030.[29] But that is 15 winters away, and Ukraine may well need a quicker solution. It is also pursuing a diversification strategy and is attempting to work with Azerbaijan, Qatar, Turkey, and Turkmenistan.[30] Ukraine also has conventional offshore deposits in the Black Sea that it hopes to develop with ExxonMobil and Royal Dutch Shell, having decided not to use the Russian firm Lukoil.[31] In addition, Ukraine is striving to develop LNG import facilities.[32] Compared to almost all the other countries of the world, Ukraine has the most at stake in the shale gas revolution. Developing its own resources and getting access to LNG priced competitively on a world market are vital to its future, but there remains the problem of securing these other sources before Russia completes the development of its alternative supply routes, making it free to deal with Ukraine as it wishes.

Australia

According to the 2011 USEIA estimate, Australia has over 3,000 bcm of proved gas reserves, as shown in Table 7.7, and it holds 11,213 bcm of technically recoverable shale gas as well, which is about half as much as the estimate for the United States.[33] In 2011, Australia produced and consumed about 45 and 25 bcm, respectively. It exported virtually the entire difference as LNG, with about 80% going to Japan and almost all the balance being shipped to China.

Table 7.7 Australia and Argentina: Key Natural Gas Statistics (Billions of Cubic Meters)

Reserves Rank	Country	Reserves	Production	Consumption	Production Minus Consumption
11	Australia	3,759	45.0	25.6	19.4
34	Argentina	341	38.8	46.5	–7.7

Source: BP, "Statistical Review of World Energy," June 2012.

Already the largest supplier of LNG to Japan, Australia has large plans to develop its shale gas and increase its LNG exports. Moving quickly, Australia produced its first shale gas in 2012.[34] With a small population and vast area, much of Australia's shale is located well away from population centers, a situation almost exactly the opposite of Europe's. Much of Australia's gas lies in the interior desert and near pipelines, making exploitation relatively easy.[35] However, some assessments assert that Australia faces much higher extraction costs than the United States and that real shale exploitation is a decade away.[36]

A Brookings Institution study suggests that Australia will have an LNG export capacity of 10 to 12 bcm per day by 2020,[37] while the International Energy Agency predicts that Australia will be the world's largest LNG producer by 2020.[38] Presently, there are seven LNG projects planned or in construction. One of the most interesting is Australia's Prelude LNG venture, being built by Shell. It will be a floating LNG plant on the world's largest floating structure. The surface area of the barge would accommodate four football fields.[39] All these projects are enormously expensive, especially when taken in the aggregate. The total investment may well exceed $200 billion.

As we have seen, there are successive finds of shale gas around the world, as well as constantly expanding conventional resources. These continuing finds raise the question of whether Australia's massive investment can pay off.[40] For example, we have seen that China has the world's greatest shale resources. If it develops them fully and quickly, it may not need Australia's LNG. The same kind of reflections challenge all the contemplated LNG expansion plans around the world, including those of the United States.

The Eastern Mediterranean

Even though BP's "Statistical Review of World Energy" is a wonderful resource, one may search in vain for natural gas reserves or production figures for Israel, Lebanon, and Cyprus. Even for consumption figures, BP's review shows only that in 2011 Israel consumed a modest 5 bcm in 2011, but it provides no information for Lebanon or Cyprus. One might reasonably conclude that these countries have no role to play in the world of natural gas, but such a conclusion would be completely wrong, it now suddenly seems.

The U.S. Geological Survey published an estimate in 2009 opining that the waters off the coasts of Syria, Lebanon, Cyprus, Israel, and Gaza contained 3,500 bcm of natural gas and 1.7 bcm of oil (see Plate 21). At almost the same time, in January 2009, two energy companies discovered a reservoir of natural gas, Tamar, about 55 miles off the coast of Haifa in Israeli waters. In 2010 came the discovery of the Leviathan field, also in Israeli waters. Tamar is estimated to contain 225 bcm of gas, while Leviathan, as the name implies, contains 450 bcm. Leviathan may even be as large as 675 bcm. Soon after this came the discovery of a gas reservoir north of Leviathan and Tamar, in waters off Cyprus. This Aphrodite field apparently contains 225 bcm, enough to supply Cyprus with gas for a couple centuries.[41]

These discoveries have major implications for the region and for the individual countries as well. Some of the maritime borders, such as the waters of Israel and Lebanon, are disputed. Similarly, the Palestinian authority and Syria will also surely demand a share. Israel has been producing very modest supplies of gas and obtaining 40% of its natural gas by pipeline from Egypt since the Camp David Accords of 1978. The pipeline has been very unpopular among Egyptians and was attacked at least five times in 2011.[42]

Given the fraught geopolitics of the region and the location of the resource well offshore, producing the gas and securing it for use is not automatic. As Michael Economides notes, "First, the Eastern

Mediterranean finds are buried under 6,000 feet of water and then another 14,000 feet beneath the bottom of the sea for a total approaching 20,000 feet. Had it not been for the geopolitical incentives, these finds might not be economically attractive. Certainly, there are virtually no other places in the world where natural gas (not associated with oil) is produced from such depths."[43] However, the challenges of producing from these fields have already been overcome at least to a significant degree; in March 2013, gas started flowing via a pipeline from the Tamar field to an onshore terminal in Israel.[44] Given the incentives and the good progress to date, the remaining technological problems are likely to be resolved.

The geopolitical problems may be more persistent. For example, Lebanon claims that part of the Leviathan field falls within its territorial waters. There are also fears that rogue Arab elements might attack drilling platforms, so Israel has committed to strengthening its navy. In Cyprus, the Turkish Republic of Northern Cyprus claims co-ownership of the gas find and opposes Nicosia's attempts to unilaterally access the resource.[45] Looming over the entire scene are two nations with large navies, Turkey and Russia. Turkey has the most capable force in the region. For its part, Russia maintains bases in Syria, the long-term viability of which are threatened by the civil war there. The relationship between Israel and Turkey has been tense since Israel attacked Turkish ships bound for Gaza in 2010, an attack that resulted in a number of deaths. To compose this relationship, Israel formally apologized to Turkey for the incident in 2013.[46]

Nonetheless, big plans to develop the gas fields are proceeding. The hope is that Israel and Cyprus can sell some of the gas to Europe as LNG. If these plans are successful, they will significantly offset the dependence of Western Europe on Russian gas.[47] There are almost certainly additional finds to come, given the original estimate by the U.S. Geological Survey and the now-verified tremendous endowment of the region, and some of these future finds will probably be in the territory of Syria and Lebanon, which may help to alleviate some of the current undercurrent of geopolitical envy and tension.

Mozambique and Tanzania

Like Israel, Lebanon, and Cyprus, the impoverished countries of Mozambique and Tanzania were on no radars as consequential players in world energy. They are certainly not major consumers, and no one expected them to become significant energy producers and exporters. Starting in 2006, oil exploration firms have made a sequence of large gas discoveries off the shores of Tanzania and Mozambique (see Plate 22). These are conventional deposits, with low sulfur and low carbon dioxide content, which makes them particularly valuable. New finds in this area continue, leading to successive increases in estimated resources. Thus, the total amount of gas lying in this virtually untapped region is certainly very large, but no one knows how large. Based on current estimates, there may well be 2 trillion cubic meters of gas in place or even much more.

With modest gas needs of their own, Tanzania and Mozambique, and even Kenya, stand to become significant gas exporters. They would export LNG almost exclusively, bound for destinations around the world, but particularly toward Asia. The International Energy Agency believes that exports from this region will reach 45 bcm by 2035.[48] These fields can probably support up to 12 operating LNG trains. The ultimate effects on world LNG are uncertain but are expected to be quite significant.[49]

Because these are conventional deposits in a fairly good location, gas produced from these fields should be quite inexpensive compared to shale gas. For example, one analyst, Daniel Fisher, believes that this additional supply could drive the landed price of gas in Japan from $17 all the way down to $8 per million cubic feet. This would obviously be quite bad news for Qatar and other current LNG exporters.

Further, Fisher points out that this LNG from East Africa is likely to be "bad news for the more than 20 U.S. LNG terminal projects on the drawing board that assume cheap shale gas can be exported into more lucrative markets."[50] Similarly, this East African gas could seriously impair Australia's plan to expand its LNG exports. As we have seen, these plans are well under way, with Australia already supplanting Qatar as the leading LNG supplier to Japan. One estimate suggests that gas from East Africa could cost only half as much as Australian-supplied LNG.[51] Similarly, Russia is anxious to become a major LNG supplier, and these plans, too, could be disturbed substantially.[52] Additional LNG supplies would clearly benefit all LNG importers, but one nation stands to reap special benefits. China is already Tanzania's largest trading partner and has already forged deep ties with the previously gas-poor nation. Some regard Tanzania as already constituting one pearl in China's string-of-pearls strategy. The *Indian Express* quietly understates the point: "The discovery of massive natural gas deposits off the coast of Tanzania and neighbouring Mozambique has lent a new dimension to China's strategic interest in the waters of East Africa."[53]

Argentina

As shown in Table 7.7, Argentina holds proved gas reserves of 341 bcm. In 2011, it produced 38.8 bcm and consumed 46.5 bcm, importing the balance. All of its pipeline imports, 3.58 bcm, came from Bolivia. Argentina acquired 4.38 bcm via LNG from Trinidad and Tobago and Qatar, with very small amounts coming from other sources. In short, Argentina to date has been a modest force in world gas markets, with limited production and quite minor exports.

That could change, however, as Argentina has massive technically recoverable shale gas deposits. Plate 16 shows the major shale basins of southern South America, embracing both Argentina and southern

Brazil. According to the USEIA's estimate, Argentina possesses almost 22,000 bcm of shale gas. This is more than three times as much as Brazil, South America's second largest holder of shale gas. It also puts Argentina just shy of the United States in total shale resources. Since that assessment was published, there have been large additional finds of both shale gas and oil.[54]

All this good news has proceeded against a background of other developments that threaten any idea of effective exploitation of this new resource. First, Argentina reports current inflation at slightly over 10% per year, but the official statistics are widely discredited, and nongovernmental resources put inflation at 24% per year. Argentina defaulted on its sovereign debt in 2001, and those claims are still not fully resolved. Further, in the spring of 2013, Argentina teetered on the edge of a new default. This troubled history and Argentina's current economic problems hardly create a tenable investment climate for attracting the international investment commitment and technical expertise that Argentina needs to bring its shale resources to market. But these serious problems are hardly the worst feature of Argentina's energy industry situation.

Argentina has capped the export price of oil at $42 per barrel, with the government siphoning away any amount in excess of that price. In April 2012, Argentina renationalized YPF, an oil and gas firm that it had sold to the Spanish multinational Repsol only six years before, taking 51% of YPF without compensation. Repsol sued Argentina for $10.5 billion in compensation.[55] Yet less than one year after the takeover, there was talk of reconciliation and a joint venture between Repsol and YPF to produce shale gas and to exploit the shale oil in the Vaca Muerta formation.[56] Whether and when such fruitful work might occur can only be a matter of speculation. When we recall that Argentina once had the same standard of living and the same economic prospects as the United States, it may be that Argentina is a country that has huge potential and always will.

Conclusion

There are still other nations not included in our story that continue to play an active role in the world gas markets. Algeria, for instance, has received little mention, although it has been a persistent if not gigantic contributor to world LNG markets for some time. The same is largely true of Nigeria. Some countries with very generous oil endowments play little current role in world gas markets, such as Venezuela, with its heavy oil production in the Orinoco basin. Yet some of these countries, as well as others, may someday come to the fore in world gas markets. After all, just a few years ago, the United States was cast in the role of a major importer, not as an exporter and global force in world gas markets.

But the main story of natural gas for the near and medium terms is first and foremost a story of the large economies discussed in the two previous chapters as well as the smaller contending nations of this chapter. Many of them have the capacity to change their roles in the continuing drama of natural gas. Some may do so by deciding to actively develop their own resources. Others may dramatically change their consumption and demand patterns, but the story of hydrocarbon energy has continuously evolved since humans first started to use it in a serious way in the nineteenth century.

But perhaps the story of energy revolutions is poised to accelerate, not merely to continue. As the next chapter discusses, other potential energy revolutions are in prospect that may well dwarf the natural gas revolution that already is changing the world.

Notes

1. USEIA, "Natural Gas Exports from Iran," October 2012.

2. See UUSEIA, "Natural Gas Exports from Iran," October 2012; Naturalgasasia. com, "Turkey, Pakistan Want More Gas from Iran," July 5, 2012; and Natural-gasasia.com, "Iran Plans Hike in Gas Exports, Reduce Reliance on Oil," April 7, 2013.

3. Naturalgasasia.com, "Iran to Supply 40 mcm of Gas to Iraq," April 5, 2013.

4. Jen Alic, "How Far Will the US Go to Derail Iran–Pakistan Pipeline," Oilprice. com, March 4, 2013.

5. See "Pakistan and Iran Gas, But Not the Useful Sort," *Economist*, March 16, 2013; Naturalgasasia.com, "China Offers $500 Million Loan to Pakistan for IP Gas Pipeline," March 14, 2013; and, especially, Jen Alic, "How Far Will the US Go to Derail Iran-Pakistan Pipeline," Oilprice.com, March 4, 2013. For background on the Iran–Pakistan–India pipeline, see Ariel Cohen, Lisa Curtis, and Owen Graham, "The Proposed Iran–Pakistan–India Gas Pipeline: An Unacceptable Risk to Regional Security," Heritage Foundation, May 2008; Gal Luft and Anne Korin, "Realism and Idealism in the Energy Security Debate," in Gal Luft and Anne Korin (eds.), *Energy Security Challenges for the 21st Century*, Santa Barbara, CA: ABC Clio, 2009; and Marie Lall, "India's Gas Pipeline Efforts: An Analysis of the Problems That Have Prevented Success," National Bureau of Asian Research, NBR Special Report #23, September 2010, pp. 43–54.

6. For the history and an analysis of Qatari LNG, see Kohei Hashimoto, Jareer Elass, and Stacy Eller, "Liquefied Natural Gas from Qatar: The Qatargas Project," Stanford University and James A. Baker Institute, December 2004.

7. Kohei Hashimoto, Jareer Elass, and Stacy Eller, "Liquefied Natural Gas from Qatar: The Qatargas Project," Stanford University and James A. Baker Institute, December 2004; and Justin Dargin, "Qatar's Natural Gas, the Foreign-Policy Driver," *Middle East Policy*, Fall 2007, 24, pp. 136–142. Figures on Qatar gas in this paragraph are derived from BP, "Statistical Review of World Energy," June 2012.

8. Justin Dargin, "Qatar's Natural Gas, the Foreign-Policy Driver," *Middle East Policy*, Fall 2007, 24, pp. 136–142.

9. Ariel Cohen, Lisa Curtis, and Owen Graham, "The Proposed Iran–Pakistan–India Gas Pipeline: An Unacceptable Risk to Regional Security," Heritage Foundation, May 2008. See also Naturalgaseurope.com, "Poland to Renegotiate LNG Contract with Qatar," November 23, 2012; and Naturalgasasia.com, "The National: Qatar Unfazed by Shale Gas Growth," June 9, 2012.

10. Uzbekistan heavily subsidizes the domestic consumption of natural gas. When I was traveling in Uzbekistan, one local resident told me that gas was so cheap that one would not get off the sofa to bother to close a stovetop burner just to save gas. The same intense subsidies occur in other countries, such as Turkmenistan.

11. The time from groundbreaking to completion was 28 months, with the construction started in July 2008 and finished in December 2009. See CNPC, "Central Asia–China Gas Pipeline," December 14, 2009. The second of the dual lines was completed in late 2010.

12. On this point, see Robert W. Kolb, "The Natural Gas Revolution and Central Asia," *Journal of Social, Political, and Economic Studies*, Summer 2012, 37, pp. 141–180.

13. USEIA, "Country Analysis Briefs: Turkey," February 11, 2012.

14. Naturalgaseurope.com, "South Stream Gets the Go Ahead from Turkey," December 28, 2011; and Naturalgaseurope.com, "Turkey's Bold Move Shakes up the Southern Corridor," January 8, 2012.

15. Reuters.com, "Gazprom Warns Turkey over Azeri Gas Pipeline Deal," June 29, 2012.

16. Semih Idiz, "The 'Great Game' in Levant," *Al-Monitor*, April 5, 2013.

17. USEIA, "Country Analysis Briefs: Turkey," February 11, 2012. See also Jeff M. Smith, "The Great Game, Round Three," *Journal of International Security Affairs*, Fall 2009, 17.

18. USEIA, "World Shale Gas Resources: An Initial Assessment of 14 Regions Outside the United States," April 2011, p. 4.

19. Naturalgaseurope.com, "Is Turkey's Shale Taking Off?" September 10, 2012; and Naturalgaseurope.com, "Turkey: Turns Out We Have Shale Gas After All," March 19, 2012.

20. USEIA, "World Shale Gas Resources: An Initial Assessment of 14 Regions Outside the United States," April 2011, p. 4.

21. Jan Cienski, "Poland's Shale: Enter the State," *Financial Times*, July 4, 2012.

22. Marc Lanthemann, "STRATFOR: Impact of the Poland–Russia Natural Gas Price Revision," Naturalgaseurope.com, November 7, 2012.

23. For an overall assessment of Poland's energy picture, see Dimiter Kenarov, "Poland's Shale Gas Dream," Foreignpolicy.com, December 26, 2012.

24. Naturalgaseurope.com, "Voice of Russia: Shale Gas Crisis," December 6, 2012.

25. Roderick Kefferpütz, "To Shale or Not to Shale: That Is Not the (Only) Question," Europeanenergyreview.eu, February 9, 2012.

26. Naturalgaseurope.com, "Bureaucratic Delays Impact Poland's Shale Promise," February 1, 2013.

27. Naturalgaseurope.com, "Ukrainian Energy Dependence: Kicking the Habit," May 9, 2012. See also Mikhail Korchemkin, "Gazprom to Export Gas Only by Its Own Pipelines," *East European Gas Analysis*, April 7, 2013.

28. Roman Olearchyk and Neil Buckley, "Russia Hands Ukraine $7bn Gas Bill," *Financial Times*, January 25, 2013. On the geopolitical dimensions, see Naturalgaseurope.com, "Gas as an Instrument of Russian Pressure on Ukraine," February 1, 2013; Roman Kupchinsky, "Russian LNG: The Future Geopolitical Battleground," Jamestown Foundation, June 2009; and Elena Kropatcheva, "Playing Both Ends Against the Middle: Russia's Geopolitical Energy Games with the EU and Ukraine," *Geopolitics*, 2011, 16, pp. 553–573.

29. See Naturalgaseurope.com, "Ukraine Reveals Ambitious Plans to Cut Dependence on Russian Gas," June 21, 2012; Naturalgaseurope.com, "Annual Production of Shale Gas in Ukraine Could Reach 5 Billion Cubic Meters," October 7, 2012; and Naturalgaseurope.com, "Shale Gas in Ukraine: Turning Enthusiasm into Results," April 3, 2013.

30. Oleg Varfolomeyev, "Ukraine Reveals Ambitious Plans to Cut Dependence on Russian Gas," *Eurasia Daily Monitor*, June 19, 2012, 9(116).

31. Naturalgaseurope.com, "Ukraine Moves to Escape Russia's Grip," August 20, 2012.

32. Naturalgaseurope.com, "Ukrainian PM Invites Qatar to Participate in LNG," May 11, 2012.

33. USEIA, "World Shale Gas Resources: An Initial Assessment of 14 Regions Outside the United States," April 2011, p. 4.

34. Dow Jones Newswires, "Australian Shale Gas Looms After Santos Drill Success," August 16, 2012.

35. Paddy Manning, "Why Shale Gas Is Still the Next Big Thing," smh.com.au, May 19, 2012.

36. Naturalgasasia.com, "Australian Shale Gas Faces Significant Challenges," May 16, 2012.

37. Charles Ebinger, Kevin Massy, and Govinda Avasarala, "Liquid Markets: Assessing the Case for U.S. Exports of Liquefied Natural Gas," Brookings Institution, May 2012, p. 21.

38. International Energy Agency, "Gas: Medium-Term Market Report 2012," 2012, p. 61.

39. Alex Forbes, "The Exciting Future of LNG, and How It Will Transform the Global Gas Market," Europeanenergyreview.eu, February 2, 2012.

40. A number of sources question the investment wisdom of LNG in Australia. For example, see International Energy Agency, "Gas: Medium-Term Market Report 2012," 2012; and Naturalgasasia.com, "China's Unconventional Resources to Compete with Australian LNG," April 12, 2012. See also Paul Garvey, "China's LNG Demand Questioned," *Australian*, October 10, 2011.

41. Nizar Abdel-Kader, "Potential Gas Conflict in the Mediterranean," Realclearworld.com, March 16, 2012; and Michael J. Economides, "Eastern Mediterranean Energy: The Next Game," Energytribune.com, June 5, 2012.

42. Robin M. Mills, "The Land of Gas and Honey," *Foreign Policy*, September 15, 2011; Michael Economides, "Natural Gas: Changing the Geopolitics of Eastern Mediterranean and Beyond," Energytribune.com, January 4, 2011.

43. Michael J. Economides, "Eastern Mediterranean Energy: The Next Game," Energytribune.com, June 5, 2012.

44. Naturalgaseurope.com, "Eastern Mediterranean Offshore Gas: Growth or Conflict?" February 27, 2012.

45. Yuri M. Zhukov, "Trouble in the Eastern Mediterranean Sea," *Foreign Affairs*, March 20, 2013.

46. See Semih Idiz, "The 'Great Game' in Levant," *Al-Monitor*, April 5, 2013; and Robin M. Mills, "The Land of Gas and Honey," *Foreign Policy*, September 15, 2011.

47. For a discussion of these plans for LNG, see two articles by Michael J. Economides, "Eastern Mediterranean Energy: The Next Game," Energytribune.com, June 5, 2012; and "Natural Gas: Changing the Geopolitics of Eastern Mediterranean and Beyond," Energytribune.com, January 4, 2011.

48. International Energy Agency, "World Energy Outlook 2012," OECD/IEA, 2012, p. 140.

49. See Daniel Fisher, "The Best Thing About Shale Gas: We Know Where It Is," Forbes.com, March 22, 2013; International Energy Agency, "World Energy Outlook 2012," OECD/IEA, 2012; Isabel Ordonez, "Statoil, Exxon Say Tanzania Offshore Gas Find Is Big," *Wall Street Journal*, February 24, 2012; Guy Chazan, "Africa's East Coast in Natural-Gas Spotlight," *Wall Street Journal*, November 28, 2011; and Nathanial Gronewold, "With LNG Exports in Mind, Mozambique Opens Doors to Exploration," eenews.net, May 24, 2012.

50. Daniel Fisher, "The Best Thing About Shale Gas: We Know Where It Is," Forbes.com, March 22, 2013.

51. Eduard Gismatullin, "Africa Gas Rush Imperils $100 Billion in Australian LNG," Bloomberg.com, August 30, 2012.

52. Steve LeVine, "How Mozambique Could Shake Up Putin's World," Oilandglory. foreignpolicy.com, March 28, 2012.

53. C. Raja Mohan, "Tanzanian Pearl," *Indian Express*, March 27, 2013.

54. Naturalgasamericas.com, "Huge Shale Oil Deposit Discovery for YPF in Mendoza," March 30, 2012. See also Naturalgasamericas.com, "YPF Discovers More Shale Gas; Presents 2013–17 Strategy," August 30, 2012.

55. On Argentina's shale potential and its nationalization of YPF, see Clifford Krauss, "Argentina Hopes for a Big Payoff in Its Shale Oil Field Discovery," *New York Times*, July 4, 2011; Matthew Craze and Brian Swint, "Argentina Stifles Shale Oil Interest with Seizure Threat: Energy," Bloomberg.com, April 12, 2012; Michael J. Economides, "Argentina's Re-Nationalization of the Energy Industry and What It Means," Energytribune.com, September 18, 2012; and Naturalgasamericas.com, "Argentina's Shale Gas Revolution," April 27, 2012.

56. Jude Webber, "Repsol–YPF: Burying the Hatchet?" *Financial Times*, March 4, 2013.

8

The Next Energy Revolutions

Even as the wave of the natural gas revolution continues to roll over the world, there are new swells on the horizon. Already building far at sea and promising to be larger than the natural gas revolution is a coming shale oil revolution. And some have already detected sea floor tremors that may eventually create a true energy tsunami from a most unlikely source: "fire ice" or methane hydrates. This concluding chapter explores both of these phenomena.

The Shale Oil Revolution

In the first half of the twentieth century, the United States led the world in oil production and produced the "blood of victory" for both World Wars, as we saw in Chapter 1, "To the Brink of Innovation." But U.S. oil production peaked in 1970, at slightly more than 3.5 billion barrels per year, and it began a persistent slide that hit a bottom in 2008. During this interval, production fell by almost half, down to 1.8 billion barrels per year.

Since 2008, there has been a remarkable surge in the production of oil in the United States, which is due almost exclusively to an increase in production in just two states, Texas and North Dakota. Table 8.1 shows oil production for the United States and the marked increase between 2008 and 2012. For the United States as a whole, oil production increased from 1.8 to 2.4 billion barrels, for an increase of 5.4 million barrels or 29.3%. In Texas, for the same period, production ramped up by 77.8%, from 405.8 to 721.3 million barrels. North Dakota had an even more stellar performance. North Dakota produced 62.8 million barrels in 2008 but increased this to 242.3 million barrels in 2012, for a 286.0% increase. Taken together, Texas and North Dakota increased their combined production by almost half a billion barrels. This surge in Texas and North Dakota accounts for 92.2% of the total increase in U.S. production.

Table 8.1 Oil Production: The United States, Texas, and North Dakota, 2008 Versus 2012 (Thousands of Barrels)

	2008	2012	Change	Percentage Change
United States	1,830,136	2,366,985	536,849	29.33
Texas	405,791	721,360	315,569	77.77
North Dakota	62,780	242,286	179,506	285.93
Texas plus North Dakota	468,571	963,646	495,075	105.66

Source: U.S. Energy Information Administration (USEIA), "Petroleum & Other Liquids," www.eia.gov/dnav/pet/pet_crd_crpdn_adc_mbbl_a.htm.

This has been a stunning reversal that virtually no one predicted. Further, now almost everyone expects continuing increases in production for the years ahead. What is the source of this remarkable renaissance in U.S. oil production?

This book has focused on the leading wedge of the worldwide energy revolution stemming from hydraulic fracturing, horizontal drilling, and the buildout of the international liquid natural gas (LNG) distribution system, all focused on natural gas. As we have seen, this has led to a vast increase in the availability and affordability of natural gas in the United States. This suddenly available energy has changed the energy future of the United States from being one of import dependency to possessing a nascent export industry and a resurgence in gas-intensive manufacturing. As noted in Chapter 2, "They Call It a Revolution," many of the shale beds that have proved so rich and fruitful in natural gas also contain oil. Thus, the same advanced drilling techniques of hydraulic fracturing and horizontal drilling that have proved so effective in producing natural gas are also extremely valuable in producing oil.

Because Texas and North Dakota together account for 92% of the increase in U.S. oil production, each state requires closer examination. Each state tells a similar story, with the increase in production coming from particular locales that host shale oil production. In Texas, activity has been centered in the Eagle Ford Shale, while in North Dakota, the Bakken formation has proved to be the mother lode. This is not to minimize the contribution of other fields in both states, notably the Permian Basin in Texas, but the Eagle Ford and the Bakken are clearly the exemplary producers.

The Bakken Play

Back in 1981, the peak oil production in the United States was already more than a decade in the past, but the United States was still producing robustly, and total production was considerably higher than even today. That year, total U.S. oil production was 3.1 billion barrels, of which North Dakota contributed only 45.4 million barrels, or less than 1.5% of the total. As we have discussed, from 1970 to 2008, U.S. oil production fell, and then it rebounded. Table 8.2 compares 1981 to 2012, showing the production figures for North Dakota and the United States as a whole. While total U.S. production fell by 24% over those years, North Dakota production increased by more than 400%.

Table 8.2 Annual Oil Production (Thousands of Barrels)

	1981	2012	Percentage Change
United States	3,128,624	2,366,985	–24.3
North Dakota	45,424	242,486	433.8

Source: USEIA, "Petroleum & Other Liquids," www.eia.gov/dnav/pet/pet_crd_crpdn_adc_mbbl_a.htm.

The North Dakota Department of Mineral Resources identifies 29 distinct oil-producing and 30 gas-producing formations in the state. However, actual production of both oil and gas is highly concentrated. The Bakken formation accounts for 70% of the state's gas production and 83% of its oil production.[1] Plate 6 shows the location of this critical Bakken formation, which spills into Montana and Canada. This discussion focuses on the Bakken in North Dakota. No other North Dakota formation provides more than 7% of the oil produced or more than 13% of gas production. So the Bakken formation is the overwhelmingly dominant source of both oil and gas in the state.

Because of its great importance, it is worth examining the changing estimates of the Bakken's ultimate yield. In 1995, the U.S. Geological Survey (USGS) estimated that the Bakken had a total of 151 million barrels of technically recoverable oil. But in 2008, the USGS increased its estimate to the range of 3.0 to 4.3 billion barrels, a 25-fold increase.[2] In 2011, the U.S. Energy Information Administration (USEIA) essentially confirmed the 2008 USGS estimate, giving a point estimate of 3.59 billion barrels of technically recoverable oil. April 2013 brought a radical reassessment from the USEIA, which estimated that there would be 8.1 billion barrels of oil actually produced from the Bakken during the period 2012 to 2040.[3] These radical improvements emphasize how quickly the shale revolution has emerged. As the USEIA's "2013 Annual Energy Outlook" rightly notes, "Tight oil development is still at an early stage, and the outlook is highly uncertain."[4]

The sudden surge in the Bakken's productivity caught the industry with inadequate infrastructure to allow the produced gas and oil to get to market. Chapter 4, "Environmental Costs and Benefits," noted that up to 30% of gas produced in the Bakken field was being flared away in a rush to get to the more valuable tight oil and natural gas liquids. Part of the reason for this was the typical lease contract that required drillers to start producing or lose the leasehold they had already purchased. But even the oil being produced had its own problems reaching market due to lack of transport infrastructure. For example, in February 2012, drillers found themselves selling oil at a $28 per barrel discount due to constrained transportation capacity. However, this problem seems well on its way to a solution. The USEIA reports that North Dakota's pipeline and rail capacity will be up to 1.5 million barrels per day by the end of 2013. Also, a new refinery is being built in North Dakota, the first one in the United States in the past 40 years. Notice that this transport capacity of 1.5 million barrels per day implies an annual production greater than the 151 million barrels that was the estimate of the entire resource as recently as 1995.

The Eagle Ford in Texas

Texas has a rich history of oil production, traditionally accounting for about 30% of all U.S. production, as it continued to do in 2012. To achieve that role, Texas produces oil from fields located throughout the state. While the Eagle Ford may be the most spectacular, the Permian Basin has also enjoyed a remarkable resurgence due to new technologies. From 2008 to 2012, Texas oil production increased from 405.8 million to 721.4 million barrels, a surge of 315.6 million barrels. An extremely large portion of this increase came from the Eagle Ford Shale, shown in the map of Plate 4. The Eagle Ford contains oil, gas condensates, and dry natural gas in three geographical bands ranging from north to south.[5]

From this region, oil production went from almost nothing to 130 million barrels in just four years, as Figure 8.1 indicates. In 2008, the Eagle Ford Shale was first discovered by Petrohawk Energy Corporation, and that year it produced 128,480 barrels; in 2012, production totaled 132.4 million barrels, increasing by a factor of almost 1,100. The increased production in the Eagle Ford Shale accounted for 42% of the entire increase in Texas. The Eagle Ford Shale has a particularly dramatic production payoff, but it shares characteristics with many other shale plays, including a very rapid increase in production and very large yields.

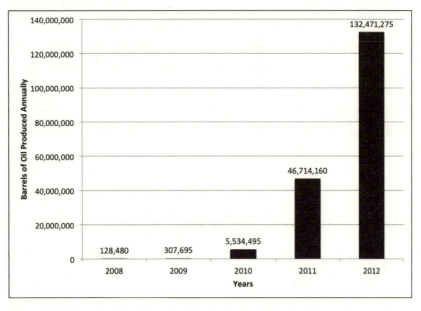

Figure 8.1 Annual shale oil production from the Eagle Ford Formation, 2008–2012.

Source: Railroad Commission of Texas, "Eagle Ford Statistics," www.rrc.state.tx.us/ eagleford/#stats.

Those skeptical of the natural gas revolution argue that yields from individual wells tend to fall quite quickly, with 30% of a well's production occurring in the first year and 75% of the total production being exhausted within 10 years, with production falling steadily over the life of the well.[6] Because the shale revolution is so new, there is little certainty about the true production curve for shale oil and gas wells. But without question, shale plays tend to have a large number of wells. In the Eagle Ford, the number of drilling permits issued increased from just 26 in 2008, the year of discovery, to more than 4,000 in 2012. In the first part of 2013, the rate of permitting implied a total of more than 9,000 for the entire year.

Estimates of technically recoverable resources and total production for the Eagle Ford Shale have tended to soar as we have learned more. This seems to be very typical of shale plays. For example, as recently as July 2011, the USEIA estimated that the Eagle Ford held a total of 3.4 billion barrels of technically recoverable oil.[7] In April 2013, the USEIA increased its estimate remarkably. For the period 2012 to 2040, the USEIA now estimates that the Eagle Ford will produce more than 6 billion barrels of oil. This 2013 estimate of actually produced oil is 76% larger than the 2011 estimate of the total resource in the entire play.[8] While these revisions of estimates have largely exhibited a history of increases, the radical changes emphasize how uncertain the ultimate yield from the shale revolution really will be.

The Monterey Shale

Nowhere is the future of U.S. oil more uncertain than in the Monterey play of California. As Plate 23 shows, this massive formation runs north to south through the central portion of the state and covers almost 2,000 square miles. The Monterey Shale has the Santos Shale as its very large, but less illustrious, companion. The Monterey formation is estimated to contain more than 15 billion barrels of oil, or more than two-thirds of all the known shale oil in the United States.[9] In spite of the overwhelming richness of this resource, it has contributed little to nothing at all to the U.S. supply of oil. Whereas Texas and North Dakota, for example, have had a remarkable increase in production, California's output has continued to dwindle. Over the past decade, oil production in California has fallen by one-fourth. In the span 2008 to 2012—the same years we have been examining for the Eagle Ford and Bakken plays—California's oil production fell by 9%.

Basically, the Monterey Shale is untouched, save for a few exploratory wells. The state that produced one-fourth of the world's oil in the 1920s now has only 50 drilling rigs operating in the entire state.[10] There are several potential explanations for the drilling reticence in California, and the importance of each is open to controversy. First, the geology of the Monterey Shale may actually be more difficult than that of some other shale plays. This means that understanding the actual deposits may be more difficult, and it may be harder for oil production companies to know where to locate their drilling rigs. Second, and related to the first point, the geology of California is certainly seismically sensitive. As we saw in Chapter 4, oil drilling and disposal of produced water can cause at least some small earthquakes. Third, nowhere in the United States are environmental pressure groups more powerful than in California, and they virulently oppose all hydrocarbon production, especially in their own backyards.[11]

While the ultimate productivity of all shale plays in the United States is difficult to estimate, the Monterey Shale presents the greatest uncertainty of all. However, if the resource is developed, it will contribute considerably to the depressed economy of Central California and the Inland Empire.[12] A study by the School of Public Policy at the University of Southern California asserts that the state could reap $4.5 billion in tax revenues from oil in 2015, increasing to $24.6 billion by 2020, if fracking were to accelerate, along with creating 500,000 to almost 3 million new jobs.[13] As we have seen with the shale revolution in general, and with the Eagle Ford and Bakken plays in particular, resource estimates have tended to increase with greater knowledge. The vast resources of the Monterey may prove to be even greater than now estimated, but that can be known only if we someday begin to develop those resources.

The Tight Oil Effect

In its "Annual Energy Outlook 2013," the USEIA focuses on its "reference case," which in its view is the most likely scenario for the future of energy. Figure 8.2 shows the future of tight oil production to be overwhelmingly dominated by the Eagle Ford and Bakken plays, with the Permian Basin making a smaller but significant contribution. The Monterey Shale is lumped in with the "other" category to make a contribution much smaller than either the Eagle Ford or Bakken. In this reference case, tight oil constitutes all the increase in production for the entire United States, per Figure 8.3. Without tight oil, the USEIA predicts stable to slightly declining production over the next 30 years.

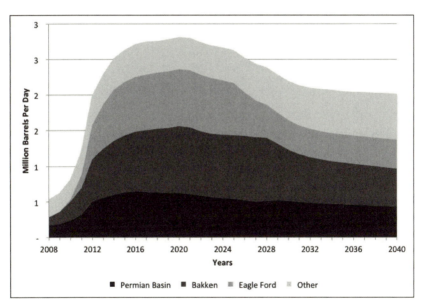

Figure 8.2 Tight oil production by geological formation—historical and forecast.

Source: USEIA, "Annual Energy Overview 2013," Spring 2013.

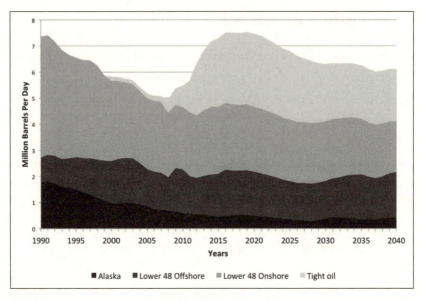

Figure 8.3 Oil production in the United States by source—historical and forecast.

Source: USEIA, "Annual Energy Overview 2013," Spring 2013.

In addition to its reference case, the USEIA also considers optimistic and pessimistic scenarios as well, by which the agency refers to high and low economic growth. Figure 8.4 shows the reference and optimistic scenarios for tight oil production. (The low economic growth, or pessimistic, case is almost indistinguishable from the reference case, so it is omitted from the figure.) The reference case shows tight oil production cresting in 2020 at about 2.8 million barrels per day and declining by 2040 to about 2 million barrels per day. The optimistic case shows tight oil production at 4.7 million barrels per day and still rising in 2020. In this case, the rate of production tops out and remains stable at slightly more than 5 million barrels per day through 2040. These estimates present radical uncertainty for the future of tight oil, with the optimistic scenario being about 150% greater than the reference scenario. But in every case, the production of tight oil makes an enormous contribution to the energy supply of the United States, and if the Monterey Shale comes into development, that contribution could be immense.

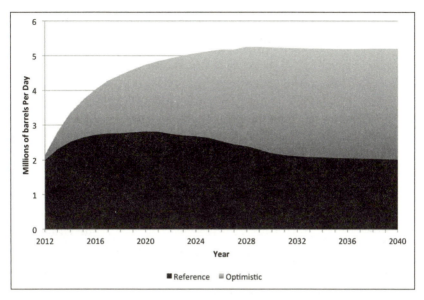

Figure 8.4 Forecast tight oil production in the United States, 2012–2040—reference and high economic growth scenarios.

Source: USEIA, "Annual Energy Overview 2013," Spring 2013.

A Methane Hydrate Energy Revolution?

While the tight oil revolution is already under way, a potentially even larger resource remains untapped but with prospects for the future that have brightened in the very recent past. This resource is "fire ice" or methane hydrate, which is discussed very briefly in Chapter 2. According to best estimates, the energy stored in the form of methane hydrates is larger than all other hydrocarbon resources in the world—coal, oil, and gas—combined. Yet not 1 British thermal unit (Btu) of usable methane hydrate has ever been produced or consumed.

Methane hydrate is natural gas encased in ice, and it lies in oceans and beneath permafrost. The methane is not chemically bound to the water that forms the ice, but rather the methane molecule is trapped in a lattice of ice crystals. Plate 24 depicts the locations in which methane hydrates reside, in arctic and marine sands and in mounds on the ocean floor. Because it depends on the encasing lattice of ice, if the ice lattice melts, the methane is released into the surrounding water or air. As a result, methane hydrate is an unstable form. Plate 25 shows the conditions under which methane hydrates can exist in water, depending on the pressure and temperature of the surrounding water. If the water temperature is below freezing, the persistence of the methane hydrate form requires a depth of 200 meters or more. Even if the water is very cold, the methane will be released, or dissociated, from the ice lattice in shallower depths. If the temperature is above 17 degrees Celsius, the methane will escape the lattice into the surrounding water, no matter how great the depth. The methane concentration is very high. One cubic meter of methane hydrate contains enough methane to constitute 160 cubic meters of gas at room temperature.[14]

As Plate 24 shows, methane hydrate can simply be heaped in mounds on the ocean floor under the right temperature and depth conditions. If the methane hydrate is suddenly brought to the surface and inspected, it looks much like regular ice. Because of the methane concentrated in the lattice, this substance can even be held in the hand and ignited with a match, hence the term "fire ice." Methane hydrate exists on land in the arctic regions of North America, Europe, and Asia. It also exists along the coasts and continental shelves of virtually the entire littoral of all the continents, although the deposits around Antarctica appear to be much smaller. There are even pockets in the Mediterranean, the Black Sea, and the Gulf of Mexico, along the coast of the United States and Mexico.[15] Approximately 99% of the resource is in the ocean, with the remaining 1% on land.[16]

As already mentioned, no methane hydrate has ever been brought into production, and it is even difficult to retrieve samples because it is so unstable. As a result, the estimates of the resource size are wildly divergent, but they all judge a tremendous quantity of methane. One estimate places the amount of methane in methane hydrate worldwide at 20,000 trillion cubic meters.[17] In 2008, the USGS estimated the total methane hydrate resource in place in the North Slope of Alaska as being 2,400 bcm.[18] The estimate for the northern Gulf of Mexico is 607 trillion cubic meters.[19] A conservative estimate judges that the methane hydrate in place is about 1,000 times the worldwide annual consumption of methane.[20]

One worry about this unstable form of methane focuses on global warming. If the earth's temperature rises too much, some methane hydrates that are currently stable will warm and release methane into the atmosphere. As discussed in Chapter 4, methane is a potent greenhouse gas, so if initial warming releases methane from the hydrate form, a feedback loop might develop in which initially dissociated methane contributes to additional warming and, with repetition, creates a climate disaster. However, this is judged to be unlikely, assuming no destructive human intervention—that is, without humans acting to cause this release.[21]

Research into accessing methane from methane hydrates is increasing both in the United States and abroad. In 2012, the United States and Japan completed a field trial in which they obtained a steady flow from a deposit of methane hydrates in the arctic, but this is very far from implying any economic viability.[22] Given the high costs of importing LNG, several Asian nations are aggressively pursuing methane hydrate as an energy source, with both Japan and Taiwan announcing recent discoveries off their shores.[23] In 2013, Japan succeeded in extracting gas from methane deposits about 30 miles offshore, in waters about 3,000 feet deep. This was a test or proof that such recovery is possible, but again, it is very far from implying economic viability.[24] However, the pace of research is intensifying and producing encouraging results. After all, only a few years ago, the shale revolution was merely a dream. If production of methane hydrates commences, the implications for the energy market and for the environment are dramatic.

A Concluding Note

The overall effect of the production of natural gas from methane hydrates on human well-being is ambiguous. We have seen that the shale revolution has come with its own uncertainty. The great increase in natural gas production has yielded great benefits to many and is causing geopolitical displacements as well. To date, the benefits have largely accrued to the United States, with reduced energy prices that have stimulated the return of manufacturing jobs from abroad. Also, the United States has increasingly turned from coal to natural gas for electric power generation, a move that has been largely responsible for falling greenhouse gas emissions. In addition, the move toward greater energy self-sufficiency can only help the standing of the United States in the world, especially at a time of economic difficulties and falling self-confidence.

The benefits of the natural gas revolution are already starting to spread to other nations, with the development of a world market for natural gas and the promise of allowing some nations to escape oil-linked contracts for their imported natural gas. Having proved the technology in the United States, it now seems clear that many other nations, perhaps most notably China, will be moving aggressively to enjoy their own shale revolution. Any change in resources as large as the shale revolution must surely create some losers as well, and Chapter 6, "The World's Other Large Economies," argues that Russia and the oil-exporting nations of the Middle East and Persian Gulf stand to lose a considerable portion of their energy export revenues. Those countries may even have to abandon their policies of buying off their populations with energy subsidies and may be forced to abandon their model of governance as resource-cursed nations.

Already the shale oil revolution seems on pace to replicate the processes this book has detailed for natural gas. If anything, the potential for shale oil may even eclipse the dramatic changes brought about by shale gas. If methane hydrates come to the fore as an energy source, the effects could be larger yet. But we must remember that all such world-altering movements are ambiguous and likely to create both winners and losers. And any dramatic changes in energy sourcing are sure to have environmental consequences as well. Perhaps *Scientific American* encapsulated the circumstances best when it wrote about methane hydrates, an outlook that pertains to the shale gas and shale oil revolutions as well: "But in principle, clean-burning natural gas from hydrates could also help displace coal consumption in places like China and India, just as cheap shale gas is now driving coal out of U.S. electricity markets. That scenario could potentially yield climate benefits and cleaner air—assuming the displaced coal stays in the ground and hydrates aren't used to simply prolong reliance on fossil fuels."[25]

Notes

1. See North Dakota Department of Mineral Resources, "2011 North Dakota Gas Production by Formation," www.dmr.nd.gov/oilgas/stats/2011gasprod.pdf and "2011 North Dakota Oil Production by Formation," www.dmr.nd.gov/oilgas/stats/2011Formation.pdf.

2. USGS, "3 to 4.3 Billion Barrels of Technically Recoverable Oil Assessed in North Dakota and Montana's Bakken Formation—25 Times More Than 1995 Estimate," Press Release, April 10, 2008.

3. USEIA, "Annual Energy Overview 2013," Spring 2013. See the discussion of Figure 97. There the estimate is for total tight oil production of 25.3 billion barrels between 2012 and 2040, with 32% coming from the Bakken/Three Forks formation, implying 0.32×25.3 billion = 8.096 billion barrels of oil produced.

4. USEIA, "Annual Energy Outlook 2013: With Projections to 2040," April 2013, p. 2.

5. USEIA, "Review of Emerging Resources: U.S. Shale Gas and Shale Oil Plays," July 2011, p. 29.

6. USEIA, "Review of Emerging Resources: U.S. Shale Gas and Shale Oil Plays," July 2011. See p. 32 for a graph of the supposed typical production experience of an Eagle Ford well with a characteristic falling production rate.

7. USEIA, "Review of Emerging Resources: U.S. Shale Gas and Shale Oil Plays," July 2011, p. 4.

8. USEIA, "Annual Energy Overview 2013," Spring 2013. See the discussion of Figure 97. There the estimate is for total tight oil production of 25.3 billion barrels between 2012 and 2040, with 24% coming from the Eagle Ford, implying 0.24×25.3 billion = 6.07 billion barrels of oil produced.

9. University of Southern California Price School of Public Policy, "The Monterey Shale and California's Economic Future," 2013, p. ii. See also Norimitsu Onishi, "Vast Oil Reserve May Now Be Within Reach, and Battle Heats Up," *New York Times*, February 3, 2013.

10. "The Energy Revolution: California Must Not Be Left Behind," *San Diego Union-Tribune*, March 2, 2013.

11. For a discussion of these issues, see Jonathan Fahey, "New Drilling Method Opens Vast Oil Fields in US," Associated Press, February 9, 2011; Norimitsu Onishi, "Vast Oil Reserve May Now Be Within Reach, and Battle Heats Up," *New York Times*, February 3, 2013; Steven Greenhut, "Californians Want Oil's Tax Revenue Without the Oil," Bloomberg.com, March 10, 2013; Elizabeth MacDonald, "The Golden State's Fracking Pot of Gold," Foxbusiness.com, April 2, 2013; and University of Southern California Price School of Public Policy, "The Monterey Shale and California's Economic Future," 2013.

12. Victor Davis Hanson writes regularly and persuasively on the self-defeating nature of politics and culture in California and the devastating results for all of the state except for the coastal strip. As an example, see Victor Davis Hanson, "It's Hard to Screw Up California—But We Try Our Best," National Review Online, www.nationalreview.com, November 28, 2013.

13. University of Southern California Price School of Public Policy, "The Monterey Shale and California's Economic Future," 2013. See also Elizabeth MacDonald, "The Golden State's Fracking Pot of Gold," Foxbusiness.com, April 2, 2013.

14. Geology.com, "Methane Hydrates," available at http://geology.com/articles/methane-hydrates/.

15. Ioannis Th. Mazis and George Sgouros, "Geographical Distribution of Methane Hydrates and International Geopolitics of Energy: Resources in the Eastern Mediterranean," *Civitas Gentium*, 2011, 1, pp. 33–40.

16. Carolyn Ruppel and Diane Noserale, "Gas Hydrates and Climate Warming—Why a Methane Catastrophe Is Unlikely," USGS, *Sound Waves*, May/June 2012.

17. National Energy Technology Laboratory, "Energy Resource Potential of Methane Hydrate," U.S. Department of Energy, February 2011, p. 5; and Timothy S. Collett, Arthur H. Johnson, Camelia C. Knapp, and Ray Boswell, "Natural Gas Hydrates: A Review," *AAPG Memoir*, 2009, 89, pp. 146–219. See pp. 149–150.

18. USGS Fact Sheet, "Gas Hydrate Resource Assessment: North Slope, Alaska," October 2008.

19. National Energy Technology Laboratory, "Energy Resource Potential of Methane Hydrate," U.S. Department of Energy, February 2011, p. 5.

20. Carolyn Ruppel and Diane Noserale, "Gas Hydrates and Climate Warming—Why a Methane Catastrophe Is Unlikely," USGS, *Sound Waves*, May/June 2012.

21. For a discussion of this issue, see Realclearenergy.com, "Arctic Methane Could Ice the Game for Global Warming," May 7, 2012; Marianne Lavelle, "Good Gas, Bad Gas," *National Geographic Magazine*, December 2012; Melissa C. Lott, "Methane Hydrates: Bigger Than Shale Gas, 'Game Over' for the Environment?" *Scientific American*, March 19, 2013; and Carolyn Ruppel and Diane Noserale, "Gas Hydrates and Climate Warming—Why a Methane Catastrophe Is Unlikely," USGS, *Sound Waves*, May/June 2012.

22. U.S. Department of Energy, "New Methane Hydrate Research: Investing in Our Energy Future," August 31, 2012, available at http://energy.gov/articles/new-methane-hydrate-research, accessed November 10, 2012; and U.S. Department of Energy, "U.S. and Japan Complete Successful Field Trial of Methane Hydrate Production Technologies," May 2, 2012.

23. Bloomberg.com, "Asians Hunt Gas Treasure Locked in Ice Beneath Seabeds: Energy," March 13, 2013. See also Naturalgasasia.com, "Taiwan Discovers Gas Hydrates in South China Sea," March 13, 2013.

24. Hiroko Tabuchi, "An Energy Coup for Japan: 'Flammable Ice,'" *New York Times*, March 12, 2013; Naturalgasasia.com, "Japan May Start Extraction of Methane Hydrates," March 10, 2013; and Naturalgaseurope.com, "Methane Hydrates and the Potential Natural Gas Boom," February 12, 2013.

25. Melissa C. Lott, "Methane Hydrates: Bigger Than Shale Gas, 'Game Over' for the Environment?" *Scientific American*, March 19, 2013.

References

Abdel-Kader, Nizar, "Potential Gas Conflict in the Mediterranean," Realclearworld.com, March 16, 2012.

Aizhu, Chen, "China's Ragtag Shale Army a Long Way from Revolution," Reuters.com, March 11, 2013.

Alic, Jen, "How Far Will the US Go to Derail Iran–Pakistan Pipeline?" Oilprice.com, March 4, 2013.

Bahgat, Gawdat, "The Geopolitics of Energy in Central Asia and the Caucasus," *Journal of Social, Political, and Economic Studies*, Summer 2009, 34, pp. 139–153.

Barcella, Mary Lashley, Samantha Gross, and Surya Rajan, "Mismeasuring Methane: Estimating Greenhouse Gas Emissions from Upstream Natural Gas Development," IHS CERA, August 2011.

Barone, Michael, "North Dakota Boom Shows Importance of Free Markets," Investors.com, July 20, 2012.

Begos, Kevin, "Marcellus Shale Study Claims Gas Drilling Did Not Contaminate Drinking Water Wells," Huffingtonpost.com, July 10, 2012.

Bellman, David K., "Power Plant Efficiency Outlook," working document of the NPC Global Oil & Gas Study, Topic Paper #4, May 8, 2007.

Blas, Javier, "Japan Pushes Asia Gas Price Close to High," *Financial Times*, May 17, 2012.

Bloomberg.com, "Asians Hunt Gas Treasure Locked in Ice Beneath Seabeds: Energy," March 13, 2013.

Boris, Joseph, "Resourceful Thinking," *China Daily*, February 8, 2013.

BP, "Statistical Review of World Energy," June 2012.

Brendon, Piers, "China Also Rises," *National Interest*, November/ December 2010, pp. 6–13.

Brennan, Elliot, "The 'Fracking' Revolution Comes to China," *Diplomat*, March 21, 2013.

Broder, John M., "U.S. Caps Emissions in Drilling for Fuel," *New York Times*, April 18, 2012.

Brown, Robbie, "Gas Drillers Asked to Change Method of Waste Disposal," *New York Times*, April 19, 2011.

Bryce, Robert, "Ban Natural Gas! No, Ban Coal!" National Review Online, www.nationalreview.com, June 11, 2012.

Bustelo, Pablo, "China and Oil in the Asian Pacific Region: Rising Demand for Oil," *New England Journal of Public Policy*, 2007, 21, pp. 171–201.

Callus, Andrew, "Schlumberger's Clever Frack Takes Aim at Gas Costs," Reuters.com, August 31, 2012.

Cantarow, Ellen, "How Rural America Got Fracked," Europeanenergyreview.eu, June 4, 2012.

Cathles, L. M., "Assessing the Greenhouse Impact of Natural Gas," working paper, June 6, 2012.

Cathles III, Lawrence M., Larry Brown, Milton Taam, and Andrew Hunter, "A Commentary on 'The Greenhouse-Gas Footprint of Natural Gas in Shale Formations,' by R. W. Howarth, R. Santoro, and Anthony Ingraffea," *Climatic Change*, 2012, 113, pp. 525–535.

Cathles, Lawrence M., Larry Brown, Andrew Hunter, and Milton Taam, "Press Release: Response to Howarth et al.'s Reply," February 29, 2012.

Chameides, Bill, "Natural Gas: A Bridge to a Low-Carbon Future or Not?" Huffingtonpost.com, July 20, 2012.

Chazan, Guy, "Africa's East Coast in Natural-Gas Spotlight," *Wall Street Journal*, November 28, 2011.

Chazan, Guy, and Gerrit Wiesmann, "Shale Gas Boom Sparks EU Coal Revival," *Financial Times*, February 3, 2013.

Cienski, Jan, "Poland's Shale: Enter the State," *Financial Times*, July 4, 2012.

Citigroup, "Resurging North American Oil Production and the Death of the Peak Oil Hypothesis: The United States' Long March Toward Energy Independence," February 15, 2012.

[CNPC] China National Petroleum Corporation, "Central Asia–China Gas Pipeline," www.cnpc.com.cn/cn/en/, December 14, 2009.

Cobb, Kurt, "How the Fracking Mess Is About to Make the Mortgage Mess Worse," *Energy Bulletin*, May 20, 2012.

Cohen, Ariel, Lisa Curtis, and Owen Graham, "The Proposed Iran–Pakistan–India Gas Pipeline: An Unacceptable Risk to Regional Security," Heritage Foundation, May 2008.

Collett, Timothy S., Arthur H. Johnson, Camelia C. Knapp, and Ray Boswell, "Natural Gas Hydrates: A Review," *AAPG Memoir*, 2009, 89, pp. 146–219.

Craze, Matthew, and Brian Swint, "Argentina Stifles Shale Oil Interest with Seizure Threat: Energy," Bloomberg.com, April 12, 2012.

Crisher, Brian, and Mark Souva, "Power at Sea: A Naval Power Dataset, 1865–2011," Florida State University working paper, 2012.

Daiss, Tim, "China's Nascent Shale Gas Industry Gains Momentum," *Energy Tribune*, July 10, 2012.

Dargin, Justin, "Qatar's Natural Gas, the Foreign-Policy Driver," *Middle East Policy*, Fall 2007, 24, pp. 136–142.

de Boerl, J. Z., J. R. Hale, and J. Chanton, "New Evidence for the Geological Origins of the Ancient Delphic Oracle (Greece)," *Geology*, August 2001, pp. 707–710.

DeSilva-Ranasinghe, Sergei, "Why the Indian Ocean Matters," *Diplomat*, March 2, 2011.

Dow Jones Newswires, "Australian Shale Gas Looms After Santos Drill Success," August 16, 2012.

Ebel, Robert E., "Energy and Geopolitics in China: Mixing Oil and Politics," Center for Strategic & International Studies, November 2009.

Ebinger, Charles, Kevin Massy, and Govinda Avasarala, "Liquid Markets: Assessing the Case for U.S. Exports of Liquefied Natural Gas," Brookings Institution, May 2012.

Economides, Michael J., "Argentina's Re-Nationalization of the Energy Industry and What It Means," Energytribune.com, September 18, 2012.

Economides, Michael J., "Eastern Mediterranean Energy: The Next Game," Energytribune.com, June 5, 2012.

Economides, Michael, "Natural Gas: Changing the Geopolitics of Eastern Mediterranean and Beyond," Energytribune.com, January 4, 2011.

Economist, "Booming North Dakota by the Numbers," March 16, 2013.

Economist, "Pakistan and Iran Gas, but Not the Useful Sort," March 16, 2013.

Edelman, Eric S., "Understanding America's Contested Primacy," Center for Strategic and Budgetary Assessments, 2010.

Eenews.net, "Ballot Measure to Ban Fracking Floated in Colorado Town," June 1, 2012.

Ellis, John, *World War II: A Statistical Survey*, New York: Facts on File, 1993.

Encyclopedia of the New American Nation, "Oil: Oil and World Power."

Entine, Jon, "Fracking Safety Improves Dramatically, Says Independent Study," Forbes.com, May 15, 2012.

Environmental Protection Agency, "Class II Wells: Oil and Gas Related Injection Wells (Class II)," available at http://water.epa.gov/type/groundwater/uic/class2/.

Erickson, Andrew S., Abraham M. Denmark, and Gabriel Collins, "Beijing's 'Starter Carrier' and Future Steps," *Naval War College Review*, Winter 2012, 65, pp. 15–55.

Esch, Mary, "For NY Farmers, Fracking Means Salvation—Or Ruin," Associated Press, May 22, 2012.

Etiope, G., G. G. Papatheodorou, D. Christodoulou, M. Geraga, and P. Favali, "The Geological Links of the Ancient Delphic Oracle (Greece): A Reappraisal of Natural Gas Occurrence and Origin," *Geology*, October 2006, 34, pp. 821–824.

Fahey, Jonathan, "New Drilling Method Opens Vast Oil Fields in US," Associated Press, February 9, 2011.

Fairley, Peter, "Fracking Quakes Shake the Shale Gas Industry," *Technology Review*, January 20, 2012.

Federal Energy Regulatory Commission, "North American LNG Import/Export Terminals: Approved," December 5, 2012.

Federal Energy Regulatory Commission, "North American LNG Import/Export Terminals: Existing," December 5, 2012.

Federal Energy Regulatory Commission, "North American LNG Import/Export Terminals: Proposed/Potential," December 5, 2012.

Fishelson, James, "From the Silk Road to Chevron: The Geopolitics of Oil Pipelines in Central Asia," School of Russian and Asian Studies, December 12, 2007.

Fisher, Daniel, "The Best Thing About Shale Gas: We Know Where It Is," Forbes.com, March 22, 2013.

Forbes, Alex, "The Exciting Future of LNG, and How It Will Transform the Global Gas Market," Europeanenergyreview.eu, February 2, 2012.

Foster, John, "Afghanistan, the TAPI Pipeline, and Energy Geopolitics," *Journal of Energy Security*, March 23, 2010.

Fountain, Henry, "Add Quakes to Rumblings Over Gas Rush," *New York Times*, December 12, 2011.

Francis, David, "How the U.S. Blew Up the Global Energy Market," *Fiscal Times*, April 5, 2013.

Friedberg, Aaron L, "China's Challenge at Sea," *New York Times*, September 4, 2011.

Friedberg, Aaron L., *A Contest for Supremacy: China, America, and the Struggle for Mastery in Asia*, New York: W.W. Norton & Company, 2011.

Friedberg, Aaron L., and Robert S. Ross, "Here Be Dragons: Is China a Military Threat?" *National Interest*, September/October 2009, pp. 19–34.

Galbraith, Kate, "As Fracking Increases, So Do Fears About Water Supply," *New York Times*, March 7, 2013.

Galbraith, Kate, "Unlocking the Secrets Behind Hydraulic Fracturing," *New York Times*, January 14, 2012.

Garvey, Paul, "China's LNG Demand Questioned," *Australian*, October 10, 2011.

Gautam, P. K., "Mapping Chinese Oil and Gas Pipelines and Sea Routes," *Strategic Analysis*, July 2011, 35, pp. 595–612.

Geology.com, "Methane Hydrates," available at http://geology.com/articles/methane-hydrates/.

Geropoulos, Kostis, "Gazelle, Nord Stream Deal Final Blow to Ukraine," Neurope.eu, January 21, 2013.

Gertz, Bill, "China's High-Tech Military Threat," *Commentary*, April 2012.

Gilbert, Daniel, and Kris Maher, "Shale Gas Fuels Legal Boom," *Wall Street Journal*, October 31, 2011.

Gilbert, Daniel, and Russell Gold, "EPA Backpedals on Fracking Contamination," *Wall Street Journal*, March 30, 2012.

Gismatullin, Eduard, "Africa Gas Rush Imperils $100 Billion in Australian LNG," Bloomberg.com, August 30, 2012.

Gjelten, Tom, "The Dash for Gas: The Golden Age of an Energy Game-Changer," *World Affairs Journal*, January 21, 2012.

Glover, Peter C., "Irony of Ironies: Europe Switches to Coal as US Gas Glut Reduces Emissions," *Energy Tribune*, July 12, 2012.

Glover, Peter C., "UK Shale Gas Green-Lighted with Tax Breaks," Energytribune.com, March 28, 2013.

Gold, Russell, "The Man Who Pioneered the Shale-Gas Revolution," *Wall Street Journal*, October 23, 2012.

Gold, Russell, and Ana Campoy, "Oil's Growing Thirst for Water," *Wall Street Journal*, December 6, 2011.

Goodell, Jeff, "The Big Fracking Bubble: The Scam Behind Aubrey McClendon's Gas Boom," *Rolling Stone*, May 5, 2012.

Gordon, John Steele, "Crucifying the Oil and Gas Industry," *Commentary*, April 27, 2012.

Gray, Louise, "Shale Gas 'Could Heat All Homes for 100 Years,'" Telegraph.co.uk, April 5, 2013.

Green, Kenneth P., "EPA Exonerates Fracking in Pennsylvania," Aei-ideas.org, July 25, 2012.

Greenhut, Steven, "Californians Want Oil's Tax Revenue Without the Oil," Bloomberg.com, March 10, 2013.

Griswold, Eliza, "Situation Normal All Fracked Up," *New York Times*, November 17, 2011.

Gronewold, Nathanial, "With LNG Exports in Mind, Mozambique Opens Doors to Exploration," Eenews.net, May 24, 2012.

Hamilton, James D., "Historical Oil Shocks," forthcoming in the *Handbook of Major Events in Economic History*. Working paper, February 2011.

Hanson, Victor Davis, "It's Hard to Screw Up California—But We Try Our Best," National Review Online, www.nationalreview.com, November 28, 2013.

Harris, Gardiner, "In Tiny Bean, India's Dirt-Poor Farmers Strike Gas-Drilling Gold," *New York Times*, July 16, 2012.

Harvey, Fiona, "Coal Resurgence Threatens Climate Change Targets," *Guardian*, October 29, 2012.

Hashimoto, Kohei, Jareer Elass, and Stacy Eller, "Liquefied Natural Gas from Qatar: The Qatargas Project," Stanford University and James A. Baker Institute, December 2004.

Healy, Jack, "For Farms in the West, Oil Wells Are Thirsty Rivals," *New York Times*, September 5, 2012.

Healy, Jack, "With Ban on Drilling Practice, Town Lands in Thick of Dispute," *New York Times*, November 25, 2012.

Herberg, Mikkal E., "Pipeline Politics in Asia: Energy Nationalism and Energy Markets," National Bureau of Asian Research, NBR Special Report #23, September 2010, pp. 1–6.

Holditch, Stephen A., "Tight Gas Sands," *Journal of Petroleum Technology*, June 2006, pp. 84–90.

Holmes, James, and Tashi Yoshihara, "Is China Planning String of Pearls?" *Diplomat*, February 21, 2011.

Hopkirk, Peter, *Foreign Devils on the Silk Road: The Search for the Lost Treasures of Central Asia*, London: John Murray Publishers, 2006.

Howarth, Robert W., Renee Santoro, and Anthony Ingraffea, "Methane and the Greenhouse-Gas Footprint of Natural Gas from Shale Formations," *Climatic Change*, 2011, 106, pp. 679–690.

Hulbert, Matthew, "Arctic Oil: Putin's Last Chance," Europeanenergyreview.eu, July 19, 2012.

Hulbert, Matthew, "Gazprom Tightens Control over European Supply," *Forbes*, November 26, 2012.

Hulbert, Matthew, "Why European Shale Is Totally 'Fracked,'" *Forbes*, July 12, 2012.

Hurdle, Jon, "New York Town Is Sued Over Ban on Fracking Discussion," *New York Times*, February 12, 2013.

Hurdle, Jon, "Utica Shale May Be Its Own Energy Game-Changer," Energy.aol.com, October 7, 2011.

Idiz, Semih, "The 'Great Game' in Levant," *Al-Monitor*, April 5, 2013.

Institute for Energy Research, "Bakken Formation Fact Sheet," 2012.

Institute for Energy Research, "U.S. Energy-Related Carbon Dioxide Emissions Are Declining," July 20, 2012.

IntelliBrief, "China: 'String of Pearls' Strategy," April 1, 2007.

International Energy Agency, "Are We Entering a Golden Age of Gas?" *World Energy Outlook*, 2011.

International Energy Agency, "Gas: Medium-Term Market Report 2012," 2012.

International Energy Agency, "Natural Gas Information, 2011," 2012.

International Energy Agency, "World Energy Outlook 2012," OECD/IEA, 2012.

International Gas Union, "World LNG Report 2011," June 2012.

Iwata, Mari, and Peter Landes, "Crisis in Japan Transforms Global Natural-Gas Market," *Wall Street Journal*, February 13, 2012.

Jaffe, Amy Myers, "Shale Gas Will Rock the World," *Wall Street Journal*, May 10, 2010.

Jaffe, Amy Myers, "The Americas, Not the Middle East, Will Be the World Capital of Energy," *Foreign Policy*, September/October 2011.

Jianjun Tu, Kevin, "China's Problem with Shale," *Wall Street Journal*, October 24, 2012.

Johnson, Kirk, "Drilling in Fast-Growing Areas Ushers in New Era of Tension," *New York Times*, October 24, 2011.

Jolly, David, "U.K. Company Suspends Controversial Drilling Procedure," *New York Times*, June 1, 2011.

Kaplan, Robert D., "Center Stage for the 21st Century: Power Plays in the Indian Ocean," *Foreign Affairs*, March/April 2009.

Kaplan, Robert D., "Geography Strikes Back," *Wall Street Journal*, September 7, 2012.

Kaplan, Robert D., "Lost at Sea," *New York Times*, September 21, 2007.

Kaplan, Robert D., *Monsoon: The Indian Ocean and the Future of American Power*, New York: Random House, 2010.

Kaplan, Robert D., "South Asia's Geography of Conflict," Center for a New American Security, August 2010.

Kaplan, Robert D., "The Geography of Chinese Power," *Foreign Affairs*, May/June 2010, pp. 22–41.

Kaplan, Robert, "The Geopolitics of Shale," Stratfor.com, December 20, 2012.

Kaplan, Robert D., "The Revenge of Geography," *Foreign Policy*, May/June 2009, pp. 96–105.

Kefferpütz, Roderick, "To Shale or Not to Shale: That Is Not the (Only) Question," Europeanenergyreview.eu, February 9, 2012.

Kenarov, Dimiter, "Poland's Shale Gas Dream," Foreignpolicy.com, December 26, 2012.

Kolb, Robert W., "Geopolitical Threats to World Energy Markets," *Journal of Social, Political, and Economic Studies*, Summer 2011, 36, pp. 154–196.

Kolb, Robert W., "Geopolitics and World Energy Markets," in Betty and Russell Simkins (eds.), *Energy Finance: Analysis and Valuation, Risk Management, and the Future of Energy*, Hoboken, NJ: John Wiley & Sons, Inc., 2013, pp. 19–48.

Kolb, Robert W., "The Natural Gas Revolution and Central Asia," *Journal of Social, Political, and Economic Studies*, Summer 2012, 37, pp. 141–180.

Kolb, Robert W., "The Natural Gas Revolution and the World's Largest Economies," *Journal of Social, Political, and Economic Studies*, Winter 2012, 37, pp. 415–467.

Kong, Bo, "The Geopolitics of the Myanmar–China Oil and Gas Pipelines," National Bureau of Asian Research, NBR Special Report #23, September 2010, pp. 55–66.

Korchemkin, Mikhail, "Gazprom to Export Gas Only by Its Own Pipelines," *East European Gas Analysis*, April 7, 2013.

Kostecka, Daniel J., "Places and Bases: The Chinese Navy's Emerging Support Network in the Indian Ocean," *Naval War College Review*, Winter 2011, 64, 59–78.

Koyama, Ken, "An Analysis on Asian Premium for LNG Price," Institute of Energy Economics, Japan, March 2012.

KPMG Global Energy Institute, "Watered-Down: Minimizing Water Risks in Shale Gas and Oil Drilling," www.kpmginstitutes.com, 2012.

Kramer, Andrew E., "As Europe Shivers, Russia and Ukraine Point Fingers Over Natural Gas Supply to the West," *New York Times*, February 3, 2012.

Krauss, Clifford, "Argentina Hopes for a Big Payoff in Its Shale Oil Field Discovery," *New York Times*, July 4, 2011.

Krauss, Clifford, "Can We Do Without the Mideast?" *New York Times*, March 30, 2011.

Krauss, Clifford, "In North Dakota, Flames of Wasted Natural Gas Light the Prairie," *New York Times*, September 26, 2011.

Krauss, Clifford, and Eric Lipton, "U.S. Is Inching Toward Elusive Goal of Energy Independence," *New York Times*, March 22, 2012.

Kropatcheva, Elena, "Playing Both Ends Against the Middle: Russia's Geopolitical Energy Games with the EU and Ukraine," *Geopolitics*, 2011, 16, pp. 553–573.

Kupchinsky, Roman, "Russian LNG: The Future Geopolitical Battleground," Jamestown Foundation, www.jamestown.org, June 2009.

Kusnetz, Nicholas, "North Dakota's Oil Boom Brings Damage Along with Prosperity," ProPublica.com, June 7, 2012.

Lall, Marie, "India's Gas Pipeline Efforts: An Analysis of the Problems That Have Prevented Success," National Bureau of Asian Research, NBR Special Report #23, September 2010, pp. 43–54.

Lanthemann, Marc, "STRATFOR: Impact of the Poland–Russia Natural Gas Price Revision," Naturalgaseurope.com, November 7, 2012.

Lavelle, Marianne, "Good Gas, Bad Gas," *National Geographic Magazine*, December 2012.

Leslie, Thomas, "As Large as the Situation of the Columns Would Allow: Building Cladding and Plate Glass in the Chicago Skyscraper, 1885–1905," *Technology and Culture*, April 2008, 49, pp. 399–419.

Levi, Michael, "Yellow Flags on a New Methane Study," Council on Foreign Relations, cfr.org, February 13, 2012.

LeVine, Steve, "How Mozambique Could Shake Up Putin's World," Oilandglory.foreignpolicy.com, March 28, 2012.

LeVine, Steve, "Is This Group Think, or Is the U.S. About to Be Energy-Independent?" *Foreign Policy*, November 2, 2011.

LeVine, Steve, "LNG: Alaska Pitches Security, Diversity in Hunt for Gas Buyers," Energywire.com, April 11, 2012.

LeVine, Steve, "The Math Doesn't Add Up on the US's Ambitions to Export Natural Gas," Quartz, www.qz.com, December 7, 2012.

Lott, Melissa C., "Methane Hydrates: Bigger Than Shale Gas, 'Game Over' for the Environment?" *Scientific American*, March 19, 2013.

Lucas Jr., Robert E., "The Industrial Revolution: Past and Future," Minneapolis Federal Reserve Bank *Annual Report*, May 1, 2004.

Luft, Gal, and Anne Korin, "Realism and Idealism in the Energy Security Debate," in Gal Luft and Anne Korin (eds.), *Energy Security Challenges for the 21st Century*, Santa Barbara, CA: ABC Clio, 2009.

Lustgarten, Abrahm, "Injection Wells: The Poison Beneath Us," ProPublica.com, June 26, 2012.

Lustgarten, Abrahm, "More Reasons to Question Whether Gas Is Cleaner Than Coal," ProPublica.com, April 12, 2011.

Luttwak, Edward N., *The Rise of China vs. the Logic of Strategy*, Cambridge, MA: Belknap Press, 2012.

Macalister, Terry, "King Coal Nears the End of the Line," *Guardian*, March 7, 2013.

MacDonald, Elizabeth, "The Golden State's Fracking Pot of Gold," Foxbusiness.com, April 2, 2013.

Maddison, Angus, *Contours of the World Economy 1–2030 AD: Essays in Macro-Economic History*, Oxford, UK: Oxford University Press, 2007.

Manning, Paddy, "Why Shale Gas Is Still the Next Big Thing," smh.com.au, May 19, 2012.

Martor, Boris, and Raphael Chetrit, "French Parliament: Blind to the Bigger Energy Picture," Europeanenergyreview.eu, September 19, 2011.

Massachusetts Institute of Technology, "The Future of Natural Gas," http://web.mit.edu/, 2010.

Masuda, Tatsuo, "Security of Energy Supply and the Geopolitics of Oil and Gas Pipelines," *European Review of Energy Markets*, December 2007, 2, pp. 1–32.

Mazis, Ioannis Th., and George Sgouros, "Geographical Distribution of Methane Hydrates and International Geopolitics of Energy: Resources in the Eastern Mediterranean," *Civitas Gentium*, 2011, 1, pp. 33–40.

McKibben, Bill, "Why Not Frack?" *New York Review of Books*, March 8, 2012.

Medlock, Kenneth B., Amy Myers Jaffe, and Peter R. Hartley, "Shale Gas and U.S. National Security," James A. Baker III Institute for Public Policy, Rice University, July 2011.

Millard, Peter, "Brazil Prepares to Surprise Drillers This Time with Gas," Bloomberg.com, February 8, 2013.

Mills, Robin M., "The Land of Gas and Honey," *Foreign Policy*, September 15, 2011.

Milner, Brian, "'Saudi America' Heads for Energy Independence," *Globe and Mail*, March 19, 2012.

Mitchell, George P., and Mark D. Zoback, "The Duty to Fracture Responsibly," Naturalgasamericas.com, February 20, 2012.

Mohan, C. Raja, "Tanzanian Pearl," *Indian Express*, March 27, 2013.

Montgomery, Carl T., and Michael B. Smith, "Hydraulic Fracturing: History of an Enduring Technology," *Journal of Petroleum Technology*, December 2010.

Mooney, Chris, "The Truth About Fracking," *Scientific American*, November 2011, pp. 80–85.

Moore, Stephen, "How North Dakota Became Saudi Arabia," *Wall Street Journal*, October 1, 2011.

Morales, Alex, "U.K. Plans to Allow Shale Gas Drilling to Resume This Year," Businessweek.com, October 16, 2012.

Morgan, Sion, "Shale Gas Extraction Could Be 'Catastrophic,'" AMs Told," Walesonline.com, March 7, 2013.

Morse, Ed, "Move Over, OPEC—Here We Come," *Wall Street Journal*, March 19, 2012.

Morse, Richard K., "Cleaning Up Coal," Foreignaffairs.com, July/August 2012.

Mufson, Steven, "In North Dakota, the Gritty Side of an Oil Boom," *Washington Post*, July 18, 2012.

National Energy Technology Laboratory, "Energy Resource Potential of Methane Hydrate," U.S. Department of Energy, February 2011.

National Petroleum Council, "Unconventional Gas," Topic Paper #29, July 18, 2007.

National Research Council, "Induced Seismicity Potential in Energy Technologies," June 15, 2012.

Naturalgas.org, "History," available at www.naturalgas.org/overview/history.asp.

Naturalgasamericas.com, "Argentina's Shale Gas Revolution," April 27, 2012.

Naturalgasamericas.com, "Huge Shale Oil Deposit Discovery for YPF in Mendoza," March 30, 2012.

Naturalgasamericas.com, "YPF Discovers More Shale Gas; Presents 2013–17 Strategy," August 30, 2012.

Naturalgasasia.com, "Australia Becomes Japan's Biggest LNG Supplier," March 7, 2013.

Naturalgasasia.com, "Australian Shale Gas Faces Significant Challenges," May 16, 2012.

Naturalgasasia.com, "China Offers $500 Million Loan to Pakistan for IP Gas Pipeline," March 14, 2013.

Naturalgasasia.com, "China Should Not Overdo Shale Gas Development," November 10, 2012.

Naturalgasasia.com, "China's First Shale Gas Next Year," October 5, 2012.

Naturalgasasia.com, "China's Unconventional Resources to Compete with Australian LNG," April 12, 2012.

Naturalgasasia.com, "Halliburton's New Technology Enables Reuse of Produced Water," March 7, 2013.

Naturalgasasia.com, "Iran Plans Hike in Gas Exports, Reduce Reliance on Oil," April 7, 2013.

Naturalgasasia.com, "Iran to Supply 40 mcm of Gas to Iraq," April 5, 2013.

Naturalgasasia.com, "Japan May Start Extraction of Methane Hydrates," March 10, 2013.

Naturalgasasia.com, "Shell Fracking with Foam," August 15, 2012.

Naturalgasasia.com, "Taiwan Discovers Gas Hydrates in South China Sea," March 13, 2013.

Naturalgasasia.com, "The National: Qatar Unfazed by Shale Gas Growth," June 9, 2012.

Naturalgasasia.com, "Turkey, Pakistan Want More Gas from Iran," July 5, 2012.

Naturalgasasia.com, "U.S. Expected to Approve Expanded LNG Exports to Japan," July 29, 2012.

Naturalgaseurope.com, "Balancing Water Risks Will Be Key to Releasing China's Shale Gas Potential," December 24, 2012.

Naturalgaseurope.com, "Bureaucratic Delays Impact Poland's Shale Promise," February 1, 2013.

Naturalgaseurope.com, "Eastern Mediterranean Offshore Gas: Growth or Conflict?" February 27, 2012.

Naturalgaseurope.com, "Fight Escalates Over Chemical Secrecy in Hydraulic Fracturing," July 2, 2012.

Naturalgaseurope.com, "Final Exam: TAP Versus Nabucco West," February 4, 2013.

Naturalgaseurope.com, "First Out of the Gates: South Stream Starts Construction," December 13, 2012.

Naturalgaseurope.com, "Full Cost of the South Stream Project to Exceed €50 Billion," February 1, 2013.

Naturalgaseurope.com, "Gas as an Instrument of Russian Pressure on Ukraine," February 1, 2013.

Naturalgaseurope.com, "Is Turkey's Shale Taking Off?" September 10, 2012.

Naturalgaseurope.com, "Methane Hydrates and the Potential Natural Gas Boom," February 12, 2013.

Naturalgaseurope.com, "No Contamination Found in Sampled Shale Gas Exploration Wells," January 10, 2013.

Naturalgaseurope.com, "Poland to Renegotiate LNG Contract with Qatar," November 23, 2012.

Naturalgaseurope.com, "Putin Says EU Energy Law 'Uncivilised,'" December 21, 2012.

Naturalgaseurope.com, "Russia Activates the LNG Sector," January 20, 2013.

Naturalgaseurope.com, "Russia Touts Unconventional Gas Promise," December 31, 2012.

Naturalgaseurope.com, "Shale Gas in Ukraine: Turning Enthusiasm into Results," April 3, 2013.

Naturalgaseurope.com, "South Stream Gets the Go Ahead from Turkey," December 28, 2011.

Naturalgaseurope.com, "South Stream Ready to Lay Pipes in 2014 South Stream," November 22, 2012.

Naturalgaseurope.com, "'The Entire Natural Gas System' Is Driving Methane Emissions: MIT Study," December 6, 2012.

Naturalgaseurope.com, "The Gazelle Gas Pipeline Has Connected the Czech Republic with Nord Stream," January 25, 2013.

Naturalgaseurope.com, "The Impact of Soaring Guar Gum Prices," June 21, 2012.

Naturalgaseurope.com, "Turkey: Turns Out We Have Shale Gas After All," March 19, 2012.

Naturalgaseurope.com, "Turkey's Bold Move Shakes Up the Southern Corridor," January 8, 2012.

Naturalgaseurope.com, "Turkmenistan Signs Major Gas Deal with India, Pakistan," May 23, 2012.

Naturalgaseurope.com, "UK: Environment Agency Backs Fracking," May 8, 2012.

Naturalgaseurope.com, "Ukraine: Annual Production of Shale Gas Could Reach 5 Billion Cubic Meters," October 7, 2012.

Naturalgaseurope.com, "Ukraine Moves to Escape Russia's Grip," August 20, 2012.

Naturalgaseurope.com, "Ukraine Reveals Ambitious Plans to Cut Dependence on Russian Gas," June 21, 2012.

Naturalgaseurope.com, "Ukrainian Energy Dependence: Kicking the Habit," May 9, 2012.

Naturalgaseurope.com, "Ukrainian PM Invites Qatar to Participate in LNG," May 11, 2012.

Naturalgaseurope.com, "Unprecedented Opportunity for NATO Allies' Natural Gas Diversification," January 17, 2013.

Naturalgaseurope.com, "Voice of Russia: Shale Gas Crisis," December 6, 2012.

Naturalgaseurope.com, "With Trans-Caspian on the Back-Burner, Turkmenistan Focuses on TAPI," February 20, 2012.

Naturalgaseurope.com, "With US LNG Exports, the EU May Not Need Nabucco," October 8, 2012.

Navarro, Mireya, "New York Sues Over a Drilling Rules Plan," *New York Times*, May 31, 2011.

Navarro, Mireya, "Report Outlines Rewards and Risks of Upstate Natural Gas Drilling," *New York Times*, September 7, 2011.

New York Times, "Floated to Victory on a Wave of Oil," November 23, 1918.

North, Douglass C., and Robert Paul Thomas, *The Rise of the Western World: A New Economic History*, Cambridge, UK: Cambridge University Press, 1973.

O'Rourke, Ronald, "Navy Ford (CVN-78) Class Aircraft Carrier Program: Background and Issues for Congress," U.S. Congressional Research Service, March 13, 2013.

Oil & Gas Financial Journal, "India's ONGC Finds First Shale Gas in Asia Near Durgapur," July 8, 2011.

Olearchyk, Roman, and Neil Buckley, "Russia Hands Ukraine $7bn Gas Bill," *Financial Times*, January 25, 2013.

Onishi, Norimitsu, "Vast Oil Reserve May Now Be Within Reach, and Battle Heats Up," *New York Times*, February 3, 2013.

Ordonez, Isabel, "Statoil, Exxon Say Tanzania Offshore Gas Find Is Big," *Wall Street Journal*, February 24, 2012.

Paleontological Research Institution, "Understanding Drilling Technology," *Marcellus Shale*, January 2012, 6.

Pant, Harsh V., "Great Game in the Indian Ocean," *Japan Times*, June 14, 2011.

Pascual, Carlos, "The Geopolitics of Energy: From Security to Survival," Brookings Institution, Research Paper, January 2008.

Patti-Guzman, Leslie, "LNG: Security of Gas Supply Will Matter in 2012," Naturalgaseurope.com, May 17, 2012.

Paul, Amanda, "Gas Is Cut While Europe Freezes," *Today's Zaman*, February 12, 2012.

Pehrson, Christopher J., "String of Pearls: Meeting the Challenge of China's Rising Power Across the Asian Littoral," Strategic Studies Institute, July 2006.

Pei, Minxin, "China's Achilles' Heel," *Diplomat*, February 8, 2012.

Peiser, Benny, "Europe 'Dithering' Over Joining Shale Gas Revolution," Publicserviceeurope.com, August 29, 2012.

Perlez, Jane, "China Shows Off an Aircraft Carrier but Experts Are Skeptical," *New York Times*, September 25, 2012.

Pfeifer, Sylvia, "Cost Advantage Fuels Demand for Coal," *Financial Times*, October 3, 2012.

Pfeifer, Sylvia, and Andrew Bounds, "Shale Gas Fracking Blamed for Blackpool Quake," *Financial Times*, November 2, 2011.

Piccardi, Luigi, Cassandra Monti, Orlando Vaselli, Franco Tassi, Kalliopi Gaki-Papanastassiou, and Dimitris Papanastassiou, "Scent of a Myth: Tectonics, Geochemistry, and Geomythology at Delphi (Greece)," *Journal of the Geological Society*, January 2008, 165, pp. 5–18.

Pinchuk, Denis, "UPDATE 1-Gazprom Sees Deal to Build Pipeline to Britain in 2013," Reuters.com, November 14, 2012.

Place, Michael, "Brazilian Shale Bigger Than Pre-Salt, Says Regulator," *Business News America*, January 17, 2013.

Plumer, Brad, "Will the U.S. Export Fracking to the Rest of the World?" *Washington Post*, July 21, 2012.

Radow, Elisabeth N., "Homeowners and Gas Drilling Leases: Boon or Bust?" *NYSBA Journal*, November/December 2011, pp. 10–21.

Rao, Vikram, *Shale Gas: The Promise and the Peril*, Research Triangle Park, NC: RTI Press, 2012.

Rao, Vikram, "Sustainable Shale Gas Production Is Feasible," Naturalgaseurope.com, August 30, 2012.

Realclearenergy.com, "Arctic Methane Could Ice the Game For Global Warming," May 7, 2012.

Reddall, Braden, "Frackers in Frantic Search for Guar Bean Substitutes," Reuters.com, August 13, 2012.

Reed, Stanley, "Oil Giants Invest Heavily in Exploration Near Shetlands," *New York Times*, March 28, 2013.

Resnkaya, Natalia, "Macedonians and the Poles Pay the Highest Prices to Gazprom in All of Europe," *Izvestia*, February 1, 2013, available at http://izvestia.ru/news/544100.

Reuters.com, "Gazprom Warns Turkey over Azeri Gas Pipeline Deal," June 29, 2012.

Richter, Wolf, "Natural Gas Is Pushing Coal Over the Cliff," *Business Insider*, August 21, 2012.

Ridley, Matt, "The Shale Gas Shock," The Global Warming Policy Foundation, GWPF Report 2, 2011.

Riley, Alan, "The New Geopolitics Shale Could Bring," Naturalgaseurope.com, December 13, 2012.

Riley, Alan, "Resetting Gazprom in the Golden Age of Gas," Europeanenergyreview.eu, September 17, 2012.

Rogers, Howard, "Shale Gas: The Unfolding Story," *Oxford Review of Economic Policy*, 2011, 27, pp. 117–143.

Romero, Simon, "New Fields May Propel Americas to Top of Oil Companies' Lists," *New York Times*, September 19, 2011.

Ruppel, Carolyn, and Diane Noserale, "Gas Hydrates and Climate Warming—Why a Methane Catastrophe Is Unlikely," U.S. Geological Survey, *Sound Waves*, May/June 2012.

Saint Jacob, Yves de, "France's 'Green Vote' Kills Shale Gas—and Targets Nuclear Power as Well," Europeanenergyreview.eu, July 21, 2011.

Sakmar, Susan L., "The Global Shale Gas Initiative: Will the United States Be the Role Model for the Development of Shale Gas Around the World?" University of San Francisco Law Research Paper No. 2011-27, 2011.

San Diego Union-Tribune, "The Energy Revolution: California Must Not Be Left Behind," March 2, 2013.

Schenk, Christopher J., and Richard M. Pollastro, "Natural Gas Production in the United States: National Assessment of Oil and Gas Fact Sheet," U.S. Geological Survey, January 2002.

Scott, David, "The Great Power 'Great Game' Between India and China: 'The Logic of Geography,'" *Geopolitics*, 2008, 13, pp. 1–26.

Seelye, Katharine Q., "Pennsylvania Hunting and Fracking Vie for State Lands," *New York Times*, November 11, 2011.

Sider, Alison, Russell Gold, and Ben Lefebvre, "Drillers Begin Reusing 'Frack Water,'" *Wall Street Journal*, November 18, 2012.

Silverstein, Ken, "LNG Export Ruling Heard Around the World," Energybiz.com, April 25, 2012.

Silverstein, Ken, "The Other F-Word of Shale Drilling," *Forbes*, September 27, 2012.

Simkins, Betty, and Russell Simkins (eds.), *Energy Finance: Analysis and Valuation, Risk Management, and the Future of Energy*, Hoboken, NJ: John Wiley & Sons, Inc., 2013.

Singh, Mandip, "China Base a Threat to India Navy?" *Diplomat*, December 17, 2011.

Smil, Vaclav, *Energy Transitions: History, Requirements, Prospects*, Oxford: Praeger, 2010.

Smith, Jeff M., "The Great Game, Round Three," *Journal of International Security Affairs*, Fall 2009, 17.

Socor, Vladimir, "China to Increase Central Asian Gas Imports Through Multiple Pipelines," *Eurasia Daily Monitor*, August 9, 2012.

Sofia News Agency, "Construction of Bulgarian South Stream Section Set for June 2013: Gazprom," Novinite.com, December 25, 2012.

Solomon, Deborah, "SEC Bears Down on Fracking," *Wall Street Journal*, August 25, 2011.

Soraghan, Mike, "EPA's Dimock Results Cloud Pa.'s Pollution Case," *E&E Reporter*, www.eenews.net, May 30, 2012.

Soraghan, Mike, "Wyoming Official Pins Pavillion Pollution Complaints on Greed," *E&E Reporter*, www.eenews.net, June 6, 2012.

State of Colorado Oil & Gas Conservation Commission, "Statement on the Documentary *Gasland*," available at http://cogcc.state.co.us/library/GASLAND%20DOC.pdf.

Tabuchi, Hiroko, "An Energy Coup for Japan: 'Flammable Ice,'" *New York Times*, March 12, 2013.

Tabuchi, Hiroko, "Japan Backs Off Goal to Phase Out Nuclear Power by 2040," *New York Times*, September 19, 2012.

Tavernise, Sabrina, "Pennsylvania Set to Allow Local Taxes on Shale Gas," *New York Times*, February 7, 2012.

Techau, Jan, "Russia's Geopolitical Gazprom Blunder," Naturalgaseurope.com, November 15, 2012.

Testosteronepit.com, "Natural Gas and the Brutal Dethroning of King Coal," August 15, 2012.

Tollefson, Jeff, "Methane Leaks Erode Green Credentials of Natural Gas," *Nature*, January 2, 2013.

Trembath, Alex, Jesse Jenkins, Ted Nordhaus, and Michael Shellenberger, "Where the Shale Gas Revolution Came From: Government's Role in the Development of Hydraulic Fracturing in Shale," Breakthrough Institute, http://thebreakthrough.org, May 2012.

U.S. Department of Defense, "Quadrennial Defense Review Report," 2010.

U.S. Department of Energy, "Modern Shale Gas Development in the United States: A Primer," April 2009.

U.S. Department of Energy, "New Methane Hydrate Research: Investing in Our Energy Future," August 31, 2012, available at http://energy.gov/articles/new-methane-hydrate-research, accessed November 10, 2012.

U.S. Department of Energy, "U.S. and Japan Complete Successful Field Trial of Methane Hydrate Production Technologies," May 2, 2012.

U.S. Energy Information Administration, "Annual Energy Outlook 2001: With Projections to 2020," December 2000.

U.S. Energy Information Administration, "Annual Energy Outlook 2012," June 2012.

U.S. Energy Information Administration, "Annual Energy Outlook 2013," Spring 2013.

U.S. Energy Information Administration, "Country Analysis Briefs: Turkey," February 11, 2012.

U.S. Energy Information Administration, "International Energy Outlook 2011," September 2011.

U.S. Energy Information Administration, "Natural Gas Exports from Iran," October 2012.

U.S. Energy Information Administration, "Petroleum & Other Liquids," available at www.eia.gov/dnav/pet/pet_crd_crpdn_adc_mbbl_a.htm.

U.S. Energy Information Administration, "Repeal of the Powerplant and Industrial Fuel Use Act (1987)."

U.S. Energy Information Administration, "Review of Emerging Resources: U.S. Shale Gas and Shale Oil Plays," July 2011.

U.S. Energy Information Administration, "U.S. Crude Oil, Natural Gas, and Natural Gas Liquids Proved Reserves, 2010," August 2012.

U.S. Energy Information Administration, "U.S. Natural Gas Markets: Mid-Term Prospects for Natural Gas Supply December 2001."

U.S. Energy Information Administration, "U.S. Natural Gas Markets: Recent Trends and Prospects for the Future," May 2001.

U.S. Energy Information Administration, "World Shale Gas Resources: An Initial Assessment of 14 Regions Outside the United States," April 2011.

U.S. Geological Survey, "3 to 4.3 Billion Barrels of Technically Recoverable Oil Assessed in North Dakota and Montana's Bakken Formation—25 Times More Than 1995 Estimate," Press Release, April 10, 2008.

U.S. Geological Survey, "Dissolved Methane in New York Groundwater," September 2012.

U.S. Geological Survey, "Fact Sheet: Gas Hydrate Resource Assessment: North Slope, Alaska," October 2008.

U.S. Geological Survey, "USGS Releases First Assessment of Shale Gas Resources in the Utica Shale: 38 Trillion Cubic Feet," October 4, 2012.

University of Southern California Price School of Public Policy, "The Monterey Shale and California's Economic Future," 2013.

Varfolomeyev, Oleg, "Ukraine Reveals Ambitious Plans to Cut Dependence on Russian Gas," *Eurasia Daily Monitor,* June 19, 2012, 9(116).

Vatansever, Adnan, and David Koranyi, "An Uphill Battle on Russian Gas Prices on the Horizon," Europeanenergyreview.eu, March 14, 2013.

Vatansever, Adnan, and David Koranyi, "Lowering the Price of Russian Gas: A Challenge for European Energy Security," Europeanenergyreview.eu, March 11, 2013.

Verrastro, Frank A., Sarah O. Ladislaw, Matthew Frank, Lisa A. Hyland, "The Geopolitics of Energy: Emerging Trends, Changing Landscapes, Uncertain Times," Center for Strategic & International Studies, October 2010.

Walsh, Bryan, "Natural Gas and the Invisible Spill: How Much Methane Is Reaching the Atmosphere?" *Time*, April 10, 2012.

Webber, Jude, "Repsol–YPF: Burying the Hatchet?" *Financial Times*, March 4, 2013.

White, Bill, "The Cold Facts About a Hot Commodity: LNG," Oildrum.com, October 4, 2012.

White, Lynn, *Medieval Technology and Social Change*, Oxford, UK: Oxford University Press, 1966.

Wolf, Martin, "Prepare for a Golden Age of Gas," *Financial Times*, February 21, 2012.

Wolfgang, Ben, "I Drank Fracking Fluid, Says Colorado Gov. John Hickenlooper," *Washington Times*, February 12, 2013.

Wrigley, E. A., *Energy and the English Industrial Revolution*, Cambridge, UK: Cambridge University Press, 2010.

Wüst, Christian, "Fear of Fracking: Germany Balks on Natural Gas Bonanza," Spiegel Online International, www.spiegel.de/international/, October 5, 2012.

Yergin, Daniel, "Stepping on the Gas," *Wall Street Journal*, April 2, 2011.

Yergin, Daniel, *The Prize: The Epic Quest for Oil, Money, and Power*, New York: Free Press, 1991.

Zeller, Jr., Tom, "Studies Say Natural Gas Has Its Own Environmental Problems," *New York Times*, April 11, 2011.

Zhukov, Yuri M., "Trouble in the Eastern Mediterranean Sea," *Foreign Affairs*, March 20, 2013.

Index